Asymmetrical Neighbors

Asymmetrical Neighbors

Borderland State Building between China and Southeast Asia

ENZE HAN

UNIVERSITY PRESS

OXFORD
UNIVERSITY PRESS

Oxford University Press is a department of the University of Oxford. It furthers
the University's objective of excellence in research, scholarship, and education
by publishing worldwide. Oxford is a registered trade mark of Oxford University
Press in the UK and certain other countries.

Published in the United States of America by Oxford University Press
198 Madison Avenue, New York, NY 10016, United States of America.

© Oxford University Press 2019

All rights reserved. No part of this publication may be reproduced, stored in
a retrieval system, or transmitted, in any form or by any means, without the
prior permission in writing of Oxford University Press, or as expressly permitted
by law, by license, or under terms agreed with the appropriate reproduction
rights organization. Inquiries concerning reproduction outside the scope of the
above should be sent to the Rights Department, Oxford University Press, at the
address above.

You must not circulate this work in any other form
and you must impose this same condition on any acquirer.

Library of Congress Cataloging-in-Publication Data
Names: Han, Enze, author.
Title: Asymmetrical neighbors : borderland state building between
China and Southeast Asia / Enze Han.
Description: New York, NY, United States of America: Oxford University Press, [2019] |
Includes bibliographical references and index.
Identifiers: LCCN 2019006330 (print) | LCCN 2019980136 (ebook) |
ISBN 9780190688301 (hardcover : acid-free paper) |
ISBN 9780190060787 (pbk. : acid-free paper) | ISBN 9780190688325 (ebook)
Subjects: LCSH: Southeast Asia—Relations—China. |
China—Relations—Southeast Asia. | Borderlands—Southeast Asia. |
Borderlands—China. | Transborder ethnic groups—Southeast Asia. |
Transborder ethnic groups—China.
Classification: LCC DS525.9.C5 H358 2019 (print) |
LCC DS525.9.C5 (ebook) | DDC 327.51059—dc23
LC record available at https://lccn.loc.gov/2019006330
LC ebook record available at https://lccn.loc.gov/2019980136

Contents

Acknowledgments	vii
List of Abbreviations	xi
Notes on Transliterations and References	xiii

1. Introduction — 1
2. The Neighborhood Effect of State and Nation Building — 20
3. The Historical Pattern of State Formation in Upland Southeast Asia — 36
4. Spillover of the Chinese Civil War and Militarization of the Borderland — 55
5. Communist Revolutions at the Borderland — 72
6. Dynamics of Transboundary Economic Flows — 92
7. Comparative Nation Building across the Borderland Area — 118
8. Continual Contestations at the China-Myanmar Border — 137
9. Conclusion — 157

Notes	165
Chinese Bibliography	205
Thai Bibliography	209
Burmese Bibliography	211
English Bibliography	213
Index	233

Acknowledgments

This book has been long in the making. After I published my first book on ethnic politics in China in 2013, which was based on my doctoral dissertation, I was lost for what to do next. Having worked on the topic of ethnic politics in China for quite some time, I became captivated by transformations underway in Myanmar, so I started to look at its changing relations with China. Because of this new interest, I decided to learn Burmese; as a staff member of The School of Oriental and African Studies (SOAS) in London, I could easily take language classes, so I signed up for Burmese 1. Thus began my journey of reconnecting with Southeast Asian Studies. I say "reconnecting" because I had an earlier encounter with Southeast Asia, when an undergraduate many years ago at Beijing Foreign Studies University. There I studied Lao and Thai. Later, when I was doing a master's degree at the University of British Columbia, I took a year-long course on Southeast Asian Politics from Diane Mauzy. But, during doctoral studies at George Washington University, my interests diverted to China's internal politics. So it was great to reconnect with Southeast Asia once again and revamp myself with a new language—Burmese.

Taking classes in Burmese is one of the best decisions I have made in the past few years. The excellent teaching of Saya John Okell and Saya Justin Watkins, as well as Sayama Tha Zin, made me realize not only how much I enjoy language study but also how fascinating Myanmar's domestic politics and foreign relations can be. Particularly, borderland issues between there and China intrigued me. Luckily, Mandy Sadan, one of the great experts on Kachin politics and society, was also at SOAS, and through her kind introduction I made my first trip to Laiza, a border town under the control of the Kachin Independence Army (KIA). With this began my research on the politics of state building in these contested borderlands. Around that time, I also made connections with scholars in Thailand and in the summer of 2013, took up a visiting fellowship at Thammasat University in Bangkok. Since then, I have become a regular traveler to Thailand. I specifically would like to thank Sorayut Aiemueayut, Virot Ali, Thanyarat Apiwong, Waraporn

Ruangsri, Yos Santasombat, and Wasana Wongsurawat for making my trips to Bangkok and Chiang Mai fruitful.

Conceptualization of the research project presented here benefited from a research fellowship at the School of Social Science, Institute of Advanced Study, Princeton. A seminar series there on borders and boundaries, under Didier Fassin, provided an excellent intellectual setting to formulate this book's theoretical framework. I also met three wonderful friends who gave company and support throughout an isolated life in the woods, namely Alice Goffman, Monica Kim, and Rhacel Salazer Parreñas. Their encouragement was crucial, and without our writing and reunion retreats in South Carolina, California, and Bangkok this book will not be what it has become. Also, Ben, Gugma, and Pangga have been indispensable companions. At Princeton, Yan Bennett opened her home to me, and I recall fondly her driving me to do grocery shopping, together with Macaela and Zoe.

Throughout the years, I benefited tremendously from excellent colleagues at SOAS. From the Department of Politics and International Studies, I would like to thank Reem Abou-El-Fadl, Fiona Adamson, Ashin Adib-Moghaddam, Rochana Bajpai, Felix Berenskoetter, Carlo Bonura, Michael Buehler, Stephen Chan, Phil Clark, Bhavna Dave, Matthew Eagleton-Pierce, Dafydd Fell, Alastair Fraser, Stephen Hopgood, Salwa Islamil, Laleh Khalili, Tat Yan Kong, Hagar Kotef, Mark Laffey, Matthew Nelson, Kerem Nisancioglu, Manjeet Ramgotra, Rahul Rao, Meera Sabaratnam, Julia Strauss, Kristin Surak, Charles Trip, Leslie Vinjamuri, and Simona Vittorini for providing me with a collegial environment. Lawrence Saez, who has sadly passed away, will also be remembered fondly. I would like to thank the following SOAS colleagues: Ernest Caldwell, Bi-yu Chang, Michael Charney, Angela Chiu, Roy Fischel, Fabio Gygi, Rachel Harrison, Zoe Marriage, and Tim Pringle. Specifically, I really treasure Timon Screech for his warm friendship and constant support throughout the years.

While doing research and writing, I have been supported by a Leverhulme Research Fellowship and the British Council Newton Fund. Both released me from teaching and gave me time and resources to undertake field research and concentrate on writing. I also would like to thank the SOAS Staff Development Office for funding two years of Burmese summer school in Yangon. I also benefited from an East Asia Institute fellowship to deliver a series of talks on my ongoing research at the East Asia Institute in Seoul, Fudan University in Shanghai, Keio University in Tokyo, and National Taiwan University in Taipei. Thanks also go to Todd Hall who arranged a visiting fellowship at St. Anne's College, Oxford, in the 2016 Michaelmas term. The final chapters of this book were written after I took up a position at the University of Hong Kong (HKU). At HKU, I would like to thank John Burns, Wildred Chow, Courtney Fung, Ian Holliday, Richard Hu, Kai Quek, Xiaojun Yan, and Jiangnan Zhu for their help and support in easing the transition to a new life in Hong Kong. Furthermore, Bruce Dickson and Harris Mylonas continue to support me whenever I need career advice or recommendation letters.

Of course, I must also thank all the informants and interviewees in Mainland China, Myanmar, Taiwan, and Thailand. It was they who provided me stories for the ethnographical component of this book. Their identities have been anonymized, so I can not name them individually. My thanks to James Brown, Sirada Khemanitthathai, Wai Phyo Maung, Ric Neo, Tinnaphop Sinsomboonthong, Tinakrit Sireerat, and Zinn Ne Win, who provided excellent research assistance. I also thank Alaric DeArment for his proofreading support. Angela Chnapko at Oxford University Press has been the best editor I can imagine. Parts of the book were presented at the Academic Sinica, Chiang Mai University, Chulalongkorn University, George Washington University, Jinan University, Kyoto University, Mahidol University, Princeton University, Torino World Affairs Institute, University of British Columbia, University of California, Berkeley, and Yunnan University. I appreciate all the comments and feedback from these talks.

There are many friends who have given companionship over the years, I would like to thank Xiaojun Li, Joseph O'Mahoney, and Christopher Paik for many discussions about our academic lives, even though we live continents apart. I also thank the following friends, no matter where you are: Wenchin Chang, Sayaka Chatani, Dong Jie, Ben Essex, Dario Adail Ferrer, Colm Fox, Gao Jing, Guo Jiahui, Jean Hong, Huang Lei, Huang Qiongyu, Jiang Anmin, Darren Johnson, Greg Leon, Li E, Lin Shijian, Liu Bo, Liu Minhong, Liu Peng, Liu Xiaohua, Liu Zuohuang, Lju Jiayu, Jin Ou, Mu Yingying Ni Hongwei, Andreas Rufer, Fang-long Shih, Sun Xin, Tao Wenjuan, Seinenu Thein-Lemelson, Wang Dian, Xu Shaojing, Yao Xin, Yao Ying, Zeng Jinghan, Zheng Pingfu, and Zhu Mengping.

Finally, my family has always been there for me. Over the years, my parents and sister have been the most important components of my life. I dedicate this book to my niece, Xu Yilin, and nephew, Xu Yikai, for making me a proud uncle.

Abbreviations

AA	Arakanese Army
ASEAN	Association of Southeast Asian Nations
BGF	Border Guard Forces
BNA	British National Archives
BPP	Border Patrol Police
CCP	Chinese Communist Party
CIA	Central Intelligence Agency
CPB	Communist Party OF Burma
CPT	Communist Party of Thailand
CR	Cultural Revolution
GMS	Great Mekong Subregion
IDP	Internally Displaced Persons
KIA	Kachin Independence Army
KIO	Kachin Independence Organization
KMT	Chinese Nationalist Party (Kuomintang)
KNDO	Karen National Defense Organization
KNU	Karen National Union
LMC	Lancang-Mekong Cooperation
MNDAA	Myanmar National Democratic Alliance Army
MR	Military Region
MTA	Mong Tai Army
NDAA	National Democratic Alliance Army (Mongla)
NLD	National League for Democracy
OBOR	One Belt One Road
PFD	Political Frontier Defense
PRC	People's Republic of China
ROC	Republic of China
SLORC	State Law and Order Restoration Council
SPDC	State Peace and Development Council
SSA-S	Shan State Army-South
SSIA	Shan State Independence Army
TNLA	Ta'ang National Liberation Army
US NAII	United States National Archive II
UWSA	United Wa State Army
YPCC	Yunnan Production and Construction Corps

Notes on Transliterations and References

For Chinese words and names in general, I use pinyin as the system of transliteration unless in direct quotes. For both Burmese and Thai, I also follow normal ways of romanization. In addition, I provide bibliographies with Burmese, Chinese, and Thai languages in their original form at the end.

1
Introduction

It was a hot July afternoon when my plane landed at Dehong Mangshi Airport. Mangshi is a small border city in Southwest China's Yunnan province, close to Myanmar. It is the capital city of Dehong Dai and Jingpo Autonomous Prefecture and about an hour's flight from Kunming. At the airport, I was greeted by two men in their late twenties; their mission was to take me across the border to Laiza, Myanmar,[1] the headquarters of the Kachin Independence Organization (KIO) and its military arm, the Kachin Independence Army (KIA). The year was 2013, and only a few months earlier several military clashes between the Myanmar military (Tatmadaw) and the KIA ravaged this borderland area. Both of the men worked for the KIO. One, whom I will call Maung, is a Kachin from Myanmar who speaks excellent English but not much Chinese, while the other, Ahua, is a Jingpo (the Chinese name for the Kachin) from the Chinese side of the border who speaks perfect Mandarin.

I got in a car with them and they drove toward the border, which is about 200 kilometers away from Mangshi airport. The highway from the airport was relatively new, fast, and smooth, thanks to the modernization of China's infrastructure. Before long, we arrived in Yingjiang, where we had a quick dinner before continuing toward the border, after dark. In the car, Maung told me that since military confrontations escalated a few months before, a Chinese military checkpoint had been set up on the way to the border, but usually the soldiers did not come out at night. Although I have a Chinese ID card, I am not from the local area, so I do not have the right paper (*bianminzheng* or "border people ID") to cross the border officially. So, it was better to go after dark, and in the unlikely event the car was stopped, I was told to say I was a businessman from Zhejiang looking for commercial opportunities in Nabang, the small town across the border from Laiza. Before long, it started raining, and the smooth highway changed to a winding mountain road that went through a dense, eerily dark forest, and also made me feel carsick. Sure enough, the checkpoint was not staffed, so the car passed quickly through. Suddenly, another car appeared ahead of us, flashing its headlights. Ahua stopped the car and we got out. He told me that in order to cross the border secretly, they could not take a car with Chinese license plates. So, we changed cars and soon turned off from the main road to a narrow muddy, side road, arriving in Laiza fifteen minutes later.

Laiza is under the de facto control of the KIA, and the Myanmar central government does not have any presence in the town itself. Even the official border crossing is manned by the People's Liberation Army (PLA) on the Chinese side, with the KIA soldiers on the Kachin side. Architecturally, the town resembles a nondescript Chinese town, although street signs are in Kachin and Burmese as well as Chinese. Here, the main currency in circulation is the Chinese renminbi yuan (RMB), and the mobile phone networks are also Chinese. KIA soldiers patrol the town with their rifles hanging loosely from their backs, while many of the shops are run by migrants from China. Certainly, although Laiza is officially part of Myanmar territory, and all maps indisputably would put it within the sovereign boundaries of the Myanmar state, in practice the Myanmar state's sovereignty does not reach it.

Along the long border between China and Myanmar, totaling more than 2,000 kilometers, there are quite a few territories like Laiza, where Myanmar's sovereignty is fragmented, although to varying degrees. In both the Kachin and Shan states, many ethnic rebel groups continue to hold pieces of territory where they maintain direct administration. This is also the case along the border between Myanmar and Thailand, although to a lesser extent. Some of these groups, such as the KIA, are still fighting the Myanmar military. Fighting started between the KIA, who refused to be disarmed, and the Myanmar military in June 2011 and occurred sporadically into 2013, when ceasefire talks resumed. Fighting intensified in December 2012 and January 2013, when the Myanmar military made heavy use of airstrikes and artillery against KIA positions around Laiza.[2]

Similarly, a few years before the Kachin conflict, the Kokang rebels' Myanmar National Democratic Alliance Army (MNDAA) was attacked by the Myanmar military, which effectively ousted the rebel army from its base. However, fighting erupted again in Kokang when Peng Jiasheng, the head of MNDAA, came back with his troops, supported by several other ethnic rebel armies.[3] In February 2015, the MNDAA attacked Myanmar government posts around Laugai (Laojie), the capital city of Kokang. Fighting lasted until May, when the Myanmar government seized the MNDAA's last stronghold.[4] In addition to the KIA and MNDAA, there are several other ethnic rebel groups, such as the United Wa State Army

(UWSA), the National Democratic Alliance Army (NDAA), the Shan State Army (SSA), and numerous others, as well as many militias, which still maintain high levels of autonomy for territories along the Kachin and Shan borderland areas.

Today, when we look at the areas along Myanmar's borders with China and Thailand, we see that both China and Thailand have clearly consolidated sovereign control in their respective borderlands, while at the same time projecting economic and cultural influence across the border into adjacent areas of Myanmar. Relatedly, both China and Thailand have carried out nation building with some success, in that ethnic minorities in the borderland area have increasingly come to identify themselves as either Chinese or Thai nationals while retaining their own ethnic identification, although certainly in different formats. On the other hand, the Myanmar government continues to face resistance from ethnic rebels opposing its own state consolidation efforts. In addition, its nation-building process has not been successful, as we can see from the various ethnic rebels who aim to maintain their autonomy, administratively but also culturally, from the Myanmar government's vision of national belonging. So how do we explain such variations in state and nation building across this common borderland territory? Why could the Myanmar state not have a monopoly on the control of violence, in a Weberian sense, within its own territory? How did such fragmentation of the state along its borderland areas come about? Why did such fragmentation not occur in China or Thailand, where state consolidation has been mostly complete? How do we explain such variations of state building and consolidation of the borderland area among the three countries?

In *The Art of Not Being Governed*, James Scott provides a rather romantic account of the stateless spaces of upland Southeast Asia spanning across mainland Southeast Asia and Southwest China. Termed "Zomia" for this part of the Himalayan and Southeast Asian Massif, this stretch of territories is mountainous, sparsely populated, and ethnically diverse.[5] Turning the conventional accounts upside down, Scott rejected the notion of the lowland valley agrarian states as the bearers of civilization and the upland nomadic slash-and-burn people as barbarians. Instead, Scott's interpretation of the anarchist nature of these "free and mobile" upland people emphasizes how they escaped the restrictive political control by the "civilized" valley states.[6] Therefore, it is not that these people remain "uncivilized" by centralized states; rather, they intentionally escaped from the states in search of freedom and mobility.

However, such free spaces, which were difficult to reach during premodern periods thanks to geographical barriers such as mountainous terrain, have become possible targets of modern state penetration since the first half of the twentieth century.[7] The combination of technological prowess and sovereign ambitions, both modernization as well as state and nation building, has significantly compromised these erstwhile stateless spaces for the benefit of the valley states. As a result, the Zomia territories have since become disintegrated parts of several modern nation-states that all tried to reach and consolidate their presence in those remote mountainous areas and make the people living there "legible."[8] Yet, the story of how these processes of modernization and state and nation building unfolded has not been comprehensively examined. Indeed, little attention has been paid to comparatively analyzing how the uneven process of state and nation building occurred in the borderlands of upland Southeast Asia and the reasons for the variations. This book is an attempt to fill this void.

This book presents a comparative historical account of the state and nation-building process in an "organic" upland area that shares lots of similarities in terms of geography and ethnic diversity, yet has become increasingly incorporated into a set of neighboring modern states. In an attempt to explain variations in state and nation building by these neighboring states, the book aims to achieve two main goals. One is to shed light on a theoretical question of how state and nation building should be conceptualized as interactive processes across national boundaries. Departing from existing approaches that look at such processes mainly from the angle of singular, bounded territorial states, the book argues that a more fruitful approach is to see how state and nation building in one country can influence, and be influenced by, the same processes across borders. For example, Daron Acemoglu and James Robinson, in their popular book *Why Nations Fail*, argue some countries are richer than others because they were founded on better political institutions.[9] Yet they fail to comprehend that, in many instances, the failure of some nations is precisely the result of others' success. One way to understand this interactive relation is to look at Angus Deaton's treatment of global inequality as a consequence of progress.[10] In *The Great Escape*, Deaton argues that in many instances "progress in one country was at the *expense* of another" (original emphasis by author).[11] In his analysis, the Industrial Revolution benefited Europe tremendously, yet European nations' progress also meant those "who were conquered and plundered in Asia, Latin America, and the Caribbean were not only harmed at the time but in many cases saddled with economic and political institutions that condemned them to centuries of continuing poverty and inequality."[12] Drawing inspiration from such an approach, this book argues that we should also explain variations in state and nation building across national borders as mutually interactive processes. Thus, the success or failure of one country's state and nation building can depend upon factors beyond its national borders in neighboring states. For this, the book proposes a "neighborhood effect" as a theoretical lens to consider state and nation building.

The other goal of the book is to present a rich and detailed account of the modern history of state and nation building in the borderland between China, Myanmar, and Thailand. Pushing through existing boundaries set up arbitrarily in area studies, with China studies separate from Southeast Asian studies,[13] this book aims to tear down those barriers. The empirical chapters in the book thus put a strong emphasis on how deeply intertwined China is with Southeast Asia. Therefore, unlike existing accounts of state and nation building in these three countries that tend to focus on each country alone, this book looks at all three together while focusing on a common borderland territory.

Before delving deeper, some conceptual clarification is in order. What do I mean by state and nation building in this book? Although conceptually different, empirically nation and state building often happen hand in hand. This is particularly true with regard to a multi-ethnic border region where consolidation of state control and building of state institutions often require simultaneously developing a sense of national belonging.[14] For these reasons, I tend to treat state and nation building as symbiotic and part of a holistic project. That said, state and nation building are often measured empirically using different indicators. For state building, the focus is on measuring how state institutions become established and embedded in a fixed territorial space, where a Weberian state in which legitimate control of violence is monopolized by the central government, and where economic sovereignty has been attempted.[15] For nation building, the emphasis is often on the making of a common people, who are bounded by an inter-subjective understanding of mutual belonging.[16] This is often achieved through projects that aim to teach the people a common language and indoctrinate them with a nationalist ideology. Paying attention to these differences between state and nation building, this book covers both processes in the empirical chapters, while noting the deeply interrelated nature of the two.

Geography, History, and People

The geographic focus of the book is on a stretch of borderland area along the China-Myanmar-Thailand border. Broadly speaking, it covers southern

Yunnan province in China, Kachin and Shan states in Myanmar, and the northern provinces in Thailand that border Myanmar (see maps 1.1 and 1.2). At the same time, these are the territories that fall along the Mekong and Salween rivers shared by the three countries and are characterized by

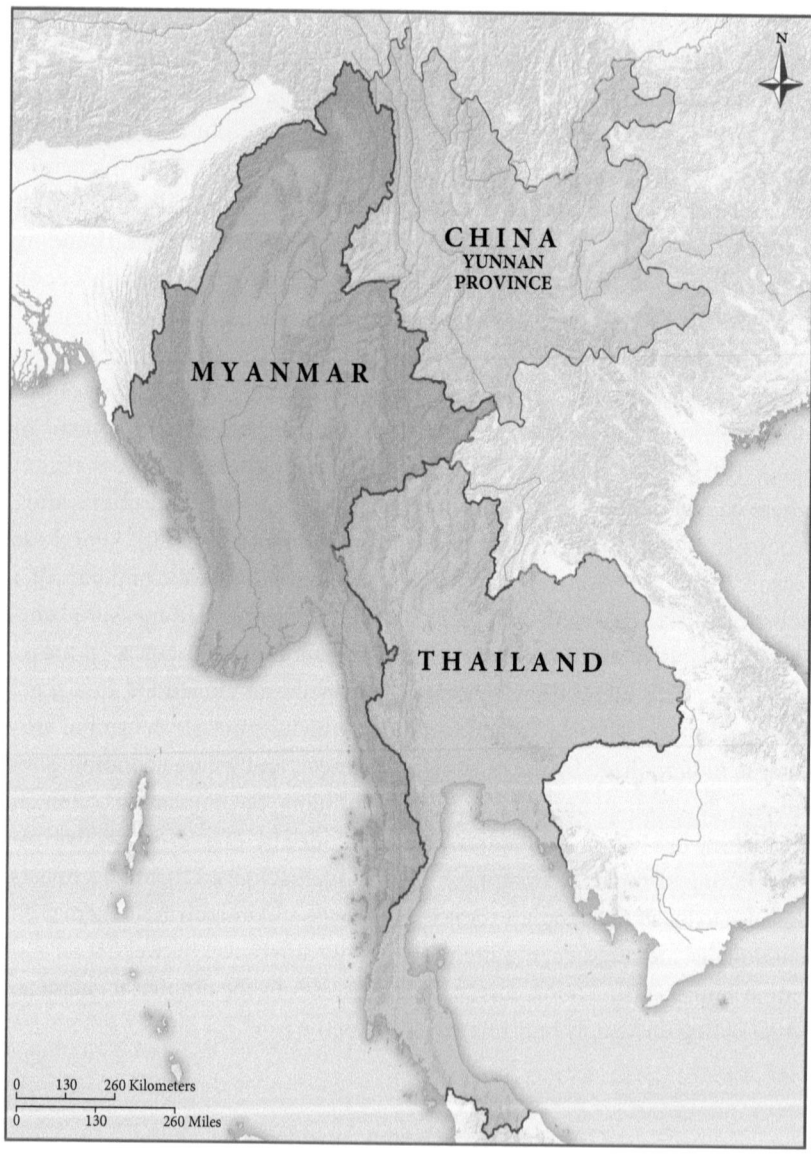

Map 1.1 Myanmar, Thailand, and Yunnan (China)

Map 1.2 Borderland Territories between China, Myanmar, and Thailand

mountainous terrain and deep river valleys that are difficult to cross. This region also includes the notorious Golden Triangle, which since the Cold War, has been a center of opium production and drug trafficking in Southeast Asia.[17]

The historical circumstances in which these areas were incorporated into the lowland states vary slightly. Southwest China was significantly subjected to tight centralized control in the mid-eighteenth century with the replacement of many local ethnic chieftains (tusi) by magistrates appointed by Beijing.[18] However, in southern Yunnan, many chieftains coexisted with the Qing and republican bureaucracies well into the mid-1950s, when the incoming communist regime formally abolished the chieftain system.[19] Many of the chieftains in the Shan and Kachin states maintained dual tributary relations with the Konbaung Dynasty in Burma as well as with Qing China.[20] After the British colonized the whole of Burma in 1885, the Kachin and Shan states were ruled separately by the British as frontier areas; Burma proper was ruled as ministerial Burma, while the country as a whole was incorporated as a province of British India.[21] When Burma achieved independence from Britain in 1948, the frontier areas were united with Burma proper, yet unification very quickly translated into a prolonged civil war that has lasted ever since.[22] For northern Thailand, the Nan kingdom used to pay tribute to both Burma and the Kingdom of Siam. After the mid-eighteenth century, it became a vassal of the Chakri Dynasty based in Bangkok. Extraterritoriality was granted to European companies, mostly British but also Danish, to exploit the profitable teak trade in northern Thailand. Eventually it was incorporated into Siam as part of the centralization that occurred during the reign of Rama V Chulalongkorn in 1899.[23]

Indeed, we can see differences at the macro level between the three cases in that only Burma was officially colonized by the British Empire. However, it suffices to say that no direct centralization in the modern sense was possible in China in the first half of the twentieth century, when the country was devastated by warlordism, the Japanese invasion, and the civil war.[24] In Thailand, European extraterritoriality was revoked in the early twentieth century, and the modern bureaucratic state only started to increase its presence then. Even though the historical incorporation of these areas into these three states varies slightly in terms of the historical context, modern nation states only started to emerge after in the mid-twentieth century, with the People's Republic of China (PRC) founded in 1949, Burma winning independence in 1948, and the 1947 military coup in Thailand.

At the same time, this borderland area covers a diverse set of ethnic groups that share strong linguistic and cultural ties across state borders.[25] Yunnan, for example, officially recognizes 25 ethnic groups in the province, which account for 34% of the total population.[26] Thailand officially does not recognize ethnic minority status, insisting everyone living within its borders is Thai, and many ethnic minority groups, especially the highlanders (hill tribes), remain stateless.[27] In Myanmar, the Kachin and Shan states are extremely diverse, although Myanmar has not released any census data about the states' ethnic compositions. Ethnic demographic data from the most recent census, in 2014, have not yet been released. However, it is generally understood that the ethnic-majority Bamar only account for about 68% of the whole population. This means ethnic minorities should account for a high percentage of the population in the borderland area, which can also be inferred from the persistence of ethnic rebel groups and the inability of Myanmar's government to impose state-building projects there. For some of the larger ethnic groups, estimates and distributions are available. There are about 1.2 million Dai in China and about 5–6 million Shan in Myanmar, both sharing strong linguistic and religious ties with northern Thailand. There are about 400,000 Wa in China and about 800,000 in Myanmar. For Kachin people, there are about 1 million in Myanmar and 150,000 in China, where they are known as Jingpo. China is home to 720,000 Lahu people, while Myanmar is home to 150,000, and Thailand 100,000. There are also 730,000 Lisu in China, 600,000 in Myanmar, and 50,000 in Thailand. Additionally, Miao (Hmong) and Yao (Iu-mien) live in the borderland area.

Interrelated Arguments

In order to explain the variations in state and nation building across the borderland area between China, Myanmar, and Thailand, the book makes two interrelated arguments. First, departing from existing literature on state building, this book proposes a novel theoretical approach that looks beyond the confines of state borders. Instead of looking at state building as a process predominantly determined by domestic factors, such as war making and preparation, political institutions, and geographic and demographic variables, the book proposes that we should look beyond the constraints of national borders. It argues that we should conceptualize state building as an interactive process heavily influenced by a "neighborhood effect" and look at how state building in one country can be influenced by the same process in the neighboring states. The book probes the conditions under which this neighborhood effect might take place. It argues that such an effect is more likely to occur in situations where there is power asymmetry between neighboring states, and its effect is further conditioned upon the nature of relations among these states. When a state borders a much stronger neighbor that is also adversarial, then the latter would have the capacity and intention to politically and militarily meddle in the mutual borderland area, which would lead to the fragmentation of the former's state building efforts in the area. If the bilateral relationship were more amicable, then the economically more powerful state would still exert significant influence on the other's borderland area. If the two neighboring states were of similar power balance and adversarial, then we would expect a mutually militarized borderland region. Finally, if such states were friendly neighbors to each other, then there would not be a "neighborhood" effect of state building.

Fashioned in a similar way concerning nation building, the book also contends that cross-border dynamics can heavily influence that process, domestically. Specifically, it looks at two ways that a neighborhood effect of nation building can occur. One is for ethnic groups that straddle national borders but have linkages with powerful ethnic-kin homeland countries that claim rights to protect them. With such external support and monitoring, these ethnic groups would have more resources and cultural repertoires to resist the nation-building projects imposed on them by the majority ethnic group in the country they inhabit. This line of argument is drawn from Rogers Brubaker's theorization of how external ethnic linkages and the support they offer for ethnic groups can fundamentally change the dynamics of nationalist politics within a country.[28] The other way concerns ethnic groups that straddle national borders but are minorities in both countries. Here, the book argues that these ethnic groups compare different nationalist ideologies to which they are subject under the neighboring nation-building projects, which influence how they perceive their own living conditions and determine which side is preferable. Thus, if they perceive their external kin groups in neighboring countries as receiving better treatment than themselves, then they are more likely to develop a grievance toward the country they inhabit. This argument was developed in my previous book on ethnic group mobilization in China, and here I am applying it to this transnational context.[29]

Thus, taken together, when the borderland area between China, Myanmar, and Thailand is concerned, the book argues that the failure of the Myanmar state to consolidate its control over its borderland area is partly due to the political and military meddling by its two more powerful neighbors during the Cold War. Furthermore, both China and Thailand, being more economically advanced than Myanmar, have exerted heavy economic influence on the borderland area at the cost of Myanmar's economic sovereignty. These two dimensions explain the variation of state building across the borderland among these three countries. Meanwhile, the Myanmar state's failure in nation building can also be explained in this way. For the Shan, because of their close ethnic ties to the Thai, historically Thailand has attempted to support their self-determination movements, while at the same time providing strong cultural capital for the Shan to resist the Burmanization process in Myanmar. For ethnic minority groups across the Sino-Myanmar border, such as the Kachin, Wa, and others, their double-minority status meant that they would compare the situations in China and Myanmar in their nationalist ideologies and policies. The more benign treatment they receive in China only feeds into their further alienation from the Myanmar state.

Methodology

The book adopts a comparative historical approach that pays attention to the interactive dynamics of state and nation building across this borderland area since the end of the second world war (WWII). In terms of examining comparative state building, it focuses on two major dimensions to measure such processes. The first is political and military and measures how states have attempted to consolidate their physical control, their varying results, and the reasons for these variations. Indeed, the book treats this dimension as the most fundamental, as it sets up the foundations of later state building efforts. The second dimension of state building is economic. Here the emphasis is on different states' efforts to achieve their economic sovereignty and implications across the borderland area when there are disparities of economic power. In terms of examination of comparative nation building, the book looks at how different models of nationalist ideology and their applications have resulted in the different responses of ethnic groups scattered across this common area.

The empirical materials of the book come from a variety of sources. Materials in English, Chinese, Burmese, and Thai have been consulted and utilized, although the weight varies depending on the amount of materials available. A majority of archival materials come from the United States National Archive II (US NAII) in College Park, Maryland, and the British National Archives (BNA) in Kew. These archives contain a plethora of internal reports on the borderland area from the US State Department and the

British Foreign Office, sent by their embassies and consulates in Rangoon, Mandalay, Bangkok, and Chiang Mai. The book also utilizes extensive Chinese-language materials published in Taiwan and the PRC, in the form of memoirs, gazetteers, newspapers, and local historical accounts in Yunnan province. It engages books and journal articles published in Thai on the Chinese Nationalist Party (Kuomintang, KMT) in northern Thailand, the Thai communist insurgency, and Shan nationalist movements. The book also uses materials published in Burmese. Additionally, three major journals published by the Burmese government in the immediate post-independence period—*Burma*, *Guardian*, and *Forward*—were consulted. Some materials at the National Archives in Yangon, which are currently made public for the period before 1953, have been utilized. Statistical books from China, Myanmar, and Thailand have also been consulted. In addition, interviews have been carried out with key informants in China, Myanmar, Thailand, and Taiwan.

Chapter Outlines

The book comprises a total of nine chapters, including the introduction and conclusion. After this introductory chapter, which lays out the book's structure, the second chapter establishes its empirical and theoretical foundations. The third chapter is a historical account of the borderland that traces the pattern of relations between valley states and upland people before the mid-twentieth century. Then the book delves into five empirical chapters that each look at different aspects of the complex state and nation building along the borderland area. Chapters 4 and 5 discuss two major political and military episodes since the start of the Cold War—the KMT troops in Burma and Thailand and communist insurgencies in the borderland—and their implications for the three states' attempts to consolidate their control over their respective borderland areas. Chapter 6 then portrays the dynamics of borderland economy and the dominance of both China and Thailand on Myanmar's borderland territory. In chapter 7, the book proceeds to a discussion of the comparative nation building among the three states and the implications for the ethnic minority groups and their national identities. Chapter 8 then analyzes the current ethnic politics along Myanmar's restive borderland with its ongoing conflict and peace negotiation process. More detailed sketches of the chapters follow.

Chapter 2: The Neighborhood Effect of State and Nation Building

The second chapter establishes both the empirical and theoretical foundations for the book. For illustrative purpose, it provides comparative statistics of how state and nation building in the borderland area differs among the three states. For state building, it offers a set of indicators, such as taxation, education, and health provisions, to measure how we can conceptualize the differences in each state's ability to provide for its citizens along the borderland area. It then offers a sketch of how nation-building efforts in the three states in the borderland area also differ from one another in both style and substance. The chapter goes on to discuss, in general, different existing theoretical approaches and proposes a novel theoretical framework that looks at state and nation building as an interactive process dependent on power balances and the nature of relations among neighboring states.

Chapter 3: The Historical Pattern of State Formation in Upland Southeast Asia

This chapter introduces readers to the historical background of the upland Southeast Asia borderland area. It analyzes how the upland area and its people were perceived by valley states, as well as attempts made by those states to approach them militarily and politically. It examines existing historiographies that originated from the perspectives of the Chinese, Myanmar, and Thai states, paying attention to how they used a variety of means—military, political, and economic—in their efforts to deal with the mosaic of people living in the upland area. At the same time, it pays attention to perspectives of the upland people themselves in terms of how they viewed their relations with those valley states, if such accounts are available. The purpose of the chapter is to put this common borderland area in a historical perspective, while emphasizing the overall lack of state and national consolidation of the territories and people there before the modern period. It thus sets up the stage for the series of major political and military upheavals that fundamentally transformed the logic of political relations in this upland area. The first of these historical events was the end of the Chinese civil war in 1949, resulting in the founding of the PRC, and the war's spillover into Burma and Thailand after the KMT's intrusion into the Shan State.

Chapter 4: Spillover of the Chinese Civil War and the Militarization of the Borderland

After the PRC's establishment, a section of the KMT army crossed the border into Burma and occupied parts of the Shan State.[30] Supported by the United States, the Republic of China in Taiwan, as well as Thailand, the KMT troops militarily destabilized the borderland area of China, Burma, and Thailand for several decades. This chapter analyzes the legacy of the KMT in the borderland area in terms of its impact on state building in the three countries.

In Burma, the KMT presence strengthened the military relative to the civilian government, which paved the way for decades of military rule in the country.[31] More directly relevant for the borderland is the militarization of many of the ethnic minority groups in the area, which led to the formation of many ethnic rebel groups fighting for independence or more autonomy from Burma.[32] Thus, the intrusion of the KMT into Burma played a sizable role in the fragmentation of that country in the peripheries, and also indirectly set in motion the militarized confrontation between the Burmese army and many of the estranged ethnic groups.

After the gradual relocation of the KMT to Thailand since the early 1960s, the Thai government recruited them for border patrol against communist infiltration. The legacy of the KMT episode for Thailand should be understood first in the context of the broader security alliance Thailand formed with the United States. By actively supporting US anti-communist activities, including the KMT, clandestine activities in Laos, and later the war in Vietnam, Thailand received large sums of economic and military aid from the United States. Later on, when Thailand faced its own communist insurgency, the KMT remnant troops also proved instrumental in Thai counter-insurgency campaigns.[33]

In the case of China, the KMT's presence in Burma presented an external threat for the new communist government. Although the KMT only managed to invade Yunnan a couple of times, in 1951 and 1952, and were easily repelled by the PLA, this nevertheless provided the rationale for militarization of the border region on the Chinese side. The communist government carried out ruthless counter-insurgency campaigns against the KMT remnants as well as other ethnic and local rebellions occurring in mountainous areas that resisted the communist regime's consolidation of power. Campaigns were also carried out to subdue the population in the name of suppressing counter-revolutionaries.[34] By the mid-1950s, however, much of the southwestern borderland area was securely under Beijing's control.

Chapter 5: Communist Revolutions at the Borderland

Chapter 5 traces the other major source of instability in the borderland area: China's support for communist insurgencies in Burma and Thailand. The domestic political radicalization in China in the mid-1960s manifested internationally in Mao's push to support the "People's War" in many Third World countries, which was also related to the PRC's competition with the Soviet Union to become leader of the international communist movement.[35] In Burma's case, it meant the PRC ramped up its support for the Communist Party of Burma's (CPB) military insurrection in 1967.[36]

The legacies of the CPB insurgency for Myanmar are profound. It meant the fundamental failure of Myanmar's state building and consolidation over the borderland territories that it claims as its own. The setup of the stable base area along the Sino-Myanmar border by the CPB prevented the Myanmar central government from accessing this area until the mid-1990s, after the collapse of the CPB in 1989 and the signing of a series of ceasefire treaties with various legacy ethnic rebel groups.[37] The most significant legacy of the CPB is the further militarization of various ethnic minority groups along the border area. Although the CPB leadership predominately comprised ethnic Bamar (the main ethnic group in the country), many of its foot soldiers were heavily recruited from local ethnic minorities in the borderland area. Therefore, after the collapse of the CPB, ethnic insurgencies continued because various ethnic rebels formed their own militant organizations.

The CCP also offered support for the Communist Party of Thailand's (CPT) insurgency starting in 1965.[38] Although the CPT also recruited heavily from various ethnic minority groups in the mountains, the Thai state was better equipped with more resources and international support for its counterinsurgency work.[39] Heavily funded by the United States, Thailand carried out military campaigns against the CPT, but also undertook many nation-building projects targeting the ethnic minority "hill tribes" in an effort to assimilate them into the Thai nation-state.[40] Thus, for Thailand, the

CPT insurgency instilled a strong sense of urgency, which led to a counteractive campaign of state and nation building by the government, with US support. The Thai nationalist emphasis on nation, king, religion, and the image of royal benevolence was imposed, and as a result, spread throughout the area.[41]

In China's own case, the initiation of the Cultural Revolution resulted in large numbers of urban Red Guards being sent to the borderland areas in Yunnan.[42] Through the settlement of Han Chinese youth in the borderland area, the Chinese state somehow created a human dimension in its consolidation of the border region. It was during this period that direct interpersonal contact occurred between various ethnic minority groups and the dominant Han Chinese, which also coincided with an education system being set up to teach the Chinese language to minorities.[43] Violence unleashed through the Cultural Revolution empowered the Chinese state to penetrate deeply into the most remote areas in Yunnan, on the one hand, while at the same time, the Han Chinese "sent-down" youth unwittingly became agents for the cultural consolidation of the borderland.

Chapter 6: Dynamics of Transboundary Economic Flows

After discussing the two main political and military incidents that set in motion the interactive dynamics of state building in the borderland area in chapter 5, chapter 6 goes on to discuss the economic logic of cross-border relations. To illustrate the economic dynamics of borderland state building as a result of economic asymmetry between Myanmar and its two more powerful neighbors, this chapter mainly examines two inter-related processes.

The first process examined is cross-border movement of goods and people between China, Myanmar, and Thailand and specifically, the phenomenon of labor migration from Myanmar to Thailand,[44] as well as the integrated trade networks across the borderland.[45] As a result of the economic disparity and political chaos in Myanmar, Thailand has been the most popular destination for Myanmar migrants, especially ethnic Shan—about one-third of the 1.5 million Myanmar migrants in Thailand come from the Shan State.[46] Meanwhile, trade networks also link China with Myanmar and Thailand. Goods made in China and Thailand go to Myanmar, and natural resource products from Myanmar flow in the other direction. Indeed, the business network in the borderland area is an organic one that is oriented toward both the Chinese and the Thai sides of the border. Border cities such as Mai Sai in Thailand and Ruili in China are centers for the cross-border movement of people and goods. More importantly, the economic gaps between China and Myanmar mean that Chinese businesspeople have started to penetrate and dominate the Myanmar market.

The chapter also discusses cross-border resource development dominated by Chinese as well as Thai capital in Myanmar. Here, it mainly looks at agribusiness as well as investment in the hydropower, lumber, and mining sectors in Myanmar's Kachin and Shan states.[47] The purpose of the chapter is to illustrate the centrifugal forces across the borderlands that reorient the local economy toward northern Thailand and southern Yunnan province in China and away from Myanmar. Thus, Myanmar's lack of economic sovereignty along the border can be attributed, to a great extent, to the economic imbalance between it and its two more developed neighbors.

Chapter 7: Comparative Nation Building across the Borderland Area

After discussing the phenomenon of state building as a neighborhood effect, chapter 7 shifts attention to nation building and specifically, to how different nationalist ideologies in these three countries have affected the politics of national identity among various ethnic minority groups living along the borders. The Chinese government recognizes 56 ethnic groups with provision of "nominal" ethnic autonomy. So, the Chinese state, at least on paper, allows for the institutional provision of autonomous government, minority language education, religious and cultural expression, and so forth.[48] The Thai national discourse, on the other hand, claims everyone living within the territorial boundaries of Thailand is Thai and does not officially recognizing ethnic minorities who live on the kingdom's peripheries. At the same time, at certain points in history, Thailand has made irredentist claims to pan-Tai ethnic groups in Myanmar as well as in China.[49] The Myanmar government officially recognizes 135 ethnic groups and established 7 ethnic states. However, the long history of military rule in the country meant that ethnic cultural expression has been highly restricted, and ethnic schools are still banned. More significantly, the state has heavily repressed its ethnic-minority groups in their fight for self-determination.[50]

The chapter then examines how close ethnic linkages between the Shan and Thai manifest in Thailand's interest in supporting the Shan nationalist movements as part of its pan-Tai sentiment.[51] Although Thailand has forfeited all its claims to other Tai territories in neighboring states since the end of WWII, it continues to heavily influence them culturally and religiously. In the Myanmar Shan State, this manifests itself in the way in which the Shan are culturally oriented toward Thailand. Shan monasteries and monks have close ties to their counterparts in Thailand, and Thai pop music is popular among the Shan.[52] Additionally, support by the Thai government and public, although mainly symbolic, is crucial for maintaining Shan nationalism against Myanmar.[53]

The chapter then compares the implications of different nationalist ideologies and practices for common cross-border ethnic minorities between China and Myanmar. Compared with China, Myanmar's treatment of its ethnic minorities has been much more brutal as the country has been engulfed in more than half a century of civil war. The military campaigns against various ethnic rebel organizations have intensified repression against ethnic minorities in the Kachin and Shan states.[54] During the past three or more decades, the contrast across the China-Myanmar borderland area has been evident in the stability and economic prosperity found on the Chinese side of the border. Many ethnic minority groups across the border see China as the place where ethnic minorities are better treated than in Myanmar. Relative depravation explains this very well.

Chapter 8: Continual Contestation at the China-Myanmar Border

Chapter 8 looks at the ongoing ethnic conflicts along the Sino-Myanmar borderland area and explores ways in which these conflicts continue to implicate Myanmar's state and nation-building process. It first discusses the ceasefires in Myanmar since the late 1980s between the central government and various ethic rebel groups. Specifically, the chapter examines three prominent ethnic rebel groups: the KIA, with which the Myanmar national army has ongoing military clashes; the MNDAA, the Kokang rebel group that the Myanmar central military has defeated twice, in 2009 and 2015, solidifying its control over the Kokang area in northern Shan State; and the United Wa State Army, which despite a 2011 break in the ceasefire between it and the

Myanmar central government, has so far not faced direct military pressure and continues to maintain a high level of political and cultural autonomy. Altogether, the chapter offers a more up-to-date analysis of the challenges facing Myanmar's state and nation-building process and its implications for bilateral relations with China and Thailand.

Chapter 9: Conclusion

The book concludes with some theoretical reflection on the neighborhood effect of state and nation building. More pertinent to the borderland area examined in this book, it also looks at recent developments in China's push for more regional economic integration and their implications for both Myanmar and Thailand.

2
The Neighborhood Effect of State and Nation Building

After half an hour on a bumpy road, the car took me to one of the largest camps for internally displaced persons (IDP) in the KIA-controlled area. It was the summer of 2013, and several thousand people who had lost their homes due to the fighting between the KIA and the Myanmar military were housed here. Throughout Kachin State, as a result of the ongoing military clashes, there were many temporary IDP camps, where after years of internal conflict, large sections of the ethnic population in the borderland area have been forced to live in those makeshift dwellings with only very basic shelter. The camp had a very limited supply of electricity, and even that was through a connection with the Chinese side of the border, across from a little creek. There were limited economic activities, and many people crossed the border to China to find temporary labor. One small school with only a couple of teachers provided very basic education for the children.

In Laiza, there are a total of seven schools, including one high school, set up by the KIO, the civilian counterpart of the KIA. Since the area is under the de facto control of the KIA, its school curricula are in both the Burmese and Kachin languages. In fact, it is only in the KIA-controlled area that the Kachin language is taught in the school system; in other parts of Kachin State under Myanmar government control, such bilingual education is banned in the state school system. Thus, ordinary Kachin people who want to learn their own language cannot do so in the state school system, except in KIA-controlled areas or informally in some Kachin churches.

Indeed, this prohibition of ethnic language education is a common practice throughout the ethnic states in Myanmar. In the neighboring Shan State, people can only learn Shan languages in monasteries or in private schools set up by Shan nationalists. In the outskirts of Kengtung, in the center of eastern Shan State, my friend Duwan, a Shan monk, once took me on a tour at a local Shan (Tai-Kuen) school with a loose connection to the SSA, where about a hundred pupils were studying. The school is a primary school built on a hilltop in the compound of a Shan monastery. Here children of school age learn three languages—Burmese, English, and Shan—and teachers in the school print their own education materials in Shan. However, due to the lack of funding and facilities, the level of education is very basic, and they run the risk of the children's education background not being recognized by the Myanmar state school system.

This chapter introduces some general descriptions of various state and nation-building efforts along the borders of China, Myanmar, and Thailand and provides a set of statistics commonly utilized to measure state and nation building. It engages with existing political science literature in general, and then proposes an alternative perspective on how state and nation building in one country can be related to events and circumstances in neighboring countries, that is, the neighborhood effect of state and nation building.

Variations in State and Nation Building across the Borderland

When we look at the three neighboring states of China, Myanmar, and Thailand, we can see that they vary significantly in terms of state capacity at the national level. One of the most commonly used indicators of this is state tax revenue as a percentage of Gross Domestic Product (GDP), which is the conventional gauge of a state's extractive capacity.[1] The tax ratio reflects its ability to extract resources from both individuals and corporate actors. As figure 2.1 shows, for a selected number of years, Myanmar's state extractive capacity has been much lower than that of either Thailand or China.[2] In 2004, only about 3% of Myanmar's GDP came from tax revenue. That same year, close to 9% of China's GDP came from tax revenue, while in Thailand the figure was 16%. Although the most recent data are not available, it is certain that, overall, Myanmar's capacity is not in the same league as its two more powerful neighbors.

From figure 2.2, we can also see that China and Thailand have become much richer than Myanmar. According to World Bank Development Indicators, Myanmar's GDP per capita barely exceeded US$1,000, while Thailand's was close to US$6,000, and China's almost US$8,000 by 2014. A few other indicators of human development in terms of education and health reveal similar differences, as we can see from table 2.1. Although Myanmar's adult literacy rate has mostly caught up with both China and

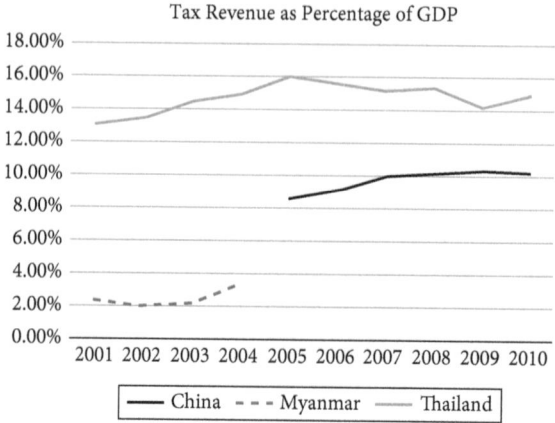

Figure 2.1 Tax Revenue as Percentage of GDP

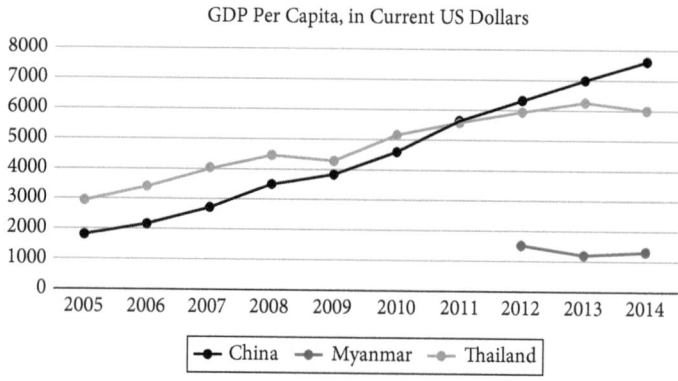

Figure 2.2 GDP per Capita, in Current US Dollars

Thailand—all three countries are in the ninetieth percentile of adult literacy at the national level—there are still discrepancies in the overall provision of education. For example, 51% of students entered secondary school in Myanmar, compared with 86% in Thailand and 96% in China. This indicates that Myanmar's education level overall is still very rudimentary, and the state has not been able to provide more than a very basic level of education. In terms of health, the infant mortality rate is much higher in Myanmar than in China or Thailand. Life expectancy is likewise much lower in Myanmar than in the other two countries. Thus, at the national level there is strong evidence

Table 2.1 Additional Indicators of Human Development in China, Myanmar, and Thailand in Selected Years

	China	Myanmar	Thailand
Adult Literacy Rate (%)	95.12 (2010)	92.79 (2013)	96.43 (2010)
Secondary School Enrollment Rate (%)	96.2 (2013)	51.3 (2013)	86.2 (2013)
Infant Mortality Rate (%)	0.92 (2015)	3.95 (2015)	1.05 (2015)
Life Expectancy (years)	76 (2014)	66 (2014)	74 (2014)

World Bank Development Indicators, bracketed numbers indicate the years most recent data are available.

showing the discrepancy in terms of state capacity and how much each state has been able to provide for its own citizens.

However, these data are at the national level and by no means represent the same levels of state building in the borderland area. There are lots of reasons to suspect that at the remote borderland territories the presence of the state might be much less evident. Especially in more remote mountainous areas that characterize the borderland among the three countries, the geographical barriers the state must overcome to penetrate society and provide for citizens can be quite formidable. However, data at the local level are very limited and inconsistent, especially in the Myanmar case. Certainly, it might be that the Myanmar government does not want to publish comprehensive data, but the more likely explanation is that for much of the borderland area discussed in this book, the central government lacks the capacity even to make its presence known—as we have already discussed in the previous chapter—let alone to provide basic infrastructure for the people living there. As a result, the data presented here are simply for illustration purposes and by no means represent a valid across-the-board comparison of state building in the borderland area.

There are other indicators to measure such differences, such as the 2009–2010 UNICEF Multiple Indicator Cluster Survey (MICS), which measures and records the situations of children and women in Myanmar, including data on the Kachin and Shan states.[3] From figure 2.3, we can see that several of the key basic development indicators, which highly correlate with state capacity, are overwhelmingly unsatisfactory. The primary school enrollment rate in Shan State is much lower than the Myanmar national average or that

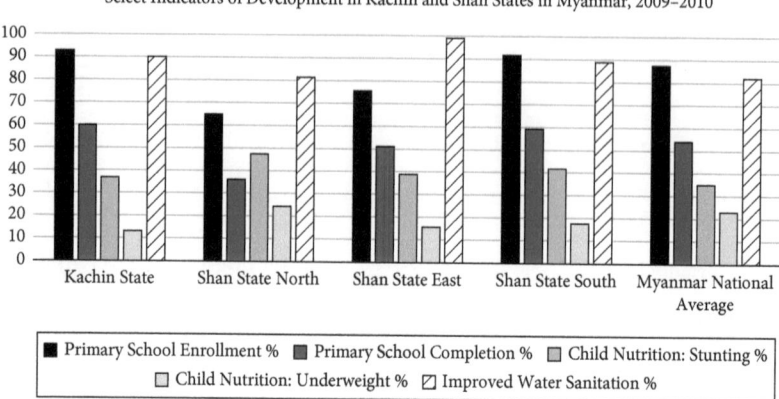

Figure 2.3 Select Indicators of Development in Kachin and Shan States in Myanmar, 2009–2010

of Kachin State. Especially in Shan State North, where it borders China, and Shan State East, where it borders China, Thailand, and Laos, enrollment rates are significantly lower. In addition, primary school completion rates are much lower overall, which indicates the rudimentary level of education in the borderland area in Myanmar. In terms of health provision for children, the conditions are quite abysmal. At the national level, about 35% of Myanmar's children are stunted. However, in northern Shan State almost 50% are. As for underweight children, the northern Shan State data indicate a higher rate there than the national average, at 24.1%.

For comparison, the UNICEF MICS of 2012 reported a much higher level of development in northern Thailand.[4] As we can see in figure 2.4, although the reported data vary slightly in terms of the measurement index, some of the comparable ones can be utilized. For example, in northern Thailand only 7.8% of children are underweight, much fewer than in Shan State. In addition, almost 98% of children in Northern Thailand are vaccinated against measles. Primary school attendance is also higher than in Shan State. But more striking is the higher rate of secondary school attendance in northern Thailand, at more than 80%. Such indicators suggest that as the level of economic development has increased in northern Thailand, the capacity of the Thai state has also improved, in its ability to provide more comprehensive education and health care for its population in the borderland area.

No such comparable MICS data are available for China. Instead, data in table 2.2 are collected from statistical yearbooks from China's Yunnan

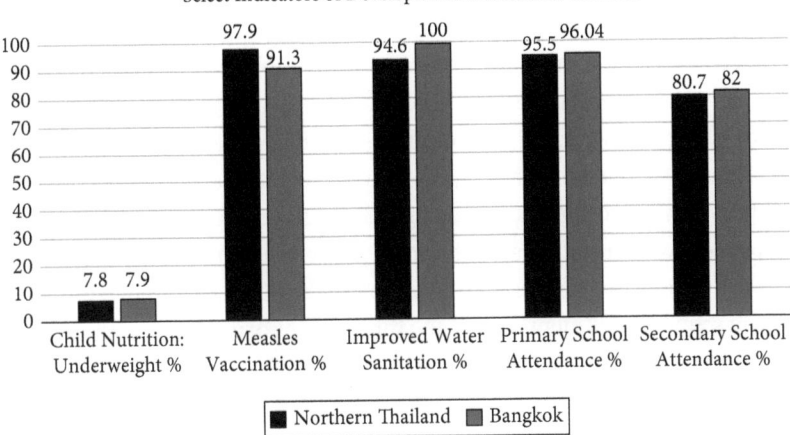

Figure 2.4 Select Indicators of Development in Northern Thailand

Table 2.2 Yunnan Province School Enrollment Rate

	Primary School (%)	Middle School (%)	High School (%)	Higher Education (%)
2007	97.59	99.63	45.71	14.61
2008	98.29	102.21	52.00	16.17
2009	98.29	103.12	58.30	17.57
2010	99.71	105.36	65.00	20.02
2011	99.61	105.24	70.00	23.00
2012	99.57	106.04	71.20	24.30
2013	99.50	106.56	72.10	25.80

Statistical Yearbook, Yunnan Province, http://www.chinadataonline.com/

province in recent years. The Chinese government has, overall, provided comprehensive education for its citizens in the borderland area. In 2013, for example, 99.5% of children were enrolled in primary school. The enrollment rate for middle school is actually higher than 100%, which means there is migration from other parts of China to this borderland area. The same can also be said of the health care and social welfare provisions. All such indicators point to the fact that China has a much higher level of state capacity than Myanmar, especially in the borderland area between the two countries.

In terms of nation building, however, comparable data to show the variations of "nation-ness" across the borderland area are much more difficult to obtain. One possible proxy is through the reach of state education, which itself is highly correlated with state capacity. Conventional literature on nation building shows that specific nationalist ideologies can be propagated among the population through state education systems.[5] While empirical data to measure the effectiveness of such nationalist education are lacking, the variations in school enrollment among the three neighboring states in the borderland can be a rough proxy measurement of its reach.

The other way to get a sense of the discrepancy in nation building is to look at existing ethnonationalist movements across the borderland. Here the only active groups are in Myanmar, where along the borderland there are still several ethnic rebel groups with varying degrees of ethnonationalist claims. Many have established special regions and vague ceasefire agreements with the Myanmar government.[6] For example, there are a few special regions along the borderland area between China, Myanmar, and Thailand, where different ethnic rebels have been holding varying degrees of autonomous control. Before August 2009, when Kokang was taken over by the Myanmar military, it was the Shan State Special Region No. 1, where the MNDAA under the leadership of Peng Jiasheng used to administer the area with strong Chinese influence. More prominent than Kokang is the Wa State, or the so-called Special Region No. 2, where the UWSA claims to be the largest non-government military force, administering two separate pieces of territory, one close to the Chinese border and the other adjacent to the Thai border.[7] There are also various Shan nationalist armed groups, such as the SSA-North and the SSA-South, who sometimes collaborate with government forces and other times clash with them. Then there is also the KIA, which has very strong Kachin nationalist claims against the Myanmar central government.[8] On top of that, several other smaller ethnic rebel groups roam the borderland area. Although it is difficult to gauge the strength of these rebel groups' ethnonationalist claims, it is reasonable to argue that various ethnic groups along the border have consistently opposed Myanmar nationalist ideology.[9]

Although China is also home to prominent ethnonationalist groups that demand more autonomy or independence, such as the Tibetans and the Uyghurs, the ethnic minority groups along its border with Myanmar are nonetheless politically inactive while reporting high levels of assimilation into the Han Chinese-dominated mainstream. In the early years after the CCP came into power, policies providing local ethnic autonomy encouraged some ethnic minority elites to join the Chinese government. During periods of political instability and repression, such as the Cultural Revolution, many ethnic minorities along the border opted to cross it and seek refuge in Burma rather than take up arms against the Chinese state. China's greater capacity to suppress such military activities thus highly restricted how much ethnic minority nationalist mobilization could occur. Ultimately, the Chinese state has been more successful in implementing its nation-building policies in southern Yunnan.

For Thailand, the only prominent ethnonationalist groups that have consistently challenged the Thai government's version of nation-building efforts are the separatist movements in the southern provinces of Pattani, Songkra, and Yala.[10] The northern ethnic minorities, which the Thai government refers to as "hill tribes" or "highland population," have been relatively successfully incorporated into the Thai nation-state for the past few decades. Except during the time of communist insurgency in the mid-1960s when some ethnic minority groups, such as the Meo/Hmong, joined the armed resistance, the highland development project sponsored by the Thai government and monarchy has made a substantial impact on incorporating the peripheral ethnic minority people into the Thai nation-state through its strong emphasis on education in the Thai language.[11] Today, in northern Thailand, there are no active ethnonationalist groups who mobilize against the state. Thus over the past few decades, China and Thailand have been more successful in their respective nation-building projects in the borderland area than Myanmar. In conjunction with the variation in state building just discussed, how does one explain such variation in nation building?

Theories of State and Nation Building

Existing literature on state building comes from different strands. The most prominent one, the so-called bellicist theory pioneered by Charles Tilly and others, looks at state building as a historical process that emerged symbiotically with war making, and has consistently emphasized the crucial role war played in the development of the European state system.[12] As Tilly argues, "To the extent that they are successful in subduing their rivals outside or inside the territory they claim, the wielders of coercion find themselves obliged to administer the lands, goods, and people they acquire; they become involved in extraction of resources, distribution of goods, services, and income, and adjudication of disputes."[13] Thus, in order to effectively fund the war making enterprise, European rulers became more efficient in their revenue collection, improved civil administration in exchange for civilian cooperation, and established nationalist symbols to unify the population they governed. In such processes, the foundations of the modern bureaucratic state were built. As the famous saying goes, "States make war, and war makes the state."[14]

The successful development of the European state system has invariably been compared with the rest of the world, where scholars have sought to explain variations in state formation. In Latin America, for example, scholars have pointed out how the lack of interstate total wars historically stunted the growth of bureaucratic states there.[15] Lacking the need for mass mobilization for total wars, "Limited wars rarely leave positive institutional legacies and often have long-term costs," such as fiscal or debt crisis, professional military rather than popular participation, alienation from patriotic symbols, and economic downturn.[16] Thus, in contrast with the European experience, strong states did not form in Latin America due to the lack of need for mass mobilization, and the easy availability of international financing also made state rulers more willing to borrow money to fund their war-making efforts rather than tax their own populations. Subsequently many Latin American governments became heavily indebted yet did not penetrate deeply into their respective societies.

Similar to Latin America, post-independence Africa has also lacked overall the total wars that Europe experienced.[17] The state system that African countries inherited from European colonization, with its fixed boundaries, meant they faced little existential pressure.[18] As Jeffrey Herbst points out, "The system that has preserved the continent's boundaries has not been significantly tested because most leaders considered it obvious that they were better off with their inherited boundaries than they would be in a chaotic war situation where sovereignty or considerable territory might be lost."[19] Instead, much of the warfare in Africa has tended to be internal and interethnic, and the African states have more difficulty building uniform national identities.[20] Furthermore, the weak bureaucracies meant insufficient capacity to extract revenue from people; instead, many governments rely on taxation of foreign goods, thus further diminishing the prospect of building strong institutions to connect the population with the state.[21]

In contrast with the Latin American and African experiences, East Asia (including both Northeast and Southeast Asia) as a region has suffered perennial devastation by both interstate and civil wars.[22] During the modern period, it has been devastated by Japanese aggression during WWII, the Chinese Civil War, the Korean War, wars in Indochina, and ethnonationalist and ideological civil insurgencies throughout Southeast Asia during and after the Cold War. With such widespread warfare in the region, both in terms of preparation for war and wars that have actually broken out, it is no wonder that quite a few strong states emerged in the region, such as several East Asian countries. Richard Stubbs, in his study of the relationship between war preparation and economic development in East Asia, points out "[Nowhere] has this lack of attention to the economic consequences of war and preparation for war detracted more from our understanding of events than in East and Southeast Asia."[23] Similarly, Doner, Ritchie, and Slater compared several Northeast and Southeast Asian states, pointing out that successful developmental states with impressive capabilities, such as South Korea, Taiwan, and Singapore, "emerged from the challenges of delivering side payments to restive popular sectors under conditions of extreme geopolitical insecurity."[24]

Other than this bellicist approach to understanding systematic development and underdevelopment in state building around the world, there is also significant scholarship on domestic factors that might facilitate or hinder state capacity building. Factors such as geography and regime types have been theorized to explain such variations. In the African context, the historically low population density meant that in much of sub-Saharan Africa, the political logic of power projection was totally different from that in either Europe or Asia. Even though many African states have made significant progress after independence, the large, sparsely populated open spaces have continued to deter effective physical control.[25] The role of political geography has also featured prominently in the civil war literature.[26] As the antithesis of state building, studies on civil wars have consistently examined factors that might facilitate the outbreak of civil wars or hinder effective consolidation efforts by the central state. For example, scholars have emphasized that rough, mountainous terrain can significantly deter the state's capacity to project centralized power, thus creating conditions conducive to civil war.[27] Furthermore, there are studies that link regime types to civil conflicts. Authoritarian systems are overall more likely to experience civil conflict than democracies.[28]

Closely intertwined with state building, nation building has also been explained through similar approaches. For example, war has a symbiotic relationship with nationalist indoctrination. Interstate wars often have a strong impact domestically on the populace, which then often creates a "rally behind the flag" effect.[29] Wartime mobilization typically has a strong dose of nationalist indoctrination. War against an external other can substantially improve internal solidarity and thus can help domestic nation building.[30] This is why wars against foreign aggression often feature prominently in nationalist education.

Regarding domestic factors, ethnic diversity and demographic patterns have been noted as crucial factors in whether nation building is successful or not. An ethnically diverse country, by its very nature, finds it more difficult to create an overarching nationalist ideology that incorporates every ethnic group without one dominating another. Thus, ethnic fragmentation and, especially, polarization have been noted as barriers to nation-building efforts to establish a uniform citizenry.[31] Similarly, ethnic demographic distribution, such as ethnic group concentration, is a crucial factor that might hinder national consolidation.[32] Economic horizontal inequality between diverse ethnic groups has also been noted as conducive for ethnic strife, leading those ethnic groups to rebel against the state.[33] Exclusion of ethnic minorities from the political process has often been noted as detrimental to nation building.[34]

The Neighborhood Effect of State and Nation Building

However, all these explanations tend to consider state building as purely confined within the territorial boundaries of states. It seems that the reasons why some states are more successful than others in state building have overall been attributed to their war making capacity, geographical features, or particular ethnic population distribution. Certainly, such factors matter a great deal, as we have already seen in the vast literature that supports such arguments. However, these approaches have generally missed out an important dimension of how states undertake their state-building projects, which is the effect from neighboring states. Indeed, not many countries in the world are isolated island states, and most share borders with other states. It is not difficult to conceptualize how state building in one country might be highly contingent upon similar processes occurring among its neighbors.

For the past decade, there has been a robust trend in studying the international dimension of civil conflict: going beyond country-specific factors, scholars have examined closely how factors spanning national boundaries affect civil conflict. Using the terms "bad neighbors and bad neighborhoods," Weiner points out that for studies on refugee flows, there is a geographic cluster effect: "Regions with a number of countries in which violence and brutality impel large numbers of people to cross international borders in search for security."[35] Further studies indeed have highlighted this contagion effect of civil war, in that conflict in one country easily spills over into neighboring states.[36] Refugee inflows can increase the burden on the neighboring host state. Worse still, militants can also easily cross the border into neighboring states, which can significantly destabilize them, as observed in the aftermath of the genocide in Rwanda, when Hutu militants crossed over into the Democratic Republic of Congo.[37]

Rebels in one country often use the neighboring states as sanctuaries, as "External bases are tactically desirable for rebels because the state is better able to conduct counterinsurgency operations at home than abroad."[38] Thus, if rebels can find sanctuaries across the border, they can escape the brunt of state repression, which helps them to survive. On the other hand, if neighboring states are adversaries, one might intentionally provide sanctuary for rebels so as to undermine the other. For example, Thailand provided shelter for the Khmer Rouge so as to weaken the Vietnamese-supported government in Cambodia in the late 1970s.[39]

Other than hosting rebels, states might meddle in each other's domestic affairs if they are adversaries. Often, the intervening party uses its military and economic capacity to influence the conflict mechanism in its neighbors so as to produce an outcome it considers favorable.[40] Meddling in neighbors' domestic affairs thus serves a variety of domestic and foreign policy purposes, such as "ideological contestation, regime change, the protection of kin group, the pursuit of disputed territory, competition between rivals for regional status and influence, and so on."[41] Other than direct military and economic support, states can also use a variety of subversive measures to undermine their neighbors. Indeed, Lee finds consistent evidence around the world in supporting how hostile neighbors can weaken each other through subversive meddling.

Therefore, if we accept that civil conflict and state building are antithetical to each other, then theoretically speaking we should pay attention to how state building in one country can influence the same process in neighboring states. We should treat state building as an interactive process between domestic politics in one state and the international dimension that relates to its neighbors. Having said that, we need to acknowledge that not every neighboring state is equally endowed in influencing state building in other states, and thus this neighborhood effect would take on different shapes under various configurations of relations among neighboring states. Here, I propose to examine two aspects of the international relations among neighboring states to theorize under what conditions different forms of neighborhood effect of state building can take place.

The first aspect is power symmetry among neighboring states, for which we can broadly categorize a dyad of countries as either asymmetrical or at parity with each other in terms of power capabilities.[42] The other aspect is the overall relation between two neighboring states, for which they can be coarsely defined as adversarial or amicable to each other. By juxtaposing these two aspects, we have a rough projection of conditions under which different forms of neighborhood effect on state building can take shape (see table 2.3).[43]

In the context where there is power asymmetry between two neighboring states, the more powerful one essentially has greater capability to influence the state-building process in the other state. If these two states were on adversarial terms with each other, either due to historical feuds, territorial disputes, or ideological differences, then the more powerful state would intend influencing the other according to its own interests. Here, therefore, we

Table 2.3 Theories of Neighborhood Effect of State Building Dynamics as Dyads

	Asymmetrical (state A more powerful than state B)	Parity (state A and B with similar power capability)
Adversarial	State A: political/military meddling State B: fragmentation of state control of the borderland	States A & B: confrontation and militarization of the mutual borderland
Amicable	State A: economic domination State B: diminished economic sovereignty over the borderland	States A & B: low neighborhood effect over the borderland

are more likely to observe a case of intensive meddling by the more powerful state in its neighbor's state-building process along the borderland region. There are many historical cases of this, Germany's military aggression toward the Sudetenland in Czechoslovakia during WWII being an excellent example.[44] If, on the other hand, these two states were amicable to each other, then the powerful state would have less incentive to change the other one according its own liking. Yet, due to power asymmetry between the two, the more powerful state's influence on its neighbor's state-building process would still be felt, although to a lesser extent and often in a more benign way than in the first scenario. Barring political meddling, the most likely dynamic in this scenario is the extensive economic influence of the more powerful state on the lesser states, whereby the latter lose much or parts of their economic control over the borderland area. For example, the relationship dynamic between the United States and Mexico and Canada fits well with this scenario, where the United States exerts significant dominance over the borderland economies.[45]

If the two neighboring states were of relatively equal power capabilities, then the dynamic between them would also be different. If the two states were adversarial to each other, then we would most likely observe heightened tension between them. However, due to the relative equal capability of both countries, neither would be able to overpower the other in the borderland area. Therefore, the most likely outcome is militarization along the border with significant military coercion and destruction. For example, during the war between Iran and Iraq in the 1980s, Iran supported the Supreme Council for the Islamic Revolution in Iraq while Iraq supported the Mujahedin-e-Khalq in Iran, with the goal of sabotaging each other's domestic politics and scizing control of the borderland territory.[46] On the other hand, if the two states are friendly to each other, then we would have a case of relatively peaceful coexistence, and the neighborhood effect on the borderland would be low, which is the case for many European states under the Schengen Agreement.[47]

When nation building is concerned, the neighborhood effect is closely intertwined with the state building dynamic just laid out, yet it is also conditioned upon specific ethnic group distribution and relations with external kin groups. Specifically for ethnic groups across the border, their ability to resist the nation-building projects of the respective states where they reside depends on whether they have a more powerful external kin state. If they do not, it depends on whether they have external kin groups in neighboring states who experience better treatment than themselves (see table 2.4).

The first set of scenarios deals with ethnic minority groups that have external kin state relations, that is, ethnic groups straddling national borders but with linkages to external kin states. External kin states that are more powerful than the countries in which these ethnic groups reside are more likely to provide support for these ethnic groups, who would subsequently have more resources and cultural repertoires to resist the nation-building projects imposed on them by the majority ethnic group in the country where they live. This line of argument is drawn from Rogers Brubaker's theorization of how external ethnic linkages and the support they offer for ethnic groups can fundamentally change the dynamics of nationalist politics within a country.[48]

In *Nationalism Reframed*, Brubaker introduces a conceptualization of nationalism as a triadic relationship between a nationalizing state, the substantial, self-conscious, organized, and politically alienated national minorities in the state, and the external kin state of the minority group. In this conceptualization, there is a nationalizing state, in the image of the majority group, that uses state power to promote its specific interests in ethno-cultural terms, such as giving its own language, culture, or religion official status at the national level. There is also the minority group, which tries to defend its cultural autonomy and resist the majority's nationalizing and assimilation efforts. Furthermore, the external kin state of the minority group also purports to "monitor the condition, promote the welfare, support the activities and institutions, assert the rights, and protect the interests of 'their' ethnonational kin."[49] Thus, ethnic minority groups that have stronger external kin states would be better prepared to resist the nation-building project imposed on them by the nationalizing state. On the other hand, if the external kin state is similar or even weaker, then it would have much less capacity to support and

Table 2.4 The Neighborhood Effect of Nation Building on Cross-Border Ethnic Minority Groups

	Asymmetrical	Parity
Ethnic minority group with external kin state	More external support	Less external support
Ethnic minority group without external kin state	More cross-border comparison	Less cross-border comparison

monitor the situation of the ethnic minority group, and thus would be less relevant in determining how the minority group would be able to mobilize politically.

The other set of scenarios involves ethnic groups across the borders of two neighboring states who are minorities in both, meaning they do not have external kin states. For these ethnic groups, a comparison between the different nationalist ideologies and practices they are subject to under the nation-building projects of the neighboring states will influence their evaluation of their respective living conditions and determine their preference for one situation or the other. Thus, if they perceive that their external kin groups are treated better in the neighboring state, then they are more likely to develop grievances toward the state they inhabit. In this situation, for ethnic groups that have external kin living in a more powerful and developed state, then these groups are more likely to develop negative perceptions of their home state, complain about their own situation, and subsequently demand more political representation.[50] Additionally, their external kin, even though they do not have the backing of a state, might still have more resources to help their less fortunate brethren by mobilizing to support them.

Concluding Remarks

This chapter presents some illustrative statistics about the comparative state and nation building across the borderland area between China, Myanmar, and Thailand. It then proceeds to offer a novel theoretical framework to analyze the neighborhood effect of state and nation building, and how power balance and relations among neighboring states can have substantial influences on the outcome. Before we proceed to the empirical chapters discussing how this neighborhood effect plays out in this specific borderland area, the next chapter provides a historical perspective of the state and nation formation process in the three neighboring countries of China, Myanmar, and Thailand as it relates to the borderland.

3

The Historical Pattern of State Formation in Upland Southeast Asia

In the center of Kengtung (Chiang Tung) stood a big hotel complex, the Amazing Kengtung Resort, which was until recently called the New Kyiangtong Hotel.[1] This multi-storied hotel complex features Burmese-style rooftops together with a swimming pool and huge gardens. The hotel is built on the grounds of the last Kengtung sawbwa's palace, which was built in 1905 in the Imperial Indian style and demolished by the Myanmar military in 1991.[2] Although there is an airport in Kengtung that serves domestic flights, I arrived at the city by crossing the Thai-Myanmar land border from Mae Sai to Taichileik where I took a bus. The bus trip was long and bumpy, over a mountain road first built by the invading Thai army in 1942. Despite its historical prominence as a rival of Lan Na (now in Northern Thailand) and Chiang Rung (now Jinghong in southern Yunnan's Xishuangbanna[3] prefecture), modern-day Kengtung has become a nondescript backwater with drab architecture and a depressed economy, especially in comparison to Chiang Mai and Jinghong.

The last sawbwa of Kengtung was Sawbwa Sailong, who was crowned in 1947 after years of education in Britain and Australia.[4] However, after the signing of the Panglong Agreement in 1947, the Shan states and Burma proper together gained independence from Britain as a union republic, which meant the power of the Kengtung sawbwa was significantly reduced starting in 1948. In 1959, all the Shan sawbwas lost most of their authority and privileges after the first coup of Ne Win, whereby the military caretaker government arranged the handover of power from the hereditary sawbwas to the Union of Burma government.[5] Finally, after the coup of 1962, Ne Win abolished the entire sawbwa system in the Shan states and the last Kengtung sawbwa, Sailong, was imprisoned for six years. After his release, he lived in Rangoon until his death in 1997. Most of the family members of the Kengtung sawbwa are now in exile in North America or Thailand, with little connection to their ancestral homeland. And in today's Kengtung, the city has undergone significant Burmanization.

Because of the sizable Myanmar military force stationed there, little of local Tai Khun cultural expression can be easily observed, except in rural areas outside the city limits.

The demise of the sawbwa system in Burma represented formally the final elimination of the myriad Tai principalities in upper mainland Southeast Asia.[6] Historically, many of these Tai principalities, called muang, dotted the lowland valleys that stretched from Southwest China to mainland Southeast Asia and all the way to India's Assam.[7] At the same time, there were large numbers of other ethnic groups living in mountainous areas who sometimes fought with these Tai principalities and at other times remained far from any state power. Furthermore, these Tai principalities all had different relationships with larger and more powerful political entities around them, namely the Chinese dynasties, Burmese kingdoms, and the Kingdom of Siam. How such premodern transnational relations functioned and how they were transformed before the mid-twentieth century is the topic of this chapter.

This chapter discusses the historical links between three main Tai principalities in upland Southeast Asia: Chiang Tung, as representative of the modern Burmese Shan states; Chiang Rung, as representative of the Tai principalities in contemporary southern Yunnan; and Lan Na, centered in Chiang Mai, and representative of the Tai principalities in modern-day northern Thailand. It also examines their relationships with Burma/Myanmar, China, and Siam/Thailand, as a proxy for understanding the workings of premodern transnational relations in upland mainland Southeast Asia. There is a short section on the political situation of the ethnic groups in the mountains, and their relationship with lowland polities will also be discussed in tandem. The chapter then examines how European colonialism in Southeast Asia generated a new dynamic of state formation in the upland Southeast Asia borderland. Finally, the chapter discusses the process of state consolidation by each of three states since the early twentieth century that set the stage for the post-WWII abolition of the sawbwa system in Burma, the elimination of the tusi system in China, and the consolidation of the Siamese bureaucratic state in the north.

The Tai Principalities

The Tai political system throughout upland Southeast Asia has been described as a loose set of polities, or muang, with complex relationships among themselves as well as with the larger political entities around them. The system was mandala-like, comprising concentric circles of political power, which meant "a particular and often unstable situation in a vaguely definable geographical area without fixed boundaries and where smaller centers tended to look in all directions for security."[8] In this muang system, there was a hierarchical relationship between the greater and lesser principalities, cemented through some sort of ritual of submission, but there was also significant autonomy for the local rulers (chao fa) of the smaller principalities to maintain their "own court, administrative and financial system, tax collection, army and judicial system."[9] While larger Tai principalities had their own subordinates, they themselves were also in tributary relationships with more powerful polities around them. It was common for these Tai principalities to pay tribute to more than one external overlord, and indeed historically, several of the major Tai principalities had to maneuver simultaneously among Burma, China, and Siam, while occasionally playing one off against the other.

In Chiang Rung, located in what is today the Xishuangbanna region of southern Yunnan, there is a telling saying about its relationship with China and Burma: "*Ho bien po, man bien mae*," which literally means China is the father and Burma is the mother.[10] This refers to the fact that before the late nineteenth century, Chiang Rung paid tribute to both China and Burma because of its geopolitical location between the expanding Qing Empire and the militarily powerful Konbaung Dynasty.

Chinese rule over the southwestern borderland had been carried out through an indirect tusi system since the Yuan Dynasty, when the Mongol empire extended its territorial reach to upland Southeast Asia.[11] During the Ming and Qing dynasties, local chieftains were conferred with the title of tusi in areas where the Chinese civilian administration was not yet consolidated. Especially in the tropical lowland valleys of southern Yunnan where malaria was rampant, Chinese military forces encountered great difficulty trying to physically conquer and occupy the area.[12] Therefore, even though during the early eighteenth century the Qing government carried out a series of administrative reforms (gaitu guiliu) to replace local tusi with appointed magistrates in parts of southern China, its reach in the southern Yunnan borderland area was still very limited.[13]

In Chiang Rung, the Chinese Ming Dynasty first bestowed on the local Tai Lue ruler (chao paendin) the status of Cheli Pacification Commission (cheli xuanweisi) in 1384.[14] During the Ming Dynasty, delegations bearing tribute were sent periodically to Beijing, and the Chinese emperor also issued an official seal for the Chiang Rung chao paendin to use as proof of political recognition; tribute from other Tai principalities such as Chiang Tung and Lan Na had to be stamped with this before proceeding to Kunming.[15] However, the Ming and later Qing courts did not interfere much with Chiang Rung's internal governance and in fact tolerated the tributary relationship it maintained with the powerful Burmese Kingdom from the mid-sixteenth century onward.[16]

Burma's rising power, starting in the mid-sixteenth century, shifted the balance of power in upland Southeast Asia. King Bayinnaung united the central parts of Burma and also subjugated the Shan states to the west of the Salween River.[17] After his troops conquered Chiang Mai and Chiang Saen, the Lan Na kingdom fell under Burmese suzerainty around 1560. The dominance of the Burmese Kingdom in upland Southeast Asia also coincided with the weakening of the Ming Dynasty. From the early seventeenth century, Chiang Rung gradually came under the direct influence of the Burmese Kingdom, based in Ava. At this time, after the Chinese conferred the tusi title (xuanweishisi) on the local Tai Lue ruler, the latter would then also have to seek consent for accepting the title from the Burmese court.[18]

As a result, Chiang Rung formed a dual tributary relationship with both China and Burma. The Qing court began interfering more directly in the internal politics of Chiang Rung starting in the mid-eighteenth century, for example by setting up a short-lived military battalion there and even abolishing the Tai Lue chao paendin for a few years between 1773 and 1777.[19] This interference in Chiang Rung's internal politics was part of the overall military campaign the Qianlong Emperor initiated against Burma along the borderland area.[20] In Chiang Rung, the Qing military occupation failed due to tropical disease, and the Qing court also realized the need to keep the local tusi so as to appease the local population.[21]

The expansion of the Konbaung Dynasty in Burma also directly threatened the Qing's dominant position in several of the Tai principalities in northern Shan states, which led to a direct military confrontation between the Qing and the Burmese. However, the military adventure of the Qing troops in the unfamiliar tropical terrain in the Shan states led to disaster, and the Burmese emerged victorious in several of their border wars. In the late-eighteenth and early-nineteenth centuries, the Qing also experienced increased domestic instability with several major uprisings, including the White Lotus, absorbing most of their military power, which explains the more hands-off approach Beijing took toward the Tai principalities that were formerly its dominions. Thus, in Chiang Rung, the Qing had to tolerate the increasing Burmese domination over local affairs, including the latter's influence in the power struggles in succession politics.[22]

Indeed, the Burmese military was extremely effective in conquering upland Southeast Asia, including all the major Tai principalities such as Chiang Tung and Lan Na. Chiang Tung in the rugged mountainous areas between the Mekong and Salween rivers is one of the largest Tai principalities and has historically been a strategically important region populated by the Tai Khun people.[23] Although Chiang Tung also sent tribute to the Chinese emperor during the Ming period, its missions were far less frequent than those of Chiang Rung.[24] After Bayinnaung's conquest of the Shan states, Chiang Tung was increasingly controlled by the Burmese. Starting in 1564, Chiang Tung became a vassal state of Burma and also a key force aiding the Burmese conquest of other parts of the Shan states and upland Southeast Asia.[25] However, being a vassal state for the Burmese did not translate into direct rule, and Chiang Tung's chao fa maintained high levels of internal autonomy. Throughout the Shan states, the Burmese king did not interfere with the feudal relations between local chao fas and their subjects and allowed the chao fas to keep their royal regalia and conduct traditional Shan spiritual rites.[26] However, as tributaries of the Burmese, they were required to provide military conscripts and send silver and gold trees, ceremonial bowls, and silk and other precious items to the Burmese court. Intermarriage between the Shan and Burmese royalties was also actively encouraged, and Shan princesses were often taken as consorts for Burmese kings. In addition, the Burmese insisted some sons and brothers of the Shan chao fas join the Burmese court, which allowed their use as hostages.[27]

Thus, in the two hundred years since its subjugation by the Burmese, Chiang Tung remained loyal, overall, to the Burmese and the Chiang Tung Chronicle did not report any obvious conflict with Burma.[28] With the exception of fighting with some other small Shan/Tai principalities, Chiang Tung's chao fas maintained their rule relatively peacefully, with a clear and linear succession of rulers, many of whose reigns were relatively long.[29] However, from the mid-eighteenth century onward, Chiang Tung became involved with a string of wars that devastated the region, including fighting with other Tai principalities, as well as battles with the Burmese, Chinese, and Siamese.

The Chiang Tung Chronicle noted that between 1730 and 1740 there was a civil war between competing princes who contested the throne of the Chiang Tung chao fa. One of the contending princes first sought military help from Chiang Mai and later fled to Chiang Rung before the Burmese finally confined him at Ava.[30] Later, Chiang Tung was directly involved in the war between Burma and China. After the founding of the Konbaung Dynasty, the Burmese launched a series of military campaigns in upland Southeast Asia. The Burmese first occupied Chiang Mai and Lamphun in 1763, attacked Luang Prabang in 1765, and finally laid siege to and sacked the Siamese capital of Ayutthaya in 1767.[31] During the border wars between Burma and China, Chiang Tung was used as passage to attack Chiang Rung. A tug-of-war between Burma and China ensued, with each side occupying and retaking Chiang Tung multiple times.[32] The decades of war directly led to the decline of Chiang Tung in the latter half of the eighteenth century.

More wars were to come to Chiang Tung. The Siamese, having regrouped from their defeat by the Burmese and reconstituted their kingdom in Bangkok, quickly carried out a series of military expeditions to the north and by the end of 1770s started to gain dominance over Lan Na.[33] After consolidating its dominance over Chiang Mai, Siam sent troops to assist local Lan Na forces in attacking Chiang Saen for the first time in 1803, when they besieged the city for three months. The following year, they finally managed to defeat the Burmese military stationed there and expel the Burmese from Chiang Saen, formerly the seat of Burmese power in Lan Na.[34] In this way, Burmese dominance over Lan Na ended and Bangkok set up its own tributary relationship with the Tai principalities there. The Siamese style of tributary relations with Lan Na was quite distinct from that of the Burmese, however. Instead of posting governors, Bangkok maintained the relationship primarily through close familial connections, rewards for loyalty, and the implicit threat of punishment for any unruly vassal.[35] The security guarantee offered by Siam generated a period of stability in Lan Na, and the region's Tai principalities became militarily powerful enough to act for themselves, without direct support from Bangkok.[36]

Thus, from the early nineteenth century on, the main competition in upland Southeast Asia was between the Burmese and the Siamese and their associated Tai principalities, while Qing China gradually withdrew its direct involvement in borderland affairs. Chinese non-interference was due partly to internal turmoil but also to the perception that the Burmese and the Siamese could check each other's expansion.[37] Siam's consolidation of its domination over Lan Na posed more of a threat to the Burmese, and increasingly the Chiang Tung area became the direct point of confrontation between the two.

Then the British came. Disputes between Burma and British India in Manipur and Assam led to the First Anglo-Burmese War, which lasted from 1824 to 1826 and resulted in the defeat of the Burmese.[38] Burma's loss not only led to Britain consolidating its control over northeast India but also forced the Burmese to cede their territories of Arakan and Tenasserim. The British control of the Tenasserim range thus brought it directly in contact with Siam and the Lan Na principalities. The British presence in mainland Southeast Asia, however, generated a totally different political logic where the Tai principalities were concerned. A post-Westphalian European power with an understanding of exclusive territorial control, Britain's expansion in mainland Southeast Asia signaled the beginning of a long process during which it would clearly demarcate the boundaries of its colonial possessions with Siam and later with China.

However, one immediate effect of the First Anglo-Burmese War is that it effectively weakened the once-powerful Burmese Kingdom. The diminishing Burmese power fostered a sense of opportunity among many Tai principalities that had been subjugated by the Burmese and encouraged Siam to be more interventionist in the politics of upland Southeast Asia. From the 1830s on, a series of succession crises within the Chiang Rung ruling houses led to competing factions seeking external support from Burma and Siam, which sparked a military confrontation between the two in Chiang Tung in the mid-nineteenth century.[39] Despite defeat by the British once again in the Second Anglo-Burmese War of 1852 and the loss of all their coastal areas in lower Burma to British India, the Burmese fought hard to maintain their position in Chiang Tung. Partly to maintain their pride and partly to prevent further territorial loss, the Burmese gathered resources to defeat the Siamese in Chiang Tung in 1855.[40] Siam's loss in Chiang Tung also ended Bangkok's military adventurism in the Shan states until WWII, when it resumed with the support of the Japanese. The Third Anglo-Burmese War in 1885 finally completed the colonization of Burma, including the Shan states. Consequently, the British then began to dominate affairs in the Tai principalities.

Western Colonialism and Local Responses

The expansion of Britain's colonial empire in Southeast Asia, particularly after its colonization of lower Burma, increased British interests in Siam.

In 1855, Bangkok and London signed the Bowring Treaty, which prompted more open trade between the two countries and granted extraterritoriality to British subjects in Siam. As a result, British subjects, including all citizens from its colonies in Asia, were exempted from Siamese law, while the British Council started to play a more prominent role in mediating their commercial interests and legal protection in the country.[41] However, the Bowring Treaty did not mention the status of the Tai principalities in the north that were under Siamese suzerainty but maintained their autonomous relations with the Western powers, and thus, it was not clear whether the extraterritoriality enjoyed by British subjects in Siam could also be applicable to Lan Na.[42]

British commercial interests were then fixated on the abundant teak resources in Lan Na, and several logging firms were expanding there from the Tenasserim range. At the same time, the British also became fascinated by the potential for the opening up of a trade route that could link Southwest China with lower Burma, hoping to send their industrial products from the port city of Moulmein up to Lan Na and then to Yunnan. As a result, the number of British subjects in Lan Na increased substantially from the mid-nineteenth century, and likewise, disputes involving British subjects also grew.[43] This created conflicts within the existing tributary relations between Siam and Lan Na, with the former under pressure from the British to put the latter under more centralized control.[44]

As mentioned earlier, under the existing tributary relations framework, the Lan Na Tai principalities enjoyed high levels of autonomy from Siam; local rulers maintained their own foreign relations and applied their own laws without much interference from Bangkok. However, Britain desired that the extraterritorial rights enjoyed by its subjects in Siam would also apply in Lan Na. This prompted Bangkok to introduce a series of administrative reforms that gradually chipped away the Lan Na principalities' autonomy. First, the Chiang Mai Treaty of 1874 between Siam and Great Britain led Bangkok to establish a dual government in the north, by installing a commissioner there.[45] The Siamese government also posted a small police force along the Salween River to regulate the teak trade between British Burma and Lan Na, which, under the treaty, also began to fall under regulation by the Siamese commissioner.[46] Additionally, the introduction of tax-farming in Lan Na led to the sharing of revenue between Chiang Mai and Bangkok.[47] Almost a decade later, the Second Chiang Mai Treaty of 1883 further strengthened Siamese control of Lan Na by stripping more of the local rulers' negotiating power.[48]

Following these two treaties, Bangkok started the process of fully incorporating the Lan Na principalities into a centralized Siam. Initiated in 1884, the administrative structure in Lan Na was reorganized: six ministries were created, with officials appointed by Bangkok to act as advisors for local rulers.[49] Finally, the issue of "The Regulation on the Administration of the Northwestern Monthon, 1900" officially integrated the Lan Na principalities as provinces within a centralized administrative system.[50] Thus ended the autonomous status of the Lan Na Tai principalities and their tributary relations with Bangkok.

After Britain's conquest of the remainder of Burma in 1885, British colonial boundaries extended to incorporate the entirety of the Shan states. Through rounds of negotiations, the British and Siamese peacefully finalized a clear demarcation of their borders in 1894.[51] On the other hand, a military confrontation between the Siamese and the expanding French imperial force in Indochina in 1893 led to the cession of territories east of the Mekong River to the French.[52] Thus, the territorial shape of modern Siam was now complete.

In contrast with Siam's relatively cordial relations with the British, Qing China had a drastically different experience dealing with the encroachment by European colonial powers. After suffering a humiliating defeat by the British during the First Opium War, China had to sign the Treaty of Nanjing in 1842, which ceded territories and opened up its coastal cities as trading ports.[53] This led to a series of military defeats of the Qing by European powers and the subsequent concessions they forced China to make. In addition to such direct external threats to the Qing's imperial rule, its domestic control was also severely tested. First there was the Taiping Rebellion, which devastated much of southern China from 1850 to 1864.[54] Then, specifically pertaining to Yunnan and Qing's relations with Burma, came the Panthay Rebellion between 1856 and 1873, during which a Muslim Sultanate under the leadership of Du Wenxiu was established in Dali.[55] The Muslim rebel forces' military campaigns against the Qing destabilized Yunnan, especially in its multi-ethnic borderland area. During this time, not only was the Qing's military capability in Yunnan significantly reduced, its former relations with the local tusi bordering Burma were also cut off by the Panthay rebels.[56]

Meanwhile, the French expansion in Indochina and the British expansion in Burma brought these two European colonial possessions into direct contact with the Qing's Yunnan frontier. In Vietnam, through the two Treaties of Saigon of 1862 and 1874, France expanded from its possessions in southern

Vietnam toward the north. Refusing to accept the French design in Vietnam, China entered the war in 1884. Although the Chinese defeated the French in their land battles, ultimately China accepted the designation of Vietnam as a protectorate of France and renounced its former claim of suzerainty.[57] The following year the Qing and French signed a border treaty that delineated Yunnan's border with French Vietnam.[58]

In terms of relations with the British, the Yunnan borderland also faced unprecedented pressure. In the aftermath of the Margary Affair of 1875 when a British diplomat was killed in the Yunnan-Burma borderland, Britain forced the Qing to sign the Chefoo Convention, which permitted the British to explore commercial opportunities in Yunnan.[59] In 1886, a year after Britain completed their colonization of Burma, Qing China and Britain signed the Convention Relating to Burma and Tibet, in which Qing China recognized the British colonization of Burma and gave up its traditional suzerain claim.[60] In addition, both countries set up a border demarcation commission and by 1899 had settled the bilateral borders, with the exception of two small sections in the north and south.[61] They also agreed to a tribunal system to manage cross-border disputes involving ethnic groups across the newly demarcated borders, which gradually started to create a sense of national belonging among the local population.[62]

Overall, despite both external threats and internal challenges, the Qing government perceived that its previous loose tributary system could no longer survive with both France and Britain now at its Yunnan border. Beijing thus tried, cautiously, to rearrange its administrative system in the borderland area by increasing centralized control. In places such as Menglian, which is a small Tai principality on the Chinese side of the border, it managed to establish a Zhengbian Subprefecture government to supervise the activities of the local Tai tusi.[63] Further efforts to increase centralized control were tried during the Republican period after 1911 as well, with the establishment of a series of counties in the borderland. However, the weak position of the Chinese governments in the face of French and British pressure in the borderland areas meant that the reactive efforts were often too feeble. Three border cities of Mengzi, Simao, and Tengyue were opened for trade with the two European powers, and their products started to dominate the Yunnan market.[64]

Unlike Siam and China, which remained independent, Burma had become a part of British India by 1885, when the last King of Thibaw was forced into exile in India. However, unlike Burma proper, which came under direct rule by the British Indian government, the Shan states were incorporated rather gradually as an appendix, and the local sawbwas were mostly spared the fate of the deposed Burmese King.[65] For the British, as well as the Burmese Kingdom before them, their priority in the Shan states was to secure the region for the security of Burma proper, especially given its long borders with China, Siam, and French Indochina.[66]

The British insisted that they had no desire to interfere in the international politics of the Shan states and that they would like to see the Shan sawbwas continue their rule, on condition that they recognized British supremacy and paid annual tribute to the British Indian government.[67] In effect, the British recognized the Shan states in the same fashion as the native states in India, and the sawbwas "were placed under the personal supervision of the Chief Commissioner (of Burma) as Agent of the Governor-General (of India)."[68] Thus, for the Shan ruling elites, at least as they thought at the beginning, they just exchanged the Burmese king as overlord for the British Crown.

However, the British did introduce several major changes in the Shan states during their rule. First, they clarified what constituted the Shan states. In addition to demarcating the borders with China and Siam, the British decided there were in total forty-eight states, although later a few of the smaller ones were merged into bigger ones.[69] In 1890, the British issued a set of notifications to the Shan sawbwas concerning the terms of their rule. The sawbwas would have to pay a fixed amount of cash tribute to the British Indian government; their traditional rights over forests, mines, and other natural resources were transferred to the British government; local laws were brought in line with the Indian penal code; and sawbwas were prohibited from contacting foreign powers outside of British India.[70] Thus, overall the British superintendents exercised greater control over the Shan states than had their Burmese counterparts.[71]

In 1922, the British government formally established the Federated Shan States, motivated by the broader political changes in British India, with the extension of the dyarchy system of limited self-governance from India to Burma.[72] With growing nationalism in Burma, the British intended that the creation of Federated Shan States would give them more control over the Shan states, which also would provide a separate institutional barrier from Burma proper.[73] The sawbwas were allowed to express their opinions through the Council of Chiefs, but real power rested in the hands of the Commissioner of the Federated Shan States. In this way, the Federated Shan States became a subunit of British Burma with its own separate administration.[74]

Appreciating the relative autonomy that the British allowed them, most of the sawbwas came to strongly support British rule.[75] Throughout the British colonial period, the Shan states remained peaceful, overall, with moderate improvement in socio-economic conditions.

On the other hand, while recognizing the Shan sawbwas' claim as local rulers, the British nonetheless realized that the ethnic demographic composition of the Shan states was more complicated and many of the sawbwas' so-called subjects did not share Shan/Tai ethnicity.[76] Believing different ethnicities were separate and difficult to assimilate, the British tried to codify and reify the ethnic boundaries between the Shan, Bamar, Kachin, and many other mountain-dwelling ethnic groups.[77] Thus, British rule contributed to the strengthening of ethnic divisions in Burma. In the 1930s and 1940s, the Shan sawbwas tried to petition the British government to make the Shan states a separate self-governing entity under the Crown, rather than including them in a federal Burma. Although the British government was sympathetic to such demands, they were constrained by the Bamar nationalists who insisted that the Shan states should be part of Burma.[78] Such was the situation when British rule was abruptly ended by the Japanese invasion in 1942 and the Shan states' future status was to be contested in the turmoil of WWII and the post-war Burmese independence movement.

Mountain People

So far, our discussion on the premodern political dynamics in upland Southeast Asia has focused predominantly on the Tai principalities, their relations with each other, and the political contestations involving the larger political powers in the region. However, the topography of upland Southeast Asia also means that in addition to those lowland people and their polities, there are also many groups of people who historically have inhabited the mountains and had complicated relations with the valley states.

A number of ethnic groups—such as the Miao/Hmong, Kachin/Jingpo, Akha, Lahu, Palaung, Wa, Yao/Mien—live at different elevations in the mountains. Such variations in elevation have historically been negatively associated with a group's level of "civilization," with those living on the mountain tops often considered the most backward.[79] Such has been the dominant discourse in the lowland valley states for the past millennia. There are also different interpretations of the origins of these ethnic groups. Classic studies by Edmund Leach, for example, argued that there are more exchanges between mountain and valley people and people's ethnic identities are in fact more flexible, exchangeable, and contingent than is often thought.[80] Following Leach's interpretation, James Scott more forcefully argues that mountain people were mainly refugees who ran away from the political domination of the lowland valley states, arguing that they were "shards of valley states: deserting conscripts, rebels, defeated armies, ruined peasants, villagers fleeing epidemics and famine, escaped serfs and slaves, royal pretenders and their entourages and religious dissidents."[81]

There are certainly some elements of truth in such an interpretation. In Yunnan, the migration of Han Chinese into the borderland and the imposition of more centralized bureaucracy in the early eighteenth century squeezed further the living space of the Luohei/Lahu, which led to years of rebellion along the Yunnan-Burma border.[82] Later, a series of major civil wars in China, such as the Taiping Rebellion and the Panthay Rebellion during the mid-nineteenth century, devastated southern China and pushed many of these mountain-dwelling people into Southeast Asia.[83] Similarly, the chronic warfare among the valley Tai principalities had a similar effect in pushing people into the mountains, as several of the main principalities such as Chiang Mai, Chiang Tung, and Chiang Rung had at one point become totally depopulated because of the wartime devastation. On the other hand, these mountain people periodically attacked the lowland valley polities and posed a significant security threat to people and goods transiting through the region. Such was the case of the Kachin, who came to dominate the upper stream of the Irrawaddy River along the Yunnan-Burma borderland area.

After the British colonization of upper Burma in 1885, the government borrowed concepts of governance from British India, such as "Backward Tracts, Excluded, Partially Excluded and Scheduled Areas," to delineate frontier regions and set up an administrative organization in the Kachin hills.[84] In 1922, the British established a new Frontier Areas Administration, which included the Kachin Hills. In the late 1930s, the Kachin hills became an "Excluded and Scheduled Area deemed to have a separate social and political development trajectory from Ministerial Burma."[85] Thus, similar to the Federated Shan States discussed earlier, the British created a separate administrative structure to rule the hill people such as the Kachin, which later became the institutional boundary for Kachin nationalism and a barrier to Burmese nationalists' goal of national unification.

State Consolidation before and after WWII

By the start of the twentieth century, the three countries had already come under heavy pressure from European colonizers in their dealings concerning the borderland. The Chinese tried to resist European pressure in Yunnan, but nineteenth- and twentieth-century internal turmoil and external aggression meant that the later Qing and Republican governments simply did not have the wherewithal to carry out much state consolidation. The Kingdom of Siam was savvier in its dealings with the European powers and the British and French design to let Siam be a buffer between the two of them meant Bangkok was left to its own devices to consolidate its northern frontier, albeit after it had already shed big chunks of its peripheral territories to the British and French. Finally, in the case of Burma, its loss of sovereignty as a British colony meant that it was the British who designed the administrative system for the management of the borderland areas, and consequently, Burmese nationalists would have to deal with these legacies in their own efforts for national self-determination.

After the Qing Dynasty collapsed in 1911, Yunnan, a province far from the capital, came under the de facto control of a series of warlords under the overall political framework of the Republic of China (ROC). During the Republican period, the Yunnan government's approach to borderland management was primarily to maintain border security and then to gradually replace the tusi system with centrally appointed officials. Thus, despite its initial goal of using military means to remove the tusi from power, ultimately the Yunnan government did not have the capacity to carry out these plans.[86] Rather, the government decided the best way forward was to install a separate civil administrative in the borderland area in addition to the existing tusi governments. It wasn't until the unification of the Republican government in the late 1920s, after years of warlordism, that the Yunnan government decided to once again tackle the tusi situation.[87]

In 1930, the provincial government carried out a census of existing tusi in the province and discovered there were still 106 in place.[88] Given that these tusi had been in power for centuries and had close relations with local populations, it was decided that educational reform was required before making changes. From 1935 onward, the government introduced a scholarship program to recruit tusi offspring to study in Kunming so as to increase their cultural affinity with Han Chinese and generate a national identification with China.[89] The government also laid out a series of ambitious programs to establish a modern school system in the borderland area.[90] However, such plans were cut short by the Japanese invasion of China in 1937 and their occupation of the Yunnan-Burma borderland between 1942 and 1945. Most of these programs were simply not implemented.[91]

During the invasion, the Republican government retreated to the southwestern city of Chongqing, and Tokyo quickly sealed off China's external supply lines by occupying its major coastal cities. In 1940, the French Vichy government ceded its control of Vietnam to the Japanese, which effectively cut off China's railway connection to Yunnan.[92] The only remaining route at this time was the Burma-Yunnan Road, commonly referred to as the Burma Road, which was constructed by the Chinese government with the help of the British Burma government during 1937–1938.[93] The Burma Road started at Kunming and cut through the mountains in Dehong before entering Burma's Shan states. Thus, from the port city of Rangoon, shipments of materiel could be sent to Yunnan to support the Chinese resistance against the Japanese.

After the Japanese attack on Pearl Harbor in December 1941, the Republican government joined the Allied Powers and, in early 1942, sent three army divisions into Burma, which started the epic Burma campaign.[94] This expedition force (yuan zheng jun) joined with the British for a couple of months, but couldn't withstand Japanese aggression. Suffering heavy casualties, the expedition force retreated back to China through the Kachin hills, while the pursuing Japanese army entered Yunnan and occupied Dehong and Baoshan west of the Salween River. Years of occupation of the borderland by the Japanese meant further destabilization and political chaos. Although some local tusi collaborated with the Japanese, most were involved in active resistance against the occupying force.[95]

After the defeat of Japan in 1945, the turmoil on the Chinese mainland continued with the resumption of the Chinese Civil War between the CCP and the KMT. Although Yunnan was under the firm control of the KMT, the party simply did not have the political will or military capacity to rein in the autonomous tusi along the borderland area. Such tasks would have to be completed by the victorious communist government in the 1950s.

To the south, Siam managed to incorporate its northern tributary states into its provincial administrative system at the turn of the twentieth century. Such incorporation, however, was carried out slowly and with moderation, with the purpose of preventing dramatic political uncertainty in the north. Therefore, the incorporation of the northern states as provinces did not lead to the removal of the traditional rulers from power, rather most were maintained in the new administrative system to create a sense of continuity, but nonetheless they became employees paid by Bangkok. With time, these local rulers were gradually replaced by royal commissioners and other appointees from Bangkok.[96] Bangkok also centralized the control of the teak forests, which deprived the northern rulers of a traditional revenue source.[97] Additionally, more reforms were carried out by creating courts in the provinces with judges appointed by Bangkok. A centralized law enforcement system was also implemented. Direct tax collection, instead of the previous tax-farming system, was instituted. Finally, the traditional corvée labor system was also abolished.[98] Thus, by 1908, Bangkok had managed to complete its control over the north.[99]

From 1908 until the abolition of the absolute monarchy in 1932, the Bangkok government reorganized the northern states into two bigger regional units called Phayap and Maharat, which were designed for further centralization of control.[100] The government also began implementing a series of economic and social reforms that aimed to modernize the north. For example, it introduced the family name system into a region where previously surnames were not used.[101] Buddhist practices in the north were integrated into the Siam National Sangha to enforce a common standard throughout the kingdom.[102] Modernization programs in the fields of education and public health were also implemented through increasing bureaucratization of the administrative system, and cultural differences between north and central Siam were reduced. The central Thai language started to dominate the political and educational system in the north.[103] It was during this period that Siam became more centralized than before and "national uniformity was emphasized at the expense of local institutions."[104]

Siam's abolition of its absolute monarchy in 1932 led to the contestation of power between civilian politicians and the military, which would characterize the nature of Thai politics for decades to come.[105] In 1938, Field Marshall Phibun Songkram became Siam's prime minister and pushed for a strong nationalist political agenda. For example, his government changed the name of the country from Siam to Thailand, meaning a country for the Thai people. In addition, his government campaigned for the return of "lost territories" from the European colonial powers, and issued irredentist claims over other Tai territories in mainland Southeast Asia.[106] Such irredentist claims eventually led Thailand to invade the eastern Shan state of Chiang Tung during WWII.

On 8 December 1941, Japan invaded Thailand after its conquest of French Indochina. Despite initial resistance by the Thai military, Phibun's government quickly decided to ally with the Japanese and let the latter use its territory to attack British Burma and British Malaya. In return for the alliance, the Thai military was permitted by the Japanese to use military force to take over the Burmese territories east of the Salween River—mostly from Chiang Tung to the Yunnan border.[107] Unlike Siam's last failed attempt to conquer Chiang Tung almost a century before, this time the Thai military only met with feeble resistance from the Chinese expedition force to Burma, whose military power was also heavily diminished by the Japanese onslaught from Mandalay.[108] After conquering Chiang Tung, in 1943 the Thai government renamed it Former United Thai States (Saharat Thai Doem) and annexed it into Thailand.[109] However, this annexation only lasted two years before Thailand had to return Chiang Tung to British Burma after the defeat of Japan in 1945.

Japanese aggression in East and Southeast Asia, however, gave hope to Burma's nationalists and its independence movement. As we discussed earlier, the British colonial administration created layers of administrative units—such as the Excluded Areas that included the Federated Shan States, Kachin Hills, and so forth—which separated Burma proper from the frontier regions. In addition, ethnic minorities, such as the Karen and Kachin, were heavily recruited into the British colonial armed forces, while the majority Bamar were prevented from joining. Such different treatment of different ethnic groups thus created different dispositions toward the British and different attitudes toward the overthrow of the British in the name of self-determination.[110]

Thus, the arrival of the Japanese during WWII, with their rhetoric of getting rid of European colonialism and restoring Asia for Asians, generated hope among Burmese nationalists for such external support. For the sake of helping the Burmese to overthrow the British so that the Burma Road supporting the Chinese would be cut, the Japanese recruited thirty Burmese nationalist youth, the so called Thirty Comrades or Thakins, for military training in Japan and on China's Hainan Island.[111] Later, these comrades went to Thailand to recruit soldiers for the Burma Independence Army, who subsequently entered Burma together with the invading Japanese army in 1942.[112]

When Japan was defeated in 1945 and the British swiftly returned, Burmese nationalists' desire for independence had already reached boiling point. Demanding immediate independence and refusing to be part of the British Commonwealth, they also demanded that an independent Burma should include all the frontier areas historically under tributary relations with Burmese kings. However, the British instead demanded that an agreement between ethnic groups in the excluded areas and Burmese nationalists had to be reached before independence would be granted.[113]

Thus, Burmese nationalist leaders such as Aung San and the Anti-Fascist People's Freedom League (AFPFL) under his leadership needed to find such a solution through negotiation with the ethnic representatives. In March 1946, the first Panglong Conference was held in the Shan states to discuss the prospect of a political union and to hear the concerns of such major ethnic groups as the Shan, Kachin, Karen, and Chin.[114] With time, however, the British came to want a quick exit from Burma, and London came around to supporting the idea of unification between the excluded areas and Burma proper, which was confirmed in the Aung San-Clement Attlee Agreement in January 1947.[115] This paved the way for the Second Panglong Conference in February of the same year, during which Aung San told the ethnic representatives that "He and his colleagues had also obtained British consent and approval to the immediate participation of the frontier areas' people in the work and responsibilities of the Executive Council and the Constituent Assembly if they so desired on terms to be agreed with the Burmese."[116]

On February 12, 1947, the Panglong Agreement was signed with representatives from the Shan states, Kachin Hills, and Chin Hills. The agreement included ethnic representation in the Executive Council, granted ethnic regions administrative autonomy, promised equal rights and privileges, and guaranteed existing financial situations in the excluded regions.[117] It was a landmark agreement that set the foundation of equality between the Bamar and the ethnic peoples, and indeed there was substantial enthusiasm about the prospect of a federated Burma, despite the exclusion of another major, dissenting ethnic group, the Karen, in the agreement. Finally, on September 24, a new Constitution was adopted for the post-independence Union of Burma, with the Panglong Agreement as its guiding principle. It set out the territorial configurations of Burma proper, as well as a list of ethnic states: the Shan, Kachin, Karen, Karenni states, and the Chin Special Division. It also granted ethnic states the right to secede after ten years, which would prove disastrous for the Shan state in the late 1950s. The assassination of Aung San in July 1947 arguably deprived the country of a respected and skillful politician needed to bridge the differences between the Bamar and ethnic minorities. However, at the dawn of Burmese independence in January, 1948, a democratic and federal state structure was set up with great promise.

Concluding Remarks

For the area of upland Southeast Asia between Burma, China, and Thailand, the lowland valley Tai principalities and the mountain people that live nearby were, historically, in one organic, regional political system. Intimate ethnic linkages and familial ties bound the different Tai principalities together despite the fact that they were under the political domination of various larger political powers in Burma, China, and Siam. Such historical divisions aside, it was the thrust of the European colonial powers into Southeast Asia that ultimately laid down a clear demarcation of borders and boundaries under the principle of post-Westphalia international law. In particular, the British were the most influential in generating reactive state building efforts by the Chinese and Siamese in this borderland area after conquering Burma, where British colonial legacies are definitely the strongest. Political chaos during WWII further destabilized the borderland region. Although colonial powers eventually departed, the intrigues of the Cold War, with further internal strife in these countries, would soon engulf the region.

4
Spillover of the Chinese Civil War and Militarization of the Borderland

In the mountain town of Mae Salong, in Thailand's northernmost Chiang Rai province bordering Myanmar, stands a memorial plaque with an inscription in Chinese that reads, "After the Yunnan Kunming Incident of December 9, 1949, the celestial land turned red. Sons and daughters of Chinese people who could not tolerate Marxism, for lofty ideals and for survival, endured much hardship and ended up in the mountainous areas in the borderland area between Yunnan and Burma, remaining there for several decades." Mae Salong, although in Thailand, is a town with a distinctly Chinese character. Despite the prominent display of the Thai national flag, most of the street signs are in Chinese, and locals, especially the older generation, speak the Yunnan dialect of Mandarin instead of Thai. Throughout the Northern Thai provinces of Chiang Mai, Chiang Rai, and Mae Hong Son, there are many such Chinese villages, hosting remnants and descendants of KMT troops resettled in Thailand in the early 1960s after their retreat from the Shan State in Burma, which they occupied for almost a decade after fleeing Yunnan.[1]

I met Ahzhong in Chiang Mai in the summer of 2016 when he took me for a short tour of several KMT settlement villages in Northern Thailand. After explaining to me the complex history of migration from China to Burma and then to Thailand, he told me his family story, which is indicative of the trauma of war and displacement of soldiers and their families in this area. Born in the Shan State in the early 1960s, Ahzhong is the youngest of four children. His parents were originally from a town in Yunnan close to the Sino-Burmese border, which they fled with the KMT troops. But, because of the haste of the retreat, they couldn't take their oldest daughter, who remained in Yunnan. Ahzhong's other siblings were all born in Burma. When he was four, as part of the resettlement deals agreed upon by the two governments, Thai and ROC in Taiwan, the family settled in a village in Chiang Mai province. Raised in Thailand and educated in local Chinese schools, his second sister went to study in Taiwan and, after relations across the Taiwan Strait improved, moved to Shanghai for business. She has lived in mainland China for more than ten years. His other brother also went to Taiwan for study and has remained there since. Both of his siblings have acquired ROC citizenship. Ahzhong, on the other hand, did not go to Taiwan for school but remained in Thailand and became a Thai citizen.

It has been more than six decades since the end of the Chinese Civil War in 1949. For Ahzhong and his family, that past has receded into memory, while they have moved on with life across multiple national boundaries. Having said that, the KMT's retreat from Yunnan and its continued military presence in the Burmese Shan State and later in Thailand has had tremendous implications for the processes of state building along the borders of the three countries. This chapter will discuss first the military dimensions of the KMT troops in this borderland area and then, in the three subsequent sections, their legacies and implications specific to state building in China, Burma, and Thailand.

Spillover of the Chinese Civil War

When Mao Zedong declared the founding of the PRC on October 1, 1949, Yunnan was still under the control of the KMT government, whose troops were stationed across the province preparing their defense against the approaching PLA. On December 9, Yunnan Governor Lu Han defected to the communist side. After failing to recapture Kunming, sections of the KMT troops retreated south, with the PLA in pursuit. By February 1950, two remaining sections of the Eighth and Twenty-sixth armies, approximately two thousand soldiers, crossed the border into Burma's Shan states, and occupied part of a triangular area around Kengtung and Tachileik, bound by the Mekong River to the east, and Thailand and Laos to the south.[2] Under the leadership of Li Mi, they would remain in the eastern part of the Shan State[3] for almost a decade.[4]

The presence of the KMT troops in Burma irked the Chinese and Burmese governments. Rangoon certainly did not like having a foreign army on its soil, especially while it was working toward diplomatic relations with Beijing as well as dealing with the reality of its own emerging civil war with various ethnic rebellions. On June 8, Beijing and Rangoon exchanged embassies, and Burma became the first non-socialist country to recognize the Chinese communist government. Subsequently, Beijing notified the Rangoon government that if the latter could not expel the KMT troops, the PLA was willing to do it for them.⁵ Worried about the prospect of a Chinese communist military intervention in its territory and fearing that the troops might not leave afterward, the Burmese government stepped up its own military offensive against the KMT troops. In mid-June, the Burmese government carried out airstrikes and a ground attack, yet its forces were no match for the KMT troops and were defeated in Tachileik.

The Burmese government understood that the United States held sway over the ROC government in Taipei, and thus diplomatically requested that the US government pressure Chiang Kai-shek to remove the troops, otherwise it would appeal to the United Nations.⁶ The Burmese government justified its request on the grounds that the KMT presence in its territory diverted its own military resources from countering internal communist and ethnic rebellions, which at first drew sympathy from the United States who did not want to see a domestically unstable Burma.

However, the outbreak of the Korean War in October 1950 and Chinese support for North Korea fundamentally altered the US strategic outlook in East Asia. Fearing the "domino effect" of communist expansion in the region, and deeming the Chinese communist government its primary adversary, the US government changed its previous cautious approach toward the KMT troops in Burma.⁷ The CIA, without the Department of State's knowledge, covertly initiated Operation Paper to provide weapons, equipment, and other logistical support for Li Mi's troops to attack Yunnan, hoping that they would be able to hold down the Chinese military in the southwest so as to reduce pressure on the United States in Korea.⁸

In order for Operation Paper to succeed, the United States needed the support of the Thai government. At this time, the government of Phibun Songkram was also actively seeking international support to strengthen the position of the Thai army against other competing power bases, such as the navy, which supported Phibun's rival Pridi. Phibun succeeded in winning over the United States by publicly declaring himself a staunch anti-communist strongman and presenting Thailand as the ideal base for US anti-communist activities in Southeast Asia.⁹ When the Korean War started, Phibun's government quickly pledged support for the United States, first by announcing the delivery of rice and then by sending troops to Korea.¹⁰ For Operation Paper, Thailand quickly offered itself as a base for US covert operations against China. Allowing military logistical support to transit through

Thai territories into Burma's Shan State, Thailand became a crucial link between the KMT and the CIA.[11]

Thus, with US support, Li Mi actively recruited soldiers in the borderland area, many of whom were former militiamen, mabang bandits, and local chieftain tusi soldiers. By the end of 1950, he claimed to have amassed around 12,500 soliders, which was many times more than the initial number of troops that crossed the border.[12] Li Mi's troops made the first major attack on Yunnan in May 1951. After initial success capturing several counties along the border, the operation was quickly repelled by the PLA, and in July Li's troops retreated to Burma once again. Even though it did not achieve military success against the PLA, in Burma Li's military bases started to grow and dominate the eastern part of Shan State. In October 1951 the Yunnan Anti-Communist and Anti-Soviet University (Yunnan Fangong Kang'e Daxue) was established and began recruiting students that December.[13] A new airport was also constructed at Mong Hsat that could receive military equipment from Taiwan.

The expansion of the KMT in the Shan State fundamentally changed the domestic military balance within Burma. By March 1953, it was estimated that 80% of the Burmese government military force was engaged in fighting the KMT rather than fighting communists and other insurgents.[14] Indeed, in the United States the Eisenhower administration concluded that supporting the KMT in Burma did more harm than good to US security interests in Southeast Asia, because it not only consumed the Burmese military force but also created a possible pretext for military intervention by the PLA. This prompted the United States to put pressure on the ROC to withdraw the KMT from Burma. In March 1953, the government of Burma submitted a complaint to the United Nations (UN), and the following month the UN General Assembly adopted a resolution demanding the KMT "be disarmed and either agree to internment or leave the Union of Burma forthwith."[15] Around the same time, Burma also agreed to join a committee together with Taiwan, Thailand, and the United States to oversee the evacuation of the KMT from the Shan State. However, although Taipei agreed to such a move, it was not genuinely willing to evacuate the troops, at least not initially. During the first round of evacuations in November 1953, evacuees were not soldiers but the elderly and disabled, the women and children, and the KMT troops failed to turn in weapons in working condition.[16]

In the end, the United States succeeded in pressuring the ROC to carry out more meaningful evacuations. By October 1954, nearly seven thousand KMT personnel had been evacuated, although several thousand more remained,[17] partly because Chiang Kai-shek was unable to compel everyone to leave, and because many of the KMT were by this time engaged in the lucrative opium trade and had little reason to move to Taiwan. In 1960, Beijing and Rangoon reached a bilateral agreement on border demarcation and signed the "Treaty of Friendship and Mutual Nonagression."[18] Thereafter, Rangoon agreed to Beijing's proposal for joint military action with the PLA against KMT troops, which eventually succeeded in defeating and driving them from Burma in 1961.[19] Afterward, the remaining KMT troops, also known as "Chinese Irregulars," relocated to Thailand and in the following years were sustained by the opium trade between Thailand, Burma, and Laos, as they continued to roam along the porous mountainous borderland region unchecked.

Solidification of the Chinese Border Region

The new communist government secured control over most of the Chinese mainland in 1950. However, it faced strong resistance, especially in the south and southwest, areas where it historically lacked popular support and which were mostly "liberated" through military means. In the rough mountainous terrain of Southwest China, sporadic military resistance by bandits (tufei), KMT remnants (jiangfei canyu), and ethnic rebels persisted. For example in Guizhou, bandits still partially controlled nearly half of the province's counties in August 1951.[20] As in other revolutionary movements, the Chinese Communist Party (CCP) would use state terror to subdue and pacify those resisting the new order. For that purpose, an extensive Campaign to Suppress Counter-Revolutionaries (zhengya fageming) took place from 1950 to 1953, violently eliminating many real and imagined enemies of the new regime, with at least 700,000 executed, 1.2 million imprisoned, and another 1.2 million brought under state surveillance.[21]

Right after the outbreak of the Korean War and the Chinese People's Voluntary Army's entry into the war to "Resist the United States and Assist Korea" (kangmei yuanchao), Mao signed a new directive to suppress counter-revolutionaries. The war effort in Korea stimulated strong domestic patriotic support for the CCP, which the party sought to take advantage of to eliminate many of its internal enemies.[22] In April 1951, Minister for Public Security Luo Ruiqing, made a speech on the need to resolutely suppress counter-revolutionaries,[23] pointing out that this was the necessary condition for supporting Chinese military activities in Korea and carrying out domestic land reforms. Luo also emphasized how the campaign needed to defeat the KMT bandits (jiangjieshi feibang) who would like to retake the Chinese mainland with the help of US imperialists (meiguo zhuyi).

Indeed, the CCP government put strong emphasis on pacifying Southwest China, particularly the borderland area between Yunnan and Burma. A report submitted to Mao Zedong by He Long and Deng Xiaoping in January 1951 summarized the military's success against bandits there, but also outlined the major challenges remaining along the border.[24] According to a report prepared by the Southwest Bureau of Public Security in 1952, an estimated 13,000 of Li Mi's troops remained in Burma constantly, carrying out sudden night attacks, propagating slogans against the CCP's suppression of counter-revolutionaries, and killing soldiers, militia members, cadres, and local activists.[25] The same report also noted that the KMT and its "imperialist supporters" had set up 21 posts along the border, including espionage stations, liaison offices, and training centers. Supposedly, the spy stations were involved in collecting information from the Chinese side of the border, organizing rebellions, and sabotaging interethnic unity. For example, in Longling County, Baoshan District, bandits across the border killed more than 80 cadres and local activists.[26] According to another internal party document released by Xinhua in 1954, between November 1953 and March 1954, there were 2,200 cases of sabotage, which led to the death of 102 people, 94 injuries, and financial losses of 1.4 billion yuan.[27] It noted how the counter-revolutionaries spread anti-communist slogans, such as "socialism is suffering," "Socialist transition only leads to hunger," and so forth. Assassination attempts were made against the party secretaries of Mojiang and Ludian counties. There were also many popular protests against the Chinese government's grain procurements, ostensibly also orchestrated by the counter-revolutionaries.[28]

Facing such challenges, the Chinese government responded in various ways. The first method was violent suppression. By October 1951, about 23,000 people had been executed in Southwest China, with another 62,000 imprisoned, and 15,000 under surveillance. In total, 190,000–200,000 people were executed between 1950 and 1953, constituting 0.21% of the region's population.[29] Indeed, throughout the Campaign to Suppress Counter-Revolutionaries, Mao decreed that executions should be carried out by quota, designated as 0.1% of the population.[30] Thus, the execution rate in the Southwest seems to have been double the national average, which perhaps indicates the more serious resistance faced by the new communist government there, though it might just be the case that the government was more ruthless and indiscriminate in the application of state violence, which certainly included many errors.[31]

The situation in the borderland was also more complicated than in inland areas, as the CCP realized. The long and porous border provided an exit option, so using violence alone risked driving people across the border into Burma. The multiethnic composition of the population was also a complicating factor. Indeed, many local ethnic chieftains and community leaders, fearing an uncertain future under the CCP, left. In Xishuangbanna, the reigning Dai king's father, Dao Dongting, escaped to Burma's Shan State in 1949 in anticipation of the PLA's arrival.[32] In Baoshan District, Silashan, a Jingpo Christian pastor, fled to Burma in August 1952 because of the Chinese state's campaign of suppression against counter-revolutionaries and the associated negative implications for the Christian religion among the Jingpo people.[33] The CCP government wanted not only to prevent such an exodus of ethnic leaders, but also to avoid creating ethnic problems that external enemies might exploit. It realized its policies and practices in the borderland area were deeply intertwined with the need to prevent external meddling and sabotage,[34] and so it would need to approach the solidification of borderland area with some moderation.[35]

In a June 1952 decree on land reform in Yunnan, Liu Shaoqi emphasized the need to maintain social order, increase interethnic unity, and win the support of ethnic leaders, in addition to rooting out bandits and counter-revolutionaries.[36] For that reason, land reform was not initially carried out in twenty-six counties along the border, according to the decrees. In counties close to but not directly on the border, land reform was to be carried out in moderation and was only suitable for lowland areas where interethnic relations were good and the task of suppressing counter-revolutionaries was complete.[37] Such moderation was emphasized because the CCP realized the complexities of the borderland area and the danger of rushing such sociopolitical transformations. It wasn't until 1955–1957 that land reform was gradually implemented in these areas.[38] Such "Peacefully Negotiated Land Reform" (Heping Xieshang Tudi Gaige) was relatively peaceful, that is, without the excessive violence and killing of landlords that occurred in most provinces.[39] For the same reason, the CCP decided not to carry out religious reforms for existing Protestant and Catholic churches as it did in other parts of China, in order to gradually win over the loyalty of borderland ethnic minorities, such as the Jingpo and Lisu, who had converted to Christianity as a result of the efforts of Western missionaries.[40]

In order to avoid ethnic problems, ethnic leaders were actively courted, the CCP having realized that in order to solidify its control in these areas, cooperation with existing social hierarchies was necessary.[41] Guidance issued by the Southwest Bureau instructed lower-level party organizations to maintain long-term unity with ethnic leaders, reasoning that only through such a cooperative relationship could the party carry out its work locally, because these ethnic leaders were targets of competing influence with the KMT "bandits" and the "imperialists" across the border.[42] Therefore, in Xishuangbanna, Dai aristocrats were co-opted into the new government after the establishment of the Xishuangbanna Dai Autonomous Region[43] in 1953, and "many preexisting cultural and political structures were left intact and even subsumed into the party-state structure."[44] In Dehong, a Dai and Jingpo Autonomous Region was established in 1953, with Dai tusi Dao Jinban as the chairman and several Dai and Jingpo ethnic leaders as vice chairmen, including Silashan, the Jingpo Christian pastor who had fled to Burma and was later convinced to come back to China by the CCP.[45] The party also carried out active recruitment among ethnic populations in the borderland area. In Dehong, by the end of 1958, members of ethnic minorities accounted for 25% of local CCP cadres.[46] In Xishuangbanna, about 30% of the cadres were ethnic minorities by 1955.[47]

It was through such a mixed approach to borderland management that the new communist government established and consolidated its rule in Yunnan. By the mid-1950s, most opponents of the new government had been removed through the Campaign to Suppress Counter-Revolutionaries. The moderate approach to land reform and ethnic and religious matters also won people's support for the new government. Politically, the CCP established a series of ethnically autonomous governments along the border. In addition to Xishuangbanna and Dehong, a few other county-level autonomous areas were established in places such as Menglian and Gengma, where a modern bureaucracy was introduced in the form of a people's government. The party also carried out active recruitment locally, especially in the rural areas.[48] In Dehong, by mid-1955, extensive party cells had been established in many townships, through which land reform was achieved by peaceful means.

Economically, the new government worked to improve the dominant position of the new currency, the RMB, in the borderland market and gradually diminish circulation of Burmese kyats and Indian rupees. For example in Dehong, the Burmese kyat was banned by mid-1954, and by mid-1955 the RMB's market share had increased to 70%.[49] The new government also banned the planting of poppies, recommending tea as a substitute, although poppy cultivation was not eradicated until the early 1960s.[50] It took measures to establish health facilities, and by the early 1960s, every district in Yunnan had at least one health clinic, and malaria and other tropical diseases had been brought under control.[51] New school systems were set up along the border, and by the early 1960s primary school enrolment among children reached 57%.[52] Thus, throughout the 1950s, the CCP government gradually built and consolidated state institutions in the borderland area. Although political radicalization from the Great Leap Forward on would once again destabilize the borderland area—for example in 1958 there was a great exodus of borderland people to Burma driven by a shortage of grain and the consequent famine[53]—the CCP state's control of the Chinese side of the border became entrenched and unchallenged.

Militarization of the Borderland and Fragmentation of the Burmese State

Burma's independence from Britain in 1948 did not bring with it the hoped for post-independence unity and solidarity among its diverse ethnic population as promised in the 1947 Panlong Agreement. The assassination of Aung San in July 1947 deprived independent Burma of a unifying figure. But fundamentally, many of the problems the Union of Burma faced had deep colonial legacies of fracture that were by no means easy to overcome. Ethnic minorities such as the Karen and Kachin who had staffed the colonial army now faced the political reality of the ethnic Bamar claiming sole possession of the country after independence. Communal violence toward the Karen soon intensified, and as a result the Karen National Defense Organization (KNDO) rebelled against the Rangoon government in January 1949. Later, the First Kachin Rifles defected from the Burmese Army. A communist insurgency had been brewing since the first half of 1948, there were ethnic rebellions in several states, and within a year of independence Burma found itself in a bitter civil war that engulfed much of its territory.[54]

Indeed, by the end of the 1949 rainy season the government of Prime Minister U Nu controlled little more than the capital Rangoon. Appealing for support, U Nu called for the nation to unite behind his slogan "Peace

Within One Year."[55] After a year and half of bitter fighting, the tide started to turn against the various insurgencies. With the expansion of the Burmese Army, which consumed 40% of the national budget, military success against various rebels meant a general improvement of the internal situation.[56] In an interview with a British newspaper, the *Observer*, on May 21, 1950, U Nu expressed his confidence that the civil war in Burma was approaching its end.[57]

Although the propaganda purpose in such self-congratulatory reports is clear, it is certainly an exaggeration that "Peace Within One Year" was in sight, but there is no denying that by 1950 the central government had significantly recovered from its previous position of weakness. Throughout 1950, the Burmese Army achieved significant military success against the KNDO. For example, a report in the government journal *Burma* titled "Drive towards Peace" reads: "On the morning of March 19, Government forces, making a lightening thrust from Zeyawaddy and Nyaungchidauk, broke through to Toungoo the same evening, capturing the former 'Kawthulay Capital' without meeting any opposition."[58] And by November, the same report states, "there was practically no insurgent activity of importance in any sector."[59] However, the KMT's invasion and occupation of the Eastern Shan States significantly disrupted the ongoing military balance within Burma. Most importantly, the security threat posed by the KMT in the context of great-power competition during the Cold War meant the Burmese government had to divert its attention and resources from fighting the CPB, KNDO, and other ethnic rebellions. Thus, the KMT incursion offered breathing room for these internal insurgencies to hide and regroup in rural and jungle areas. In a report sent from the US Embassy in Rangoon to the US State Department, the first secretary Albert Franklin noted the negative consequences of the KMT presence in Burma, writing that it "compounds the effectiveness of the Communist threat, not only by diverting a portion of the Burmese armed forces, and by affording a horrible example of 'Western disruptive and warmongering techniques,' but also by casting doubt on the Burmese government's sincerity as a bulwark against Western exploitation."[60]

Worse still, the KMT also began establishing links with the KNDO and other ethnic rebel groups. Bertil Linter points out that in January 1952 KMT troops collaborated with "Karen and Karenni rebel forces and reoccupied the mining town of Mawchi in the Karenni hills, which had served as the Karen rebel headquarters for a brief period in 1950."[61] The US Embassy in Rangoon was also aware of the assistance the KMT was giving to the KNDO, and it seems the United States worried that US military aid to Taiwan would end up in the hands of the Karen rebels.[62] In addition to the KNDO, KMT aid also went to ethnic Mon rebels, in the hope that the KMT could gain access to the Tenasserim Coast through the Mon State to obtain more aid from Taiwan.[63]

In addition to collaborating with ethnic rebels, the KMT also actively recruited soldiers from indigenous ethnic minority groups in the Shan states. Since the original soldiers escaping China were limited in number, they would need local recruits to expand their military presence. Lintner points out that, "since the beginning of 1951, the KMT generals in the Shan hills had been drafting more soldiers from the villages in the border areas: Lahus, Shans, Was, Palaungs and Sino-Shans. These fresh recruits were trained at the KMT's new base at Mong Hsat and armed with weapons that arrived on nightly flights from Taiwan."[64] At the same time, the KMT was also reportedly cruel to local communities. Burmese military historian Maung Maung wrote about the atrocities committed by the KMT: "Strength made the KMT arrogant. Their parties who periodically combed Kengtung for food became hostile. From theft and robbery they advanced with rapid steps to raid and plunder; occasionally they would rape and kill, and kidnap for ransom."[65] With martial law and military administration imposed over much of the Shan State in the name of fighting the KMT, the Burmese Army also behaved brutally toward the local Shan population and became increasingly unpopular and resented.[66] In one report, the second secretary at the US Rangoon Embassy, William Hamilton, discussed his interview with the Mahadevi of Yawnghwe who berated the misbehavior of Burmese troops toward the Shan population and accused the Burmese government of "not bombing KMTs, they are bombing Shans."[67] Linter also comments on the fact that "Shan politics had become more intense because of the KMT invasion, and the subsequent massive influx of the government forces."[68] Thus, the KMT presence in the Shan State indirectly and directly paved the way for the nationalist reaction and mobilization among the Shan.

The Shan nationalist movements obviously had a lot to do with domestic political changes in Burma. The Shan State had been promised the right to secede ten years after the independence of the Union of Burma; to prevent that from happening, by 1958 the Burmese government had been working to get rid of the Shan sawbwas through constitutional change. In April 1959, while Ne Win's Caretaker Government was in power, all thirty-four sawbaws formally surrendered their hereditary rights and power in a public ceremony in Taunggyi.[69] Although some Shan strongly supported deposing the sawbwas on anti-feudal grounds, dissatisfaction with being part of the Union of Burma had also begun to spread, and demands for secession had gained momentum. One year before the sawbwas were stripped of their power, the Shan militant group Noom Suk Harn (Young Brave Warriors) was formed in the jungles along the Thai-Burmese border. A year later, the Shan State Independence Army (SSIA) was founded and began launching military attacks against the Burmese army in December 1959. A leaflet distributed by the SSIA claimed its military actions would be "a beginning that would fire sparks and smolder on the Burmese scene, for, Independence is not an empty theory to the Shans, it is an ideal since time immemorial by which Shans or Tais as they are called, have lived and for which they are willing to die."[70] In 1962, several of the existing Shan rebel armies merged to form the SSA, which continued its armed resistance against the Burmese government along the border over the next several decades.[71] Although the Shan nationalist insurgency has been characterized by fragmentation and regrouping, armed resistance to the Burmese government has persisted along the Thai Burma border area up to today.

The emergence of the Shan rebels along the border created an opportunity for the remaining KMT troops to have "a front behind which it could hide to deflect international criticism."[72] Both groups met to find a way to coexist. By this time, the remaining KMT troops in the Golden Triangle were predominantly engaged in opium smuggling between Burma and Thailand, the huge profits from this trade being one of the main reasons why thousands had refused to be repatriated to Taiwan. Commenting on the relationship between the KMT invasion and opium production in Burma, Linter states:

> At Burma's independence in 1948, the country's opium production amounted to a mere thirty tons, or just enough to supply local addicts in the Shan states, where most of the poppies were grown. The KMT invasion changed that overnight. The territory they took over—Kokang, the Wa hills and the mountains north of Kengtung—was traditionally the best opium growing area in Burma. Gen. Li Mi persuaded the farmers to grow more opium, and introduced a hefty opium tax, which forced the farmers to grow even more in order to make ends meet.[73]

Thus, the KMT war economy of opium smuggling has played a leading role in the Golden Triangle becoming one of the main sources of drug trafficking in the world.

Finally, we can also argue that the KMT presence in Burma was one of the factors that led to the expansion of the Burmese military's institutional and personnel capacity.[74] From the time of Burma's independence to 1955, the army grew from a mere few thousand to more than forty thousand.[75] A larger share of the country's budget was allocated to the military, and General Ne Win grew more powerful than the civilian leaders of the Burmese government. As tension between the two wings, military and civilian, built up, a coup, the first, in 1958 resulted in the Caretaker Government that held power between 1958 and 1960. After briefly restoring a civilian government following the 1960 election, in 1962 Ne Win instigated another coup in an attempt to forestall secessionist movements in the Shan State and elsewhere. Thus the long history of military rule in Burma persisted until the twenty-first century, one of the longest-lived military dictatorships in modern history.

Irregular Force along the Thai Northern Borderland

The communist victory in the PRC also sent powerful shockwaves through the Kingdom of Thailand, especially in 1950, after China's military annexed Tibet and entered into the Korean War. The perception that a militarily aggressive communist regime in Beijing might intend to invade Thailand created strong fear in Bangkok,[76] especially since Field Marshall Phibun Songkram's archrival, Pridi Banomyong, reportedly went to China seeking asylum after a failed coup against Phibun. Three years before, in 1947, Phibun had returned to Thai politics with the help of the "Coup Group" that ousted Pridi and his supporters in the Thai government.[77] Thus, Phibun was worried that the PRC would use Pridi, who enjoyed public support in Thailand, to overthrow his government. Indeed, the new PRC government did publish a series of scathing editorials in the *People's Daily* against the Phibun government. For example, on January 27, 1950, the newspaper carried a piece denouncing the "fascist Phibun clique brutally oppressing overseas Chinese in Thailand."[78] Earlier the same month, another piece in the *People's Daily* accused Phibun's government of embracing US imperialists.[79] Although the threat of military invasion by the PRC was perhaps played up in the Thai press for anti-communist propaganda purposes, Beijing was nonetheless highly critical of the Thai government for Thailand's foreign policy orientation toward the United States, as well as the critical role Thailand played in US support for the KMT.

Thailand positioned itself as the crucial link between the KMT troops in Burma, the CIA, and the ROC government. Many of the liaison meetings between Li Mi, the ROC representatives, and the United States were held in Bangkok and Chiang Mai. Logistical support for the KMT also transited via Thailand. After President Truman approved Operation Paper to support the KMT's military campaigns in Burma, the CIA secretly solicited support from the Thai government to use Thailand to supply weapons and materials to Li Mi's troops. More importantly, Thailand also provided necessary diplomatic coverage for these covert actions so that the United States would not be dragged down by KMT affairs if things went awry.[80] The *People's Daily* reported, from a source in Bangkok, in June 1961 that the United States was shipping weapons and Thai rice to the Thai-Burma border to support the KMT troops. The KMT also reportedly set up a recruitment office in Bangkok for its activities in Burma. The same report also alleged that the United States requested that the Thai government set aside areas in Thailand's Nan Province where KMT troops could find sanctuary.[81]

Thailand's support for the KMT should be understood in the broader context of its pursuit of military cooperation with US anti-communist activities in Southeast Asia. It was part of Thailand's broader commitment to US security interests in the region. As discussed earlier, Phibun actively lobbied for US military aid to strengthen the power of the army that supported him. He succeeded in winning over the United States by publicly declaring himself a staunch anti-communist strongman and presenting Thailand as the ideal ally of US anti-communist activities in Southeast Asia.[82] As a result, Thailand received a tremendous amount of US aid. For example, at the request of the US government, Phibun's government recognized the Bao Dai regime in South Vietnam, this action deemed strategic to "acquire merit in American eyes and thereby to qualify for material aid in arms and equipment and also in the economic sphere."[83] Indeed, the Thai government received US$10 million in US military aid, as well as US$11.4 million in economic and technical assistance.[84] When the Korean War started, Phibun's government once again quickly pledged support for the United States, first by announcing the delivery of rice and then by sending troops to Korea.[85] In return, in August 1950 the World Bank, under the auspices of the United States, approved US$25 million in development aid for Thailand, the first funding the bank authorized for an Asian country.[86] Domestically the Phibun government also passed stringent anti-communist measures, beginning with the Alien Registration Act in 1950, ostensibly aimed at repatriating the left-leaning overseas Chinese back to the PRC.[87] The Anti-Communist Act, passed in 1952, gave the government sweeping powers to define and punish communist-related activities.[88] Thus both internationally and domestically, the Phibun government committed itself to the US anti-communist grand strategy in Southeast Asia, which paved the way for Thailand to join the Southeast Asian Treaty Organization (SEATO) in 1954.[89]

It was also within this general anti-communist environment that the Thai Border Patrol Police (BPP) was conceived. The United States was initially interested in setting up a network of defense in Thailand in the event of a Chinese invasion.[90] In 1953, the new Eisenhower administration approved the use of psychological warfare in Thailand, given the intensifying communist insurgency in Indochina.[91] Thus, through General Phao the CIA put into action the training of a select group of police in May 1953, initially termed the Border Defense Police General Headquarters in the Northeast Region and officially changing its name to the BPP in January 1955.[92] The establishment of the BPP represented a close working relationship between the CIA and relevant parties in Thailand for unconventional warfare in the country.[93] The BPP was not simply a law enforcement unit, as its name suggests, but rather it undertook a whole set of state- and nation-building duties, including building roads and schools, teaching the Thai language in a school system it controlled, fostering highland economic development, promoting "Thainess" among the highland ethnic minorities with significant royal involvement, and much more.[94]

Furthermore, through aiding US covert activities against China, key figures in Thailand's military and police forces benefited personally from US military aid as well as from the lucrative opium trade that the KMT engaged in. As the number of poppy planations grew astronomically in the war economy in the Shan State, the KMT's military superiority and close relationship with the Thai police force and military solidified its near-exclusive control of opium smuggling between Burma and Thailand. With the support of the CIA, the head of the Thai police, Phao, significantly expanded the force's size and capacity. He also managed to establish a virtual monopoly on the Burmese opium trade in Thailand due to his extensive contacts with the KMT.[95] McCoy points out that Phao "supported KMT political aims in Thailand and its guerrilla units in Burma . . . [he] protected KMT supply shipments, marketed their opium, and provided . . . miscellaneous services [for the KMT]."[96] Later, when Field Marshall Sarit ousted both Phao and Phibun in a 1957 coup, he continued to rely upon the lucrative opium trade to fund the fast-growing Thai army.[97] By the early 1960s, Thailand became the world's largest distributor of opium from Burma's Shan State, the opium having been smuggled from there into Thailand by the KMT.

As a result of their final 1961 defeat by the Burmese-Chinese military coalition, all remaining KMT troops relocated their main bases to Thailand while continuing to roam along the borderland areas, using caravans to smuggle opium into Thailand, thanks to their military organization and deep connection with the Thai military and government. The most prominent among them were the Third Army under the leadership of Li Wenhuan, based around the town of Tam Ngob, Chiang Mai Province, and the Fifth Army under the leadership of Duan Xiwen and based in Mae Salong, Chiang Rai Province. The Thai government tolerated the KMT for many reasons. One was obviously the lucrative opium trade from which key figures in the border police and military benefited. In fact, it was reported that Li Wenhuan threatened to expose Thais complicity in this trade if his troops were ordered to leave.[98]

The KMT presence created other opportunities for the Thai government. Because of their extensive caravan networks and close working relations with many ethnic groups in mountainous areas, the KMT troops were an excellent source of intelligence on the political situations in China and Burma's tumultuous Shan State.[99] And more importantly, the Thai government tolerated the existence of the KMT in the hope that their familiarity with and presence in the rugged mountains could be a barrier and buffer against possible communist infiltration from China. An article published by Taiwan's *China News* on November 9, 1968, reported specifically that "although Bangkok has said nothing officially, it is no secret that the Thai military forces have welcomed the so-called irregulars as an advance guard of anti-Communist defense. Stepped-up Communist infiltration recently has made the arrangement more important than ever."[100] Indeed, after the start of the CPT insurgency in northern Thailand, both the US and Thai governments came to the conclusion that "the KMT could usefully be employed against dissident hill tribes in the North and that this had overtaken their earlier desire to get rid of the KMT altogether."[101] It seems that in the late 1960s, the KMT was willing to help with Thai anti-insurgency efforts on condition that they would be supplied with sufficient funding and equipment.[102] Chapter 5 will discuss in more detail how the KMT offered its military service to the Royal Thai Army in its campaigns against the CPT insurgency and how in return many soldiers and their family members were granted Thai citizenship.

Concluding Remarks

The end of the Chinese Civil War has had deep repercussions in Southeast Asia. Not only did it generate momentum for other communist movements in the region it also attracted a robust anti-communist response from the United States and its allies. Specifically, in the borderland area between China, Burma, and Thailand, the KMT presence has created different outcomes for each of the three countries. Of the three, obviously Burma was the most adversely affected. Bearing the brunt of the devastation resulting from the KMT invasion and occupation, Burma's Shan State has followed the road of fragmentation ever since. The new Communist government in China also took notice of the KMT presence across the border and demonstrated both ruthlessness and sensitivity in its military campaigns and recruitment of local ethnic-minority elites, thereby successfully consolidating its control over the borderland area. The Thai government was the most opportunistic in taking advantage of US security interests in the region and benefited from both US largess and the KMT presence along its northern border. Yet, the KMT unleashed the trade and smuggling of opium in the Golden Triangle, flooding Southeast Asia and the rest of the world with drugs. Therefore, the end of the Chinese Civil War set in motion a series of developments in the borderland area that defined its post-WWII history. For Ahzhong, mentioned at the start of the chapter, his family's fate became involuntarily intertwined with Burma and Thailand. While many of these KMT descendants tend to romanticize their sacrifices for the "noble" anti-communist cause, often emphasizing their martyr-like experiences surviving in the tough mountainous areas, their overall legacies in the borderland area are nonetheless negative.

5
Communist Revolutions at the Borderland

The afternoon I met Dongfang at a coffee shop in Bangkok was hot and humid. In his thirties, Dongfang is quite thin and speaks Mandarin with a strong southern Chinese accent. Although he is a Chinese citizen, Dongfang has a unique family background rooted in the history of communist insurgencies in Thailand: his father was a CCP agent in Thailand while his mother is an ethnic Hmong CPT soldier from northern Thailand's Nan province. Over coffee, Dongfang recounted his life story to me, which sheds some light on the mysteries surrounding a period of communist intrigues at peak of the Cold War in Southeast Asia.

Dongfang's parents were both part of the CPT insurgency that spread across Northern Thailand in the mid-1960s. His father was part of the overseas Chinese community in Thailand and was recruited by the CCP as an agent to support the CPT. While in Nan, he met Dongfang's mother, who was an ethnic Hmong; revolutionary comrades, they married in the mountains along the Thai-Lao border. In the late 1970s, as part of the withdrawal of CCP support for the CPT, they returned to China and settled in Yunnan province. Dongfang was born and grew up in a compound in Kunming. He remembers his childhood years when his friends in the compound were all children of former communist party members from Burma, Thailand, and Malaysia. Many of his childhood friends still remain in China, but many others have gone to work and live in Southeast Asian countries where they speak the local languages, because of mixed parentage and schooling in Southeast Asian languages such as Thai, Burmese, and Bahasa Melayu, and where their parents used to fight for the communist cause. Dongfang is one such: he is now branch head of a Chinese investment firm in Thailand. He joked that the Chinese used to try sabotaging the Thai economy during the CPT insurgency years, but now they have become some of the largest investors in the kingdom. During a recent trip to visit his grandmother in the mountains of Nan, his parents also remembered vividly the battlefield locations where they used to fight the Thai government troops.

Today, this history of communist intrigues in Southeast Asia seems long gone, and China has transformed itself from a radical communist revolutionary state to a state that is mainly interested in economic development. Beijing might still have ambitions of regional domination, but now sees the way to do so as no longer through sabotage and support for communist insurgencies but through economic expansion. However, its past involvement in exporting revolution has had serious consequences in the countries that were affected. In both Burma and Thailand, the communist insurgencies received direct support from China and lasted for more than a decade in the common mountainous borderland area, with significant but varying legacies in all three countries.

This chapter traces the history of these insurgencies since the mid-1960s, resulting from domestic radicalization in China when Mao initiated his foreign policy of supporting People's Power revolutions in the Third World, as well as launching the Cultural Revolution domestically. It specifically examines the implications for state building in the three countries and discusses how much impact communist revolutions had on the political and social landscapes of the borderland area. The chapter first reviews the general outline of the Cultural Revolution in China and the domestic political radicalization initiated by Mao. It then looks at Yunnan as a province that suffered more disorder than most other provinces in China, partly due to its proximity to the border.[1] The chapter then focuses on the experiences of the tens of thousands of sent-down youth from big cities in China and the effect of their presence on the multi-ethnic borderland area. In the sections on Burma, the chapter first discusses the history of the CPB in the first decade of the country's independence and then focuses on its insurgency along the Sino-Burmese border from 1967 to 1989. It goes on to examine the CPB legacy of ethnic rebellions resulting from the ceasefire process between them and the Myanmar central government. In the Thai context, the chapter examines the CPT insurgency since the mid-1960s and how the international political situation between China and Indochina deeply affected its political fortunes.

Cultural Revolution and Yunnan

The Chinese Cultural Revolution marked the most violent and frantic decade in modern Chinese history.[2] As part of a push for another revolution to remake Chinese society in his utopian vision and to consolidate his dictatorial rule to eliminate potential challengers within the CCP, Mao unleashed the Cultural Revolution in May 1966. With the mindset that capitalist revisionists had penetrated the CCP, Mao called upon the people to rise up and oust those in power. To do that, Mao established a Cultural Revolution Committee as a separate powerbase away from the party, and appealed to the public, especially students—the so-called Red Guards—to rebel against authority. Particularly between 1966 and 1968, Chinese society experienced widespread violence, with factions battling in the streets as the whole country was literally in a state of civil war. Throughout the Chinese government and the CCP, most of those who were previously in power had been "struggled" (publically humiliated and sometimes tortured), demoted or arrested, and many of those arrested died. The economy crashed because of the political chaos, and China's industrial output became negative. The national education system came to a halt as well, with much of the student body heavily politicized and radicalized. Indeed, those middle and high school students who were out of school but without employment exceeded the urban job supply, especially after Mao's initial goal of purging the party had been accomplished. In this context, Mao delivered a directive published in the *People's Daily* in December 1968 calling for educated youth to go to the countryside and be re-educated by the peasants. Thus, started the movement "Up to the Mountains and Down to the Villages (*shangshan xiaxiang*)," through which urban students and former red guards were sent to the countryside and to the peripheral borderland areas of China.[3] Many went to Yunnan.

Of all the provinces, Yunnan was arguably one of the most negatively affected by the Cultural Revolution. Multiple factors made it so, many related to the topics of discussion in the previous chapter. The first factor was the KMT. When the PLA took over Yunnan in late 1949 and early 1950, the handover to the communists was relatively peaceful, through the defection of the KMT governor Lu Han.[4] With the exception of those who fled to Burma, hordes of KMT troops surrendered to the PLA, which was militarily far superior.[5] Except for those branded counter-revolutionaries and subsequently persecuted, most former KMT members were initially left alone or even wooed as targets for co-optation when the communist regime was still consolidating its power. Therefore, when the KMT troops in Burma were harassing the Chinese borderland in the early 1950s, the Communist government tried to introduce its social transformation programs in the region gradually. The ethnic mosaic of Yunnan province also made the communists wary of being too aggressive in their policies. As discussed in chapter 4, for the sake of borderland ethnic stability, land reforms were not carried out immediately, and many ethnic elites were co-opted into the party.

But, the moderation of the early 1950s came back to haunt Yunnan. When radicalism took hold with the start of the Cultural Revolution, those who were previously spared became targets of attack in the name of ridding the party and society of "capitalist revisionists." First, moderate leaders were removed from the provincial party and government. The First Secretary of the CCP in Yunnan, Yan Hongyan, who previously advocated adjusting the party's borderland politics to accommodate special local conditions, was the first to fall from power. Since November 1966, at a series of meetings held in Kunming, Red Guards attacked Yan for carrying out policies in Yunnan province that were "capitalist and counterrevolutionary." Pressure on Yan continued to build, and on January 8, 1967, he committed suicide.[6] Before the situation in the province went out of control, the PLA took over control through the Kunming Military Region (MR).[7] By the time the Yunnan Provincial Cultural Revolution Committee was established in August 1968, the province had been engulfed in two years of military clashes that led to more than five thousand deaths.[8]

However, radicalization in the province continued. For the purpose of "fighting the enemy, defending the frontier and doing work in relation to national minority affairs and building up the border regions," the Yunnan Cultural Revolution Committee together with the Kunming MR launched the Political Frontier Defense (PFD) initiative in April 1969,[9] which included five measures. First they pushed for utmost personal worship of Mao through quasi-religious propaganda throughout the province. Anybody with grudges against Mao or showing disrespect of his images was simply branded as a counter-revolutionary. The second called for cleansing of the class ranks in Yunnan. As we have seen in chapter 4, due to the moderate policies of the 1950s the Yunnan borderland areas did not go through a rigid categorization of classes, and land reform did not proceed as it did elsewhere in China. Through PFD, this policy was reversed, and many ethnic minorities in the borderland area received their official class categorizations, which in many localities were carried out arbitrarily.[10] Third, the PFD called for the establishment of "People's Communes" in the borderland to bring the "backward" ethnic minority societies into the advanced socialist stage.[11]

The fourth mobilized the masses to topple the ruling elites of ethnic minorities. Previously, many of these ethnic leaders were targeted for co-optation and many had escaped the political repression of the 1950s. This time, all the former ethnic leaders and their families were sent down to their ancestral villages to be struggled, many violently.[12] In Dehong, many of the former tusi were brutally attacked. For example, the former Longchuan Jingpo tusi and former vice governor for Dehong prefecture, Duo Yongan, was beaten to death at one of the struggle sessions. Another former Zhefang tusi Duo Peiying also died a day after being severely beaten.[13] According to a report submitted to the CCP central committee by the Kunming MR and Yunnan RC in March 1970, during the previous year, a total of 8,115 "counter-revolutionary" former tusi or headsmen were politically struggled. In several places, these struggle sessions were carried out by ethnic Han, which significantly worsened tension among ethnic groups.[14] The sessions represented the overall tone of the Cultural Revolution, which treated ethnicity as politically irrelevant but ignored the complexities of interethnic relations in the borderland area. As a result, interethnic relations in the borderland significantly deteriorated during the Cultural Revolution years. The most violent interethnic confrontation occurred in Shadian, where Hui Muslims staged an armed rebellion in November 1974 in response to years of targeted repression of Islam. The Shadian rebellion ultimately faced PLA military suppression, with more than a thousand deaths.[15]

Finally, the PFD called for the elimination of nine types of "bad elements" from the borderland, including "special agents, renegades, arch-unrepentant capitalist roaders, KMT dregs of the old society and unreformed landlord, rich peasant, counter-revolutionary, bad and Rightist elements."[16] Many former KMT members and their families, people with family ties with Taiwan, and even some of the CCP leadership were accused of being KMT spies and arrested. In the mission to "investigate KMT spies in Yunnan," for example, more than 500,000 people were affected in Baoshan and Dehong regions alone.[17] The scale of violence unleashed by the PFD was unprecedented in Yunnan, with the number of deaths estimated in the range of 17,000 to 37,000.[18] The political chaos also made ordinary people's lives on the Chinese side of the border unbearable. In Dehong alone, the implementation of the PFD greatly destabilized the borderland region, with more than 17,000 residents fleeing to Burma.[19]

While such violent political transformations were carried out by the CCP in the borderland, the peripheral nature of the province also made it one of the top destinations for demobilized urban youths after the first two years of violent street battles among the Red Guards. Those two years of political chaos and factional violence had fundamentally put the whole Chinese economy into a stall, raising the question of where these youth should go when schools and universities were closed and no employment opportunities were available in the cities. Mao sent them to the countryside to be "re-educated" by the peasants, and many came to Yunnan. From 1968 to 1980, when this policy was reversed, more than three hundred thousand urban youths were working in the rural areas of Yunnan's borderland, more than one hundred thousand of whom came from Beijing, Shanghai, and Sichuan. Most were forced to relocate as a test of their loyalty to Mao and the Cultural Revolution, and it was their first time in the remote peripheral borderland areas of Yunnan.

In order to host such large numbers of urban youths in the borderland area, the Chinese State Council and the Central Military Commission approved the establishment of a PLA Yunnan Production and Construction Corps (YPCC), under the auspices of the Yunnan Cultural Revolution Committee and the Kunming MR.[20] The YPCC comprised one hundred state farms within four main divisions at Xishuangbanna (Simao), Lincang, Baoshan, and Honghe. With the exception of Honghe, which borders Vietnam, the other three all have long borders with Burma. At its official founding in early 1970, the YPCC employed more than one hundred thousand people under a military-style administration.[21] In 1974, the YPCC was transformed to a government bureau, at which time the military components of the state farms were removed.

In these state farms, urban youths were made to transform the borderland geographical landscape through hard labor.[22] They cut down forests and reclaimed them for agricultural plantation. In Xishuangbanna, the YPCC No. 1 Division, a total of 52,941 urban youths were settled by the end of 1972—more than 50% of the workers. Of these, 30,245 were from Shanghai, 15,548 from Chongqing, 4,097 from Kunming and 3,051 from Beijing.[23] Ever since the early years of the PRC, because of its international isolation and the embargo of key industrial materials imposed by the United States on the Beijing government, Xishuangbanna was tasked with developing rubber plantations to supply this key commodity for China's industrialization plan. These were set up with a strong ethnic bias, in that they employed exclusively Han Chinese workers, apparently because of the ideological conviction that industrial development of this key commodity had to be carried out by the more advanced Han labor rather than the primitive local ethnic workers.[24] So when these urban youths from big cities were sent to Xishuangbanna, many ended up on those state farms, planting rubber to further strengthen Han Chinese control of the borderland human geography.[25]

Thus, the Cultural Revolution represented the most dramatic episode of Han Chinese migration or settlement to the borderland areas, and the population of Han Chinese in places such as Xishuangbanna grew substantially in the 1960s. According to census data, in 1953 there were only 147,000 Han Chinese in Xishuangbanna, which grew to 831,000 in 1964. In the 1982 census, the Han Chinese population had more than doubled again to 1.86 million.[26] The 1982 data did not account for the majority of the sent-down Han Chinese youth who left Xishuangbanna after 1979, which means that the actual number of Han Chinese in this borderland region during the Cultural Revolution was much higher. Thus, during the Cultural Revolution the interaction between local ethnic groups and Han Chinese was quite extensive; this is also when many of the urban Han Chinese youth came into direct contact with non-Han ethnic groups for the first time. On the one hand, such encounters offered a chance for the Han to re-evaluate the restrictive socialist moral code they were under and compare it with the "free nature" of the local ethnic people.[27] On the other hand, the Han Chinese youth also acted as "civilizing agents" that brought Chinese culture and language to the borderland area and increased the assimilative pressure on the local population.

The Cultural Revolution was also the period when direct assault on local ethnic culture was the most intense. In places such as Xishuangbanna, this came in the form of destroying local ethnic cultural artifacts, such as Buddhist images and temples and books written in traditional Dai Lue scripts. The teaching of the Dai language was prohibited in the school system, and the whole monastic education system was also abolished.[28] All novices and monks were forced to defrock to return to secular life, and many in fact fled to Burma. Teaching of the Chinese language was intensified, because most teachers in local schools were now Han Chinese due to the demographic shift in the borderland.[29] Indeed, while many Han Chinese see the Cultural Revolution as a regrettable period of excessive violence and repression of ethnic minorities in the borderland area, they also see that it increased the influence of the Chinese language and culture and accelerated the decline of ethnic traditions among the local population.[30] Although in the post-Cultural Revolution period, ethnic cultures in Yunnan's borderland area as well as in other parts of China have been revived,[31] the Han Chinese culture and language have successfully established hegemony.

Finally, many of the tens of thousands of Han Chinese youth, former red guards, who came to Yunnan's borderland were inspired to cross the border and support the military insurgency of the CPB. Motivated by Mao's slogan "Liberate the Whole of Mankind, Support World Revolution (*jiefang quanrenlei, zhichi shijie geming*)," and inspired by the spirit of Che Guevara, who died in 1968, and perhaps also to escape the tedious hard labor at state farms, thousands of these Chinese revolutionary youths participated in the military campaigns of the CPB. After they crossed the border and reached CPB camps, they received military training and weapons to carry out guerrilla warfare. Many died on the battlefield in Burma, while many others returned after a few years, and others still remain in Burma to this day. The story of the CPB insurgency and China's role in it will be discussed in the following section.

CPB Insurgency along the Borderland

The CPB was founded in August 1939 as part of the wide-scale political awakening of Burmese society under British colonial rule. In fact, many of the early founders of the CPB held memberships in multiple political organizations, including the Dobama Asiayone,[32] and even the future leader of the Burmese independence movement, Aung San, was a member of the CPB at the time.[33] During that period, leftist ideologies such as communism were inspiring many Burmese youth and deprived workers who, at the same, time craved national self-determination and independence from repressive British rule. Therefore, during the early years of the CPB, its activities were more nationalist than ideological.[34] However, after the Japanese invasion of Burma in 1941, the CPB worked with the British to oppose the Japanese. Two prominent leaders of the CPB, Thakin[35] Than Tun and Thakin Soe, issued an "Insein Manifesto," which called for cooperation with the British forces against the Japanese. Indeed, its anti-Japanese stance won the CPB a high amount of popular support, which also helped to increase its strength as it came to control around thirty thousand guerrilla forces.[36]

The Second Party Congress in July 1945 marked the first time that the CPB came out as an open, legal party in Burmese politics.[37] At the congress, the 120 delegates represented more than 6,000 party members throughout the country, electing Thakin Than Tun as chairman of the Politburo and Thakin Thein Pe as general secretary.[38] However, internal divisions along ideological lines started to threaten its unity. Thakin Soe accused the party leadership of compromising with the imperialists, and instead he called for a hard-line People's War. This led to the split of the party in July 1946 when Thakin Soe set up his own Communist Party, commonly known as the Red Flags, which he led in a guerrilla war.[39] The CPB itself also gradually became more radical and started to change from a legal opposition party to an underground insurgency.[40] The party agitated, in particular, against the AFPFL-led government, opposing its agrarian policies as well as some of the post-independence agreement with the British through which the AFPFL maintained some privileges.[41] In late March 1948, the government ordered the arrest of the CPB leaders; after this, from April 1948—perhaps following Mao's doctrine of rural guerrilla warfare—the CPB retreated to rural areas to take up arms against the newly independent union government.[42] Thus started the long insurgency of the CPB.

The period between 1948 and 1955 witnessed the CPB's intensive insurgency against the Burmese government as the CPB's military forces occupied large swamps of rural areas in central Burma. CPB's People's Army failed to take urban centers as a result of the government troops' counteroffensives and instead concentrated its efforts on establishing rural guerrilla zones.[43] Indeed, CPB agrarian policies in rural areas at the time, such as the confiscation of land from big landowners and its redistribution to poor peasants, were quite popular. According to a report by the *Times*, "Villagers often join one or other of the Communist parties, knowing nothing about Communism but with a vague belief, arising from communist propaganda, that if the Communists were in power every villager would get land free and not have to pay rent or land revenue."[44] However, the incursion of the KMT into the Burmese Shan State in 1950 caused the CPB leadership to rethink its relationship with the Rangoon government. Naively believing the need to form a united front with the government against the foreign invaders, the CPB reversed its previous agrarian policy by returning land to the landlords. This created strong discontent among its rank and file, and almost half of its fighting force defected, while the Rangoon government never accepted its reconciliatory gesture.[45] This strategic mistake was a huge blow to the CPB insurgency, and in a press conference in November 1952, Burmese Prime Minister U Nu expressed satisfaction at the rapid extinction of the Communist revolt.[46] From the mid-1950s to the early 1960s, the CPB suffered major defeats, partly due to its own strategic mistakes and partly due to the government's military offensives.

It wasn't until the military coup of 1962 that the CPB was reinvigorated by the arrival at its headquarters in Pegu Yoma of young intellectuals interested in joining the armed struggle against the military regime.[47] The rise to power of the military government in Burma, wishing to pursue a "Burmese Road to Socialism," and a strict, neutral foreign policy somehow did not sit well with the Beijing government.[48] Beijing perceived Ne Win's military government as upsetting the regional balance of power and saw him as an ambitious and unpredictable leader.[49] Ne Win's nationalization of the Burmese economy also hurt Chinese economic interests in the country and cut off China's relations with and influence among Burma's overseas Chinese community.[50]

The Sino-Soviet split in 1961 created a dynamic of competition between the two communist giants, struggling for influence in the Third World, on the basis of their differences over how global communist movements should be organized. In June 1963, the CCP issued *A Proposal Concerning the General Line of the International Communist Movement (guanyu guoji gongchan zhuyi yundong zongluxian de jianyi)*, in which the CCP attacked the Communist Party of the Soviet Union's principle of peaceful coexistence as an excuse to justify its collusion with the United States.[51] The proposal specifically called for communist movements around the world to use armed struggle to defeat counter-revolutionary forces.[52] Indeed, it was around this time that the CCP started to set the ground for supporting communist movements abroad, especially in Southeast Asia.

In late 1963, CPB members who were already in China were tasked with surveying possible infiltration routes from Yunnan to northeastern Burma. The Chinese government also built a new network of roads that linked to the borderland area with Burma.[53] Despite such preparations, direct support for the CPB did not come until after 1967, when bilateral relations between China and Burma fundamentally broke down.

The trigger for the collapse of bilateral relations was anti-Chinese riots in several major cities in Burma. There are many interpretations of the causes of these riots, but most agree they were directly related to the export of Cultural Revolution to the overseas Chinese communities in Burma.[54] After the start of the Cultural Revolution in China in 1966, the Chinese Foreign Ministry was radicalized. One of the main missions for Chinese embassies abroad was to propagate Mao's philosophy and distribute *Quotations from Chairman Mao Tse-Tung*, commonly known as the little red book.[55] Their diplomatic missions were also actively involved in recruiting red guards among overseas Chinese communities.[56] In Burma, sections of the overseas

Chinese community started to wear badges depicting Mao, many defying the government's ban on the badges with the support of the embassy staff in Rangoon.[57] The radicalization of the overseas Chinese community also occurred at a time when Burma was facing severe economic problems with a bad rice harvest and a breakdown in the distribution of many of its economic necessities.[58] As a result, a string of anti-Chinese riots broke out that led to the burning and looting of Chinese businesses and associations and the killing of scores of Chinese people.[59]

The riots fundamentally shattered the bilateral relations between the two countries; Beijing was extremely angry about the treatment of Chinese people, and a rally of more than two hundred thousand people was organized in Beijing as a protest against the riots.[60] In many places in Yunnan, protests were also organized to denounce Ne Win as the Chiang Kai-shek of Burma and call for making Burma the new battlefield in the war against US imperialism and Soviet revisionism.[61] In order to retaliate against Burma, the CCP supported the CPB's plan to open a base in northeast Burma, across from the Chinese border.

On New Year's Day 1968, a small troop comprising many CPB cadres, including many Kachin soldiers under the leadership of Naw Seng, who had retreated into China during the previous decades, crossed into Mong Ko, a small border town in the Muse district of the Shan state, which the CPB designated as Base 303.[62] A separate attack was also carried out by the Kokang Chinese under the leadership of Peng Jiasheng to the east of the Salween River, which the CPB designated as Base 404.[63] Closely following the CPB troops was a much large number of Chinese Red Guards who supported the CPB in the name of international solidarity (guoji zhizuo).[64] Later, the CCP also sent into Burma two PLA Special Forces units to reinforce the militarily inexperienced CPB. The Chinese soldiers were all recruited from among ethnic minority groups in Yunnan and were militarily superior to the Burmese government troops. PLA support helped the CPB troops consolidate their military success, and the CPB's base area in the northeast of Burma started to expand.[65] In a speech published in the *People's Daily* in March 1969, then-CPB Vice Chairman Thakin Ba Thein Tin said the year 1968 witnessed large-scale battles in the Burmese Shan State, and the Burma People's Army achieved a significant victory by defeating Burmese government troops.[66]

The CPB's battlefield success was also due to the logistical support that China provided across the border. Between 1968 and 1973, China supplied the CPB with enough arms and ammunition to equip ten thousand soldiers, along with two million Chinese Yuan per year for general military expenditures, and Chinese hospitals along the border were opened for use by the CPB. In 1971 Beijing also set up a radio station called *People's Voice of Burma* for the CPB to disseminate propaganda.[67] It was first located in Kunming and later moved to the Sino-Burmese border city of Mangshi before moving to Pangsang, the headquarters of the CPB, in 1979.[68] As a result of such generous support, the CPB first established four main bases—101, 202, 303, and 404—and from there its troops conquered several territories. Within six years, it managed controlled over twenty thousand square kilometers of "liberated" areas along the Chinese border, "stretching uninterruptedly from the Mekong River and the Lao border up to the border town of Panghsai (kyu-hkok) where the Burma Road crosses into Yunnan."[69]

Thousands of Chinese Red Guards, in particular, made a huge contribution to the CPB's military campaigns. According to one former participant's account of events, there was a whole division of Chinese sent-down youth (zhiqing) among the CPB ranks. In the 3301 Brigade, half were from Kunming, and the other half came from overseas Chinese communities. In the 3302 Brigade, almost all came from Sichuan. In addition, there was a Women's Special Force made up of Chinese youth. These former Red Guards were highly capable and also heavily indoctrinated in Mao's revolutionary fervor. Of the thousands of Chinese Red Guards who fought for the CPB, many returned to China within a few years, many others died in the battlefields in Burma, and others still stayed behind in Burma and remain there to this day. For example, several of the current ethnic rebel leaders in Burma are former Chinese Red Guards, such as Lin Mingxian who is the leader of National Democratic Alliance Army in Mongla, formerly the CPB's War Zone 815.

Facing CPB advances in the Northeast, the Burmese military initially was not used to such guerilla tactics as a surprise attack with human waves. Instead of battling the CPB in the northeast, the Burmese military instead focused its attention on eliminating the older CPB headquarters in the Pegu Yoma mountains. Thakin Than Tun, the CPB chairman, was assassinated in 1968 by a government spy.[70] By early 1975, the Burmese military had wiped out the CPB presence there. On the other hand, the Ne Win government understood clearly that its problems with the CPB in the Northeast were due mainly to Chinese support for the communists. If bilateral relations between Rangoon and Beijing could improve, compared to the abyss of 1967, then the CPB presence there could be easily contained. In May 1975, Thakin Ba

Thein Tin officially announced the reestablishment of the CPB headquarters at Pangsang, with himself as the chairman. Pangsang, a border town across from China's Menglian county, is in the Wa hills, an area conducive to the recruitment of Wa soldiers while at the same time far away from Burmese military pressure.

China's domestic politic began changing in 1976 with Mao's passing and the end of the Cultural Revolution. At that time, the CPB leadership made a strategic mistake by criticizing Deng Xiaoping, whom they thought Mao had disposed of earlier that year. They clung to the idea that the Maoist style of revolution would continue in China.[71] When Deng emerged as the paramount leader in the post-Cultural Revolution reshuffle, Thakin Ba Thein Tin realized they had picked the wrong side. The last time the CPB was mentioned in Chinese news was November 1976. In 1978, CPB members on the Chinese side of the border were told to go back to Burma. Most of the Chinese Red Guards were also recalled.[72] Deng also decided to cut off funding for the CPB and told it to be self-reliant. At first, Beijing was willing to let the CPB monopolize taxation of bilateral trade. However in 1980, under its new open-door policy, the Deng administration decided to open up more border trading sites with Burma, and the CPB lost its monopoly.[73]

The financially strapped CPB had a huge difficulty finding an alternative income source to sustain itself. The mountainous areas it controlled along the border did not produce much grain, nor did they have many minerals or other natural resources, but they were historically known for producing opium. In the end, the CPB allowed opium harvesting and opened heroin refineries for drug trafficking, just as the KMT and other ethnic rebel groups had done, to sustain themselves.[74] However, the profit brought in by drug trafficking also led to corruption within the party. Many field commanders became heavily involved in the business and became increasingly like warlords and difficult to control.[75] Even though the CPB leadership later tried to reign in the scale of drug trafficking, its "rectification campaign" fell on deaf ears, and the leadership's ability to control the CPB was considerably reduced.[76]

However, the last straws for the CPB were the deep-rooted ethnic problems within the party's rank and file. While the party's upper echelon were predominantly ethnic Bamar intellectuals, the foot soldiers were mostly recruited from ethnic groups along the Sino-Burmese border. In particular, ethnic Wa soldiers accounted for a big chunk of the CPB's fighting forces that bore the brunt of war casualties. The Wa felt that the CPB leaders maintained a highly discriminatory system that prevented ethnic minority people from rising up the ranks. But in the end, it was Chinese Kokang soldiers under the leadership of Peng Jiasheng who fired the first shots challenging the CPB leadership, on March 12, 1989. A couple of days later, Wa soldiers under Zhao Nilai stormed party headquarters in Pangsang and forced the CPB leaders into exile in China.[77] In a speech at Pangsang, Zhao stated that the mutiny had been fought to remove the CPB leadership who were oppressing local ethnic people.[78] Thus, in the year that global communism started to crumble in Eastern Europe, as well as in Beijing where a student movement challenged the CCP, the CPB met its end as a political party and a military force.

CPT Insurgency in North and Northeast Thailand

The history of communist activities in Thailand, particularly in the metropolis of Bangkok, is more intimately connected with the communist movement in China as well as in Southeast Asia (nanyang), especially in comparison with Yangon. This was due in part to the large number of overseas Chinese in Thailand, which arguably had one of the largest overseas Chinese communities in Southeast Asia thanks to the long history of migration from southern China into Siam.[79] Also, as a country that remained independent while the rest of Southeast Asia was colonized by Europeans, Thailand provided a haven for political exiles of various leanings, which was why communist activists among the overseas Chinese in Southeast Asia often preferred Bangkok as a meeting place.[80] Thus, the first communist party active in Bangkok was the Siam branch of the CCP, which, along with the KMT, actively mobilized Thailand's Chinese community to achieve political objectives back home after the two parties split in 1927.[81] As such, the repressive measures taken by the Thai government in the 1930s, such as the Communist Act designed to prevent the spread of communism, was mostly aimed at controlling the Chinese community.[82]

On the other hand, a separate Communist Party of Thailand (CPT) also existed in Thailand but did not have a high profile at that time; its first party congress was in 1942, albeit under heavy influence of the local CCP branch.[83] During the Japanese occupation of Thailand, the CPT participated in the anti-Japanese resistance and organized strikes and sabotage in alignment with the Free Thai movement led by Pridi.[84] It was only after the PRC was founded and the CCP Siam Branch ceased to function that the CPT started to act more independently. In 1952 and 1961 the CPT held its second and third party congresses; it devoted most of its attention during this decade to urban mobilization, aiming for some kind of democratic revolution, but with limited success.[85] Ultimately, the CPT's political appeal to mainstream Thai society remained limited.

Indeed, outside of the closed Chinese community, communism as an ideology was not very attractive to the broader Thai society.[86] Having escaped colonial domination, Thailand's political and social structures had more continuity and durability compared with other formerly colonized countries in Southeast Asia. A simple comparison with the case of Burma is striking. In Burma, foreign domination provided the fodder for nationalist mobilization, and the destitute conditions of Burmese peasants and workers under the exploitation of the Indian rentier class called Chettiars, at least as perceived by the Burmese, made leftist ideology popular.[87] Thus, in Burma, communism and nationalism found the right combination of economic and political conditions that made them popular among the indigenous political elites and intellectuals. In the Thai case, national independence and class warfare were never viable political questions. Furthermore, the continuity of the Thai monarchy and the central role of Buddhism in Thai political culture also made communism less appealing, at least among the majority of Thais living in the central plains.[88]

The appeal of communist ideology in Thailand was, therefore, confined to communities on the fringes of Thai society. Other than the Chinese, the areas that offered the most potential for communist mobilization were in the far south, where Thailand borders Malaysia, and where the activities of the Communist Party of Malaya had spread across the border among the Malay populations.[89] In the North, where Thailand borders Burma and Laos, a variety of ethnic minorities, such as the Meo (Miao or Hmong) or as the Thai call them, Hill Tribes (chaokhao), historically roamed the mountain ranges between Yunnan and Thailand. These ethnic groups, with their slash and burn agriculture, had never been accepted by mainstream Thai society and developed serious grievances over land rights when the Thai government began implementing more stringent forest management around 1960.[90] Finally, the most significant community different from the central Thais are people in the northeast (Isan), who are linguistically and culturally similar to the people in Laos, and also economically more deprived. After the Lao Crisis of 1959, the spread of communism from Indochina to northeast Thailand became a serious concern for the Thai government.[91]

However, the country that had the most influence on the communist movement in Thailand remained the newly founded PRC. Earlier on, Beijing deemed Phibun's government hostile, especially when it passed the Anti-Communist Act in 1952 and deported much of the left-leaning Chinese community back to China. Although China granted political asylum to Pridi during the first half of the 1950s, little was mentioned in the Chinese media about supporting a communist revolution in Thailand.[92] It seems that during the early years of the PRC, Beijing spent its diplomatic efforts trying to draw the Thai government away from a close alliance with the United States. Indeed, after the Bandung Conference in 1955, when China unveiled its Five Principles of Peaceful Co-Existence, Bangkok's policy toward Beijing eased somewhat. However, after Sarit Thanarat's coup in 1957 that took out Phibun's government but was followed by another coup against Sarit himself in 1958, the new military dictatorship further deepened its relations with the United States.[93] The Sarit government not only tightened up its domestic repression against the left, but also reversed the previous trend of warming relations with Beijing.

At this time, Thailand was getting closely involved with US military activities in Indochina. And with the deterioration of the situation in Laos and Vietnam, Beijing's hostility toward Thailand also increased.[94] As we discussed earlier, domestic radicalization in the PRC and its competition with the Soviet Union had pushed Beijing to adopt a more adventurous foreign policy in the early 1960s. Certainly this explained the Chinese government's overall approach of increasing support for communist movements abroad. However, in the case of Thailand, the Chinese decision to offer direct support for the CPT insurgency was directly tied to the US escalation of the war in Vietnam between 1964 and 1966.[95] As Thailand offered itself as a base for the US military campaign in Indochina, Beijing increasingly came to view the country as a threat to its national security. Already in 1962, after the signing of the Thanat-Rusk Communiqué that committed US support for Thailand's defence, a *People's Daily* editorial on May 19 commented, "US aggressive moves in Southeast Asia are a serious threat to the security of China. The Chinese people cannot remain indifferent to this."[96] Thus, the CCP's decision to offer direct support for the CPT insurgency can be understood as a way to deter the Bangkok government from expanding its alliance with the United States.[97]

On January 31, 1964, the *Peking Review* reported that the People's Voice of Thailand (PVT) had been calling on the Thai people to rise up against

US imperialism in the country.⁹⁸ In December that year, the *Peking Review* published a manifesto of the Thailand Independence Movement (TIM), which demanded the overthrow of the Thannom Kittikachorn government and a return of Thailand to neutrality.⁹⁹ In January 1965, the PVT announced the formation of a Thai Patriotic Front (TPF), which together with the TIM established permanent missions in Beijing.¹⁰⁰ Later, the TIM and TPF agreed to merge and form a Thai United Patriotic Front (TUPF), modeled on the National Liberation Front in South Vietnam.¹⁰¹ Thus, from 1965 onwards the CPT insurgency started to spread in the rural areas of the northeast provinces.

The CPT insurgencies were mainly carried out in the peripheral parts of Thailand's south, north, and northeast, as noted earlier in the discussion on places where communist ideologies had some appeal. Initially, the CPT insurgency gained notice in the northeast, and the PVT started broadcasting in the Isan Lao dialect. The number of insurgents was estimated at around 1,500, and during the first nine months of 1967, they carried out 269 attacks in 28 Thai provinces.¹⁰² In 1968, insurgencies flared up in the north as well, predominantly among the Meo hill tribes.¹⁰³ Indeed, it was in the north that the CPT insurgency took on characteristics of ethno-nationalist liberation. The PVT started to broadcast in several hill tribe languages, and the CPT declared itself the leader of all nationalities in Thailand.¹⁰⁴ In a "Statement of Present Policy," issued by the CPT in January 1969, the party promised that "The various nationalities shall enjoy the right of autonomy within the big family of Thailand [and] economy, culture, education and public health shall be developed in the areas of all the nationalities."¹⁰⁵

Through a strategy of penetrating the rural and mountainous areas, the CPT succeeded in establishing several bases in northern Thailand, including parts of Chiang Rai, Phayao, Nan, and Thak, as well as in the tri-border area of Phitsanulok, Phetchabun, and Loei.¹⁰⁶ Other than these base areas, the CPT also established many guerrilla zones where they had some influence over the rural population. In these areas, the CPT categorized villages according to their level of control, ranging from "liberated villages," where the CPT had eliminated Thai government influence, to "infiltrating villages," which the party had recently infiltrated.¹⁰⁷ The CPT's military force comprised three types: party soldiers, local soldiers, and village militia.¹⁰⁸ Youth, both male and female, were actively recruited into the CPT armed forces.¹⁰⁹ Despite expanding its insurgency in Thailand's peripheral provinces, the CPT's urban influence since the mid-1960s had remained negligible.

By the early 1970s, Thailand had been under military rule for almost two decades, and the country was facing serious social problems, including large numbers of US troops on Thai soil resented by many, rampant corruption, and widening economic inequality.[110] The repressive government of Thanom became the target of an active student movement that demanded democracy and a fairer society and eventually brought it down in October 1973 following intense confrontations between students and the military.[111] The subsequent weak and unstable civilian governments provided a window of opportunity for the CPT to penetrate the student movement. By 1975–1976, the CPT had established firm ground within student organizations and started to shape the dynamics of the students' political activities.[112] Then, in October 1976 there was another coup, a violent change in government, with a massacre of hundreds of students at Thammasat University in Bangkok.[113] The result was a major influx of thousands of students and intellectuals into the jungles where they hoped to join the ranks of the CPT. Disillusioned by the failure of their democratic participation, these urban activists had come to the conclusion that armed struggle with the CPT against the military government was their only alternative.[114] The enlarged CPT then intensified its major offensives during 1977 and 1978, which was arguably the peak of the CPT insurgency.[115] By the end of 1978, there were an estimated "fourteen thousand armed insurgents operating in fifty-two of the seventy-two provinces."[116]

However, international political changes in China and Indochina gave a huge blow to the CPT in 1978. As mentioned earlier, the CPT as a political party was heavily influenced by the CCP. Its insurgency from the mid-1960s had also been heavily supported by the Chinese, in terms of financing, weapons, and propaganda.[117] Although such support cannot compare with the support the CCP gave to the CPB—perhaps simply because supplies had to bypass Laos, and Thailand does not share a direct border with China—the Chinese had been the fundamental source of the CPT's ideological orientation.[118] But, when Deng came to power following Mao's death, Beijing cut off support for communist movements in nearby countries, including the CPT. Worse for the CPT, the Chinese government was aligning more closely with the Thai government.

As a close ally of the United States, Thailand had refused to recognize the PRC. However, as a result of Nixon's visit to Beijing in 1972, and especially after the unification of Vietnam in 1975, Vietnam replaced the PRC as Thailand's greatest perceived security threat. Thailand established diplomatic relations with the PRC in 1975, and both countries began to find common ground for a cooperative relationship based on mutual antipathy toward Hanoi, as the latter's close alliance with Moscow caused its relations with Beijing to deteriorate further. In 1978, when Vietnam invaded Cambodia, Thailand and China formed a de facto alliance, whereby Thailand allowed Chinese materiel support for the Khmer Rouge to pass through its territory, and China promised it would help Thailand if the latter came under Vietnamese attack.[119] China's attack on Vietnam in 1979 also relieved Vietnamese pressure on Thailand.[120]

Such international changes dealt a huge blow to the CPT. China became increasingly uncomfortable maintaining support for the CPT, while bilateral relations with Bangkok had significantly improved. When Deng Xiaoping visited Thailand in November 1978, he was questioned at length at a press conference on China's support for the CPT, during which he tried to clarify the difference between state-to-state and party-to-party relations.[121] Soon after, in July 1979, the PVT, which was previously based in Kunming, was ordered to close, and from then on the CCP no longer provided aid to the CPT.[122] But, hostility between China and Vietnam also meant the CPT was caught in the middle. Because of its pro-China orientation, the Vietnamese cut relations with the CPT in 1979, preventing materiel from coming into Thailand via Laos, and some of the CPT camps in Laos were also asked to evacuate.[123] Thus, the CPT lost its external support.

Meanwhile, the Thai government had also adopted a new strategy of counter-insurgency. Traditionally, it tended to approach counter-insurgency purely through military means. But, the harsh military repression further alienated the rural population, which pushed them instead to the CPT.[124] It was Prem Tinsulanonda, who came to power in 1980, who implemented a political strategy to persuade intellectuals to return to the cities. The Prime Minister's Order Number 62/63, issued in 1980, included amnesty for communists who wanted to surrender and an offer to students of the chance to re-enroll in university.[125] Thus, loss of external support, deep internal divisions between the intellectuals and the CPT leadership, as well as the effectiveness of the Thai government's new strategy of counter-insurgency led to the quick decline of the CPT, which had lost most of its forces by the mid-1980s.

Concluding Remarks

The Chinese communist juggernaut deeply affected the countries in its vicinity. Not only did Mao's radicalization, both domestically and diplomatically, bring revolutionary change to China's borderland region, it also spilled over the border into mainland Southeast Asia. As we have seen, the trauma of colonialism made communism a more popular ideology in Burma than in Thailand, which explains the deep domestic root of the CPB both in terms of its political participation as well as the wide scale of its insurgency. Thus, the CPB insurgency should not be considered as entirely externally driven, but rather as having a strong social foundation in Burma. Certainly, the fact that China shares a long border with Burma but has no border with Thailand also meant that the logistics of supplying the CPB were much easier. On top of that, Thailand's government, with the support of the United States, was much more capable than Burma's of dealing with such internal challenges militarily. Overall, the CPT insurgency was not as widespread, and its geographical spread was more sporadic: it had a few bases in mountainous areas but never managed to establish a wide swath of "liberated territories," as the CPB did. The CPB insurgency also led to the continual militarization of the Sino-Burmese borderland area, while the CPT's re-absorption into Thai society through amnesty programs meant that its legacy remained minimal. How each of the three countries approached their own nation-building projects toward the borderland ethnic minorities, a factor that interacts with the borderland revolutions, will be discussed in more detail in a later chapter.

6
Dynamics of Transboundary Economic Flows

When I crossed the passport checkpoint on a bridge linking the Thai city of Mae Sai and Myanmar's Tachileik, I saw Duwan waiting for me on the side of the road in a bright-orange Buddhist monk robe. Duwan is from Kengtung and is himself a member of the Tai Khun ethnic group. Although from Myanmar's Shan State, his family sent him at a young age to Thailand for a Buddhist education, which is why Duwan speaks perfect Thai but not much Burmese. Indeed, ethnic Shan monks in the Shan State often wear orange robes, like their Thai counterparts, rather than the maroon robes of Bamar monks. Such deep religious and cultural connections aside, the Kengtung economy is deeply tied with Thailand's. Thai consumer products, as well as Chinese ones, dominate the local economy, as is apparent from the shelves full of imported (or smuggled) consumer goods in local shops, with package labels in Thai or Chinese, but not many in Burmese. Along the bus route to Kengtung, many roadside advertisement boards are also written in Thai, and many businesses accept Thai baht. Thai money also helps sustain local Shan cultural expression, as remittances and donations from Thailand help build and renovate Shan temples. Although the Myanmar government has effective sovereign and administrative control over this part of the Shan State, its grip on the local economy is much less solid.

Duwan's family lives in a small village outside of Kengtung city. There is still no electricity or running water in many such Shan villages, and the Myanmar state has not yet been able to provide any modern infrastructure. The only way for the village people to have access to electricity is through solar panels—from China—that residents have installed on their roofs and which provide enough power to satisfy some basic needs such as lighting lamps and charging mobile phones, but not much else. Except for rice farming, there are few economic opportunities locally, and most of the young people have left. Many Shan people go to Thailand to work as migrant laborers because of the substantially higher wages available there compared with Myanmar and also because of the perceived cultural affinities with Thailand. Some people go to Mongla, which is special region to the north of Kengtung that is under the control by an ethnic rebel group, the NDAA. Located right across from the Chinese border, Mongla is a place where an illicit economy with drugs, prostitution, and gambling, flourishes with the inflow of Chinese capital and business.[1]

Despite its overall depressed economic outlook, Kengtung is located on the historical trade route linking southern Yunnan with Thailand, and today smuggling and drug trafficking dominate this route. As part of the notorious Golden Triangle, historically the center of the world's opium production, today the Shan State still accounts for nine-tenths of Myanmar's poppy harvest, making it the second largest producer in the world after Afghanistan.[2] Linking the huge market demand in China and Thailand, the Shan State produces huge amounts of heroin and methamphetamine, and many of such operations are carried out by a variety of ethnic rebel groups, militias, and even the Myanmar army.[3] In addition to drugs, Myanmar's Shan State and Kachin State have, in recent decades, also become suppliers of raw materials and natural resources for the fast growing Chinese market. On the other hand, Chinese and Thai investments in agricultural business development have also made significant inroads in the borderland area.

This chapter analyzes the economic dynamics across the borderland between China, Myanmar, and Thailand during the past few decades. As a region in which nation-state boundaries mark substantial disparities in economic development, the borderland area is nonetheless part of a larger regional order where Chinese and Thai economic dominance have reduced Myanmar's economic "sovereignty." Economically speaking, the Chinese and Thai market economies, with their more abundant capital, have spilled over the borders and have effectively subsumed the borderland economy under their respective markets while sucking up natural resources and cheap labor from Myanmar's Shan and Kachin states.[4]

The chapter is organized as follows: it begins by recounting the different trajectories of economic development across the three national borders, with special emphasis on the post-Cold War period; it then analyzes the three countries' economic development strategies or lack thereof with respect to the borderland area; it discusses how recent policy initiatives such as China's opium substitution programs as well as its push for outbound capital investment have affected the borderland economies; and then discusses the flow of major commodities—as well as human migration—across the borderland area.

Disparities of Economic Development

As we have discussed briefly in the overview of disparities in development in chapter 2, China, Myanmar, and Thailand have experienced drastically different patterns of economic growth in the recent past and have reached different stages of development at different periods of time. Chinese economic reform started in the late 1970s after the disaster of the CR. However, it was not until after Deng Xiaoping's 1992 Southern Tour that China's economy began experiencing truly fast growth. In Myanmar, Ne Win's Burmese Road to Socialism proved to be an economic disaster for that country as well. By the time another military government, the State Law and Order Restoration Council (SLORC), took over in 1988, the country's internal political instability, fueled by chronic economic deprivation, continued to sink the country further. On the other hand, Thailand, as a US ally, experienced fast-paced growth in the 1960s and 1970s, partly due to the war economy of the US war in Indochina. Thus, by the end of the Cold War, both China and Myanmar were extremely poor while Thailand had already been praised as one of the success stories of Southeast Asian little tigers. As we can see in figure 6.1, by 1990 China's per capita GDP by purchasing power parity was only US$980, while Myanmar's was US$486, but Thailand's had already exceeded US$4,700. The phenomenal growth of the Chinese economy since the 1990s quickly reduced the development gap with Thailand, and by 2016, their levels of economic development were almost identical at around US$16,000. However, Myanmar's economic growth continued to lag behind both of its neighbors, and by 2016 its GDP per capita purchasing power parity was slightly less than US$6,000, slightly more than one-third that of China or Thailand.[5]

Since China's economic reforms began in the late 1970s, the government's development strategy has focused on jumpstarting the economy on the eastern coast. Deng Xiaoping deemed it necessary to let some regions to grow their wealth first and hoped the coastal provinces would be able to absorb capital and advanced technologies which could later trickle down to other places.[6] Thus, for inland provinces in the Southwest such as Yunnan, economic liberalization initiatives did not begin until the second half of the 1980s, or even later. Far from the coast, Yunnan's geopolitical advantage

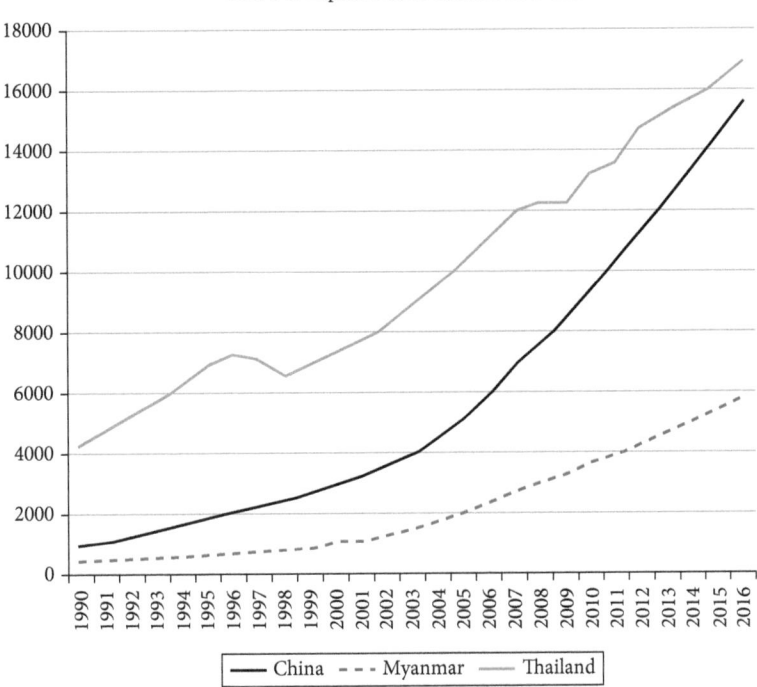

Figure 6.1 GDP per Capita PPP, in Current US Dollars

was its long borders with Southeast Asia, but before the mid-1980s these borders were effectively closed. With the winding down of the Cold War in Southeast Asia, the Chinese government abandoned its previous support for communist rebels in both Myanmar and Thailand. Relations with Laos and Vietnam also improved, after 1979, with the end of military clashes along the China-Vietnam border. The Yunnan provincial government believed that its development potential lay in increasing trade with neighboring states and positioning itself as the link between China and Southeast Asia.[7]

This positioning of Yunnan as part of a regional entity within Southeast Asia became more pronounced after the Asian Development Bank (ADB) encouraged regional economic cooperation along the Mekong River by initiating a Greater Mekong Subregion (GMS) Economic Cooperation Program in 1992, including Cambodia, Laos, Myanmar, Thailand, Vietnam, and the Chinese province of Yunnan.[8] Particular emphasis has been put on building infrastructure to improve transport links between Yunnan and mainland Southeast Asia in the name of the GMS northern economic corridor. This translates into upgrading existing road networks within the province, but also connecting these with those of neighboring states. The Chinese government, its Southeast Asian counterparts, as well as a few regional organizations have all pushed for such increasing connectivity. In addition, the ADB also hoped such increasing connectivity would facilitate more efficient cross-border movement of people and goods so that the region can realize the integration of markets, production processes, and value chains.[9]

Other than the ADB's GMS initiative, the United Nations Economic and Social Commission (ESCAP) has been pushing for an integrated Asian Highway (AH) system that would link member states' existing and future national highways. Between China and mainland Southeast Asia, for example, the AH Kunming-Bangkok Highway was finalized in 2013 after the completion of the Fourth Thai-Lao Friendship Bridge between Chiang Khong and Huay Sai, which linked Thailand, Laos, and China's Yunnan province. There are even more ambitious plans to build a railway link between Thailand and Yunnan province via Laos.[10] Commercial navigations along the Mekong River also became a topic of negotiation between regional governments. Substantial resistance from environmental groups notwithstanding, commercial shipping has already linked the Chinese city of Jinghong with Chiang Saen, Thailand.[11]

Despite the push for regional integration, Yunnan remains one of the least developed provinces in China due to its inland location and the comparatively low level of foreign investment and industrialization.[12] Aiming to readdress the imbalances between coastal and inland areas, Beijing started a grand national strategy known as the Western Development Program (WDP) (xibu da kaifa). Its primary stated aim is to integrate peripheral regions with the rest of the country, using infrastructure development to help facilitate better movement of goods and people between China's less developed western regions and its more developed and densely populated eastern "core." For ethnically diverse provinces with long international borders such as Yunnan, the WDP also has a mission to generate enough centripetal force to integrate the peripheral regions, which ostensibly carries with it a nation-building function.[13] In Yunnan, the average annual economic growth between 2000 and 2008 was 9.7%, which was accompanied by similar rates of income growth for the rural population.[14] Indeed, economic growth in the province has picked up substantially since the new millennium (figures 6.2 and 6.3).[15] Furthermore, The GMS's focus on cross-border trade and

DYNAMICS OF TRANSBOUNDARY ECONOMIC FLOWS 97

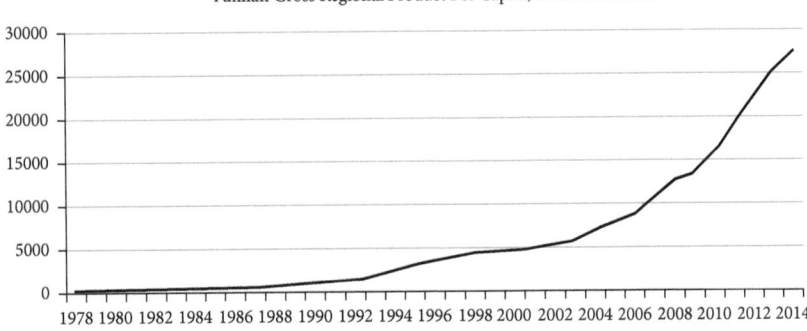

Figure 6.2 Yunnan Gross Regional Product per Capita, in Chinese Yuan

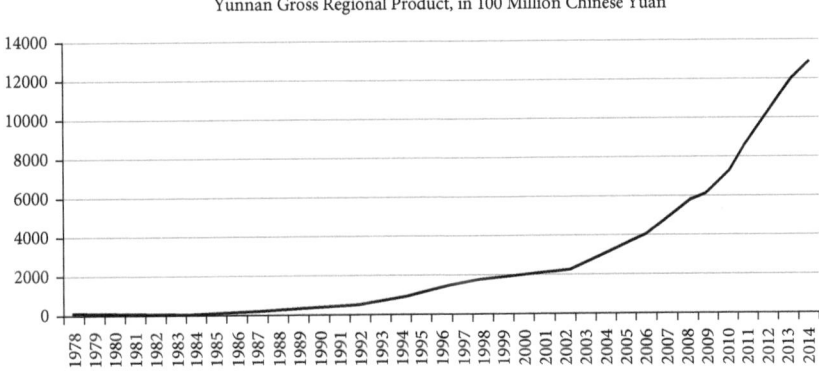

Figure 6.3 Yunnan Gross Regional Product, in 100 Million Chinese Yuan

expansion of transport links discussed earlier complements the WDP's focus on restructuring Yunnan's economy and facilitating the integration of its infrastructure with neighboring states.[16] Thus, Yunnan has taken on the role of bridgehead for outbound Chinese investment to mainland Southeast Asia.[17] On the other hand, it is worth noting that China's economic development hubs are still in its coastal areas, and the effect of such grand geo-economic development designs linking Yunnan with mainland Southeast Asia might take a long time to materialize, not least because of the political economic conditions in the neighboring states.

In the case of Thailand, its post-WWII economic boom did not start until Field Marshall Sarit Thanarat came to power in a 1957 coup. Sarit's strongman military government not only created a period of domestic political stability but also used the restored royal prestige to increase the legitimacy of his government, while promoting economic development.[18] Adding to Sarit's push for economic development was the handsome US economic assistance to Thailand when the country became the base for US military campaigns in Indochina. During this period, Thailand was "deluged with external economic resources—the result not merely of American capital investment in military bases and strategic infrastructural development, but also of direct American aid to the Thai regime, as well as substantial Japanese and American private investment in a low-wage, union-free society."[19] Between the mid-1950s and 1976, when the Vietnam conflict ended, US funds to Thailand reached US$3.5 billion, which accounted for 8.5 percent of Thailand's GNP.[20] Manufacturing expanded substantially, while agricultural production also became diversified.[21] From the mid-1980s until the mid-1990s, Thailand experienced another decade of almost double-digit annual economic growth.[22] After the devastating financial crisis of 1997, the Thai economy recovered quickly early in the new millennium, although recent political instabilities have led to economic stagnation.

For northern Thailand, especially the borderland provinces, one prominent feature of the Thai government's economic development strategy since the start of the CPT insurgency was the use of economic means, such as promoting agricultural and infrastructural modernization, to dissuade rural populations—particularly the hill tribes in remote mountainous areas—from joining the Communists, under the guidance of the CIA and the US Agency for International Development (USAID).[23] A case in point was the Accelerated Rural Development project, begun in the mid-1960s and focused on the Northern and Northeastern regions of the country, with initial emphasis on improving irrigation and road construction and, in later periods, poverty alleviation and rural welfare programs.[24]

It is in this context of development-for-counterinsurgency that the Thai royal family became actively involved in rural development projects, with the Royal Project. As the military began promoting Thai King Bhumibol Adulyadej as a symbol of national unity during the Cold War, the royal family started playing a prominent role in setting up projects in the highlands. "With the aim of improving the quality of life of hill-tribe people, to diminish their opium growing and to revive the forests and water resources," the Royal Project promoted cash crop plantation and handicraft manufacturing among highland communities.[25] In fact, successive Thai governments have propagated the Royal Project, in the form of compassionate royal patronage, for the purposes of borderland security and nation building among the hill-tribes.[26] After the devastating 1997 financial crisis, King Bhumibol called for a sufficiency economy in Thailand, which was applied to rural development with a stress on sustainable development and environmental protection.[27] Although it is difficult to verify how effective those royal projects are, at least according to official statistics, several northern provinces have experienced sustained economic growth during the past few decades (fig. 6.4).[28]

While Thailand's economic center continues to be Bangkok and its surrounding provinces, Chiang Mai, the second largest metropolitan area of the country, has become the economic center of the northern provinces and by extension, upper mainland Southeast Asia.[29] Thus, industrialization, the expansion of the agricultural sector, as well as the booming tourism and entertainment industries, have made Chiang Mai a magnet for domestic and foreign investment, and also the destination for migrant labor from neighboring countries, particularly Myanmar's Shan State. According to some statistics, about 150,000 formal refugees from Myanmar live in UNHCR (United Nations High Commission for Refugees) refugee camps in Thailand. Most other migrants from Myanmar, roughly estimated at 1.5 million, work either as registered migrant labor or remain in the country illegally. In 2004, the Thai government signed a memorandum of understanding with Myanmar, by which migrants were required to pay a fee of THB3,800 to obtain a one-year permit, along with one-year temporary permits for family

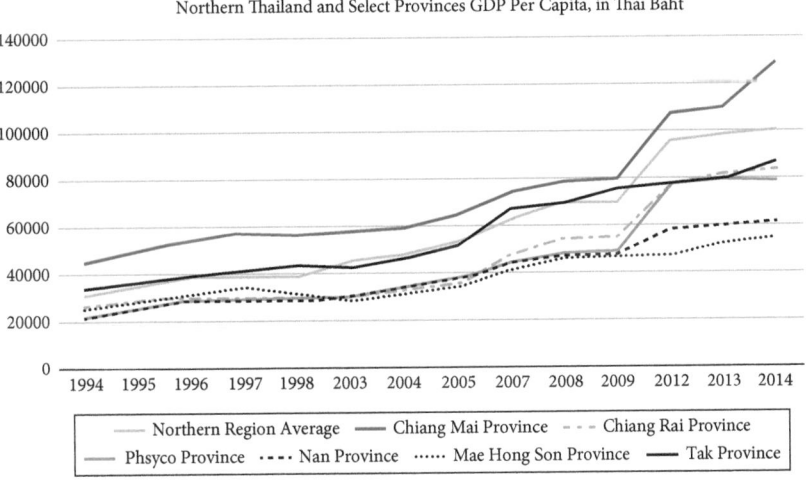

Figure 6.4 Northern Thailand and Select Provinces GDP per Capita, in Thai Baht

members to remain in Thailand. Legalized migration to Thailand has made it one of the most popular destinations for Myanmar migrants, particularly those living along the border, such as the Shan, who share close cultural and linguistic ties with northern Thais. However, the registration system is complicated and difficult to navigate, requiring migrants to apply for verification of nationality from the Myanmar government, which is why many migrants decide not to register and stay illegally.[30]

Thailand is also an active and leading participant of the GMS because of its desire to make Thailand the investment and transport hub for the region and boost growth in its northern and northeastern regions to overcome uneven development in the country.[31] Thus, similar to China's WDP, Thailand's involvement in the GMS emphasizes the building of transport infrastructure with neighboring countries so that Thailand can relocate its industries to the borderland area to take advantage of the cheap labor and raw materials available there.[32] In recent years Thailand has also flirted with the idea of setting up a series of special economic zones (SEZ) along its border, prioritizing Tak and Chiang Rai as the two main border provinces with links to Myanmar.[33] In Chiang Rai, this involves the construction of the Kunming-Bangkok Highway passing through Chiang Khong; the operation of the Chiang Saen port for Mekong River cargo ships; and the building of new customs facilities at Mae Sai to facilitate trade not only from Myanmar but also from Yunnan.[34] Despite discussions of Thailand's many plans for the GMS, progress has been slow, and its GMS designs have been criticized as being less about promoting development in the peripheral regions and more about finding cheap labor for its export industries.[35]

In 1964, the Revolutionary Council led by General Ne Win released a document titled "Specific Characteristics of the Burmese Way to Socialism," which laid out the foundation of a Burma that pursued international isolation and autarky.[36] To prevent the country from becoming entangled in the rivalries between capitalist and communist countries during the Cold War, the Burmese economy extracted itself from external involvement, and its foreign trade relative to GDP fell to one of the lowest among developing economies.[37] The Revolutionary Council also nationalized trade and industry and took over ownership of about 15,000 foreign or private firms and businesses, which fundamentally destroyed business interests that were previously in the hands of Indians and Chinese.[38] Even though Burmese agricultural output maintained basic subsistence for its population, autarky meant the overall economic condition was dire, and there was a chronicle shortage of consumer goods, which in turn fueled a rampant black market of goods smuggled from Thailand. According some estimates, the black-market economy accounted for 40% of Burma's official GDP by 1987.[39]

By the mid-1980s, the Burmese government could barely finance itself, and its management of the domestic economy was disastrous. Burma's economic growth rate during the 1970s and 1980s was around 3% annually, substantially lower than the newly industrialized countries in East and Southeast Asia in the same period.[40] Not only did the state become heavily indebted to international lenders, domestic inflation also skyrocketed in the late 1980s.[41] Unable to manage the looming domestic economic crisis, the government responded with a drastic demonetization in 1985 that removed 25% of currency in circulation, while offering only partial compensation.[42] Two years later, the government announced another, more drastic demonetization, this time without compensation, removing 60% of circulating currency and destroying any remaining popular confidence in the government.[43] A major student movement erupted in 1988, only to be ruthlessly crushed by the SLORC, which changed its name to State Peace and Development Council (SPDC) in 1997.

Although the Chinese and Burmese situations in the late 1980s were similar, with economic problems fueling student protest movements that were soon crushed by the military, ultimately the Burmese military junta took a different route from China and continued Burma's self-isolation. During the next two decades of military rule and until the change to civilian rule in 2011, its economy continued to decline, worsened by both domestic mismanagement and international sanctions. The military government's incompetence in managing the economy also meant a lack of political will to manage the borderland economy, which increasingly became dominated by expanding Chinese and Thai capital.

However, one dominant feature of Myanmar's military government's stance, since the late 1980s, toward the borderland area with China and Thailand did stand out as consequential for understanding economic changes in the borderland area. This was the government's effort to negotiate a ceasefire with various ethnic rebels and increase the state's presence there. After the CPB's collapse in 1989, the communist armies broke up into a few armed ethnic groups occupying a string of territories along the border with China. The SLORC managed to negotiate ceasefire agreements with each individual group and thereafter allowed the establishment of a series of special regions in the Shan and Kachin states, namely Shan State Special Region 1, under the MNDAA (Kokang); Shan State Special Region 2, under the UWSA; Shan State Special Region 3, under the SSA-N; Shan State Special Region 4, under the NDAA (Mongla); and North-East Kachin State Special Region 1, under the New Democratic Army—Kachin (NDA-K).[44] Between 1989 and 1995, a total of twenty-five ceasefire agreements were brokered with the government, including with the KIO in 1994.[45] Before the ceasefire agreements with the Kokang broke down in 2009 and the KIO in 2011, the military government managed to apply divide and conquer strategies toward these groups while gradually increasing state control in these areas.[46]

The ceasefires created during these two decades exchanged greater state control for greater local autonomy and economic development.[47] In a process that has been termed "ceasefire capitalism," the Myanmar government, with international capital from China and Thailand as well as local ethnic leaders and business interests, attempted to develop the borderland area through land concessions and natural resource exploitation.[48] This process—through which the Myanmar state extended its territorial presence while half-heartedly carrying out some economic development programs—will be discussed in more detail later in the chapter.

In May 1989, the SLORC established a Central Committee for Implementing Border and Ethnic People's Development, tasked with supervising agricultural assistance, forestry development, mineral extraction, education and health, road construction, and other development projects.[49] If the government statistics are to be believed, SLORC claimed that between 1989 and 1995, it established two agriculture offices in Kokang, built eighty miles of soil road, constructed five small bridges, established ten primary schools and two secondary schools, and opened three hospitals and eight clinics.[50] Similar scales of state-sponsored infrastructure development were also reported in other ceasefire areas. Although the government claims that it spent a total of US$506 million on the border areas,[51] the actual amount of money spent on improving people's living standards was abysmal.

Indeed, development amid the ceasefire did not create tangible economic benefits for the borderland population, but rather increased state control and benefited certain elites. Furthermore, within the GMS program, Myanmar was often treated as a passive target rather than an active voice for development. Indeed, it has become the destination for large quantities of foreign capital, especially from China and Thailand, to exploit the natural resources in Myanmar's borderland area. Many such investments have allegedly led to environmental degradation and land deprivation for the local population.[52]

Increasing demand for natural resources in Myanmar boosted overall bilateral trade as well as cross-border trade between Myanmar, China, and Thailand, and a few commodities from Myanmar, such as jade, timber, oil, and gas, as well as illicit drugs started to dominate such trading relationships.

Cross-Border Trade

During the past two decades, China and Thailand have become Myanmar's largest trading partners (see figs. 6.5 and 6.6),[53] even though actual trade volumes between them were also dependent on changes in bilateral relations.[54] In addition, official trade data do not include the large amount of illegal smuggling that has been historically rampant and continues in the area along the border.[55] Both countries' trading relations with Myanmar should also be seen in the context of Myanmar's international isolation since the early 1990s, when it faced economic sanctions from several Western countries. The military government's cancellation of the 1991 election results put Aung San Suu Kyi and her National League for Democracy (NLD) party in the international spotlight, and with Western sanctions and threats of regime change the Myanmar military government's reliance on its neighbors deepened.[56]

During the 1990s and 2000s, the Chinese government offered diplomatic protection for the Myanmar government in exchange for favorable trading and investment opportunities. For example, the Chinese sheltered the Myanmar government at the United Nations by vetoing a Security

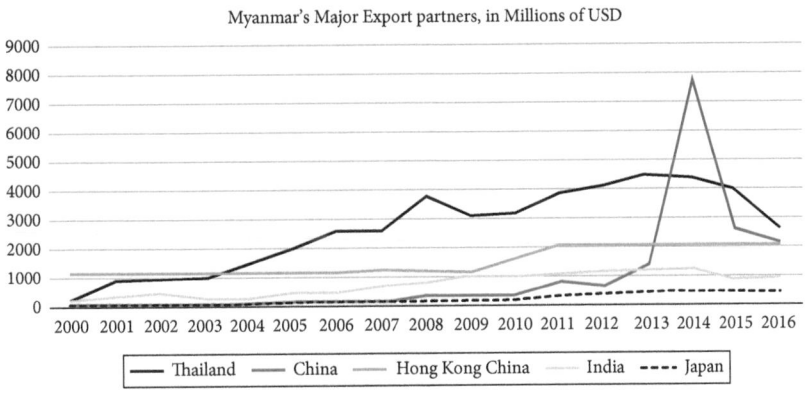

Figure 6.5 Myanmar's Major Export Partners, in Millions of USD

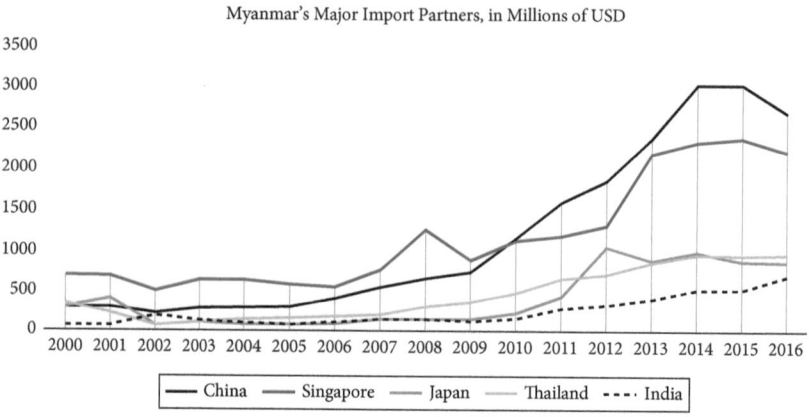

Figure 6.6 Myanmar's Major Import Partners, in Millions of USD

Council resolution in 2007.[57] Similarly, relations between Myanmar and Thailand improved after 2001, when Thaksin Shinawatra became the Thai prime minister and pursued an engagement policy that thawed bilateral relations and encouraged Thai investment in Myanmar.[58] The Thai government at the time also lobbied ASEAN on behalf of Myanmar for more economic cooperation with the country. In a way, sanctions by Western governments diverted Myanmar's trade relations to its immediate neighbors, and China and Thailand's trading relations with Myanmar have continued to grow during the past decade.[59] In particular, China's demand for raw materials and natural resources has seen exports to China skyrocket in the past few years. Overall, Myanmar exports more than it imports, in part because of its lower level of economic development and thus lower capacity for the purchase of foreign goods.

At the same time, because of Myanmar's long borders with China and Thailand, border trade accounts for a large share of overall bilateral trade volume.[60] During the Cold War, insurgencies along the Thai border by the CPB and other ethnic rebel groups such as the Karen National Union (KNU) meant that Myanmar's land border crossings with the two countries had been blocked. And it wasn't until the ceasefire agreements between the Myanmar government and the rebels that official cross-border trade between the neighboring states became possible. Additionally, formal trade agreements between Myanmar, China, and Thailand since the late 1980s also transformed the previously informal nature of such cross-border trade.[61] In particular, the 1988 opening of border trade with China, which occurred when Myanmar suffered significant shortages of consumer goods, created the foundation for cheap Chinese products to become dominant in upper Myanmar in the decades to come.[62] Despite continual smuggling and the illicit economy along the borderland area, which will be discussed later, the official border trade has created significant economic activity in several of the border towns.

Yunnan's southern borders with Myanmar, Vietnam, and Laos were effectively closed before the early 1980s, with the exception of the period when the Beijing government gave assistance to communist movements there, as discussed in chapter 5. Before China's economy opened, the area's cross-border trade volume was very small because only people living within 10 kilometers of the border zone could engage in such trade, much of which comprised limited quantities of smuggled goods.[63] It was not until the Chinese government issued in 1985 the "Temporary Policy for Small-Scale Trading along the Border Region" that the Chinese government started toying with the idea of encouraging commercial relations with Yunnan's neighbors, but domestic political tensions in the late 1980s derailed major reform initiatives.[64]

The final turning point came in 1992 when the State Council issued a policy document, "Custom Inspection and Preferential Tax Privileges Pertaining to Trading along the Sino-Myanmar Border of the People's Republic of China," which handed over rights to manage and police cross-border trade to the Yunnan provincial government.[65] Beijing also opened a few cities in Yunnan for trade, including Ruili, which became the entrepôt for commercial relations with Myanmar. Indeed, trade along the border accounted for more than half of the overall import and export between the two countries in the early 2000s,[66] and it has continued to grow at a phenomenal pace since 2010, as seen in figure 6.7.[67]

At Ruili, the Chinese government also set up the Jiegao Border Trade and Economic Experiment Zone to link with the Myanmar city of Muse.[68] Since the early 1990s, Dehong, where Ruili is located, has become the prefecture through which most Sino-Myanmar trade passes, as shown in figures 6.8, 6.9, and 6.10 with comparative statistics at several border crossing towns along the Sino-Myanmar border. In fact, despite a weak transportation infrastructure on the Myanmar side, the Ruili/Muse trade corridor has facilitated border trade between the two countries thanks to favorable institutional arrangements between the two and weak law enforcement at the border.[69] Overall, Myanmar exports food, agricultural

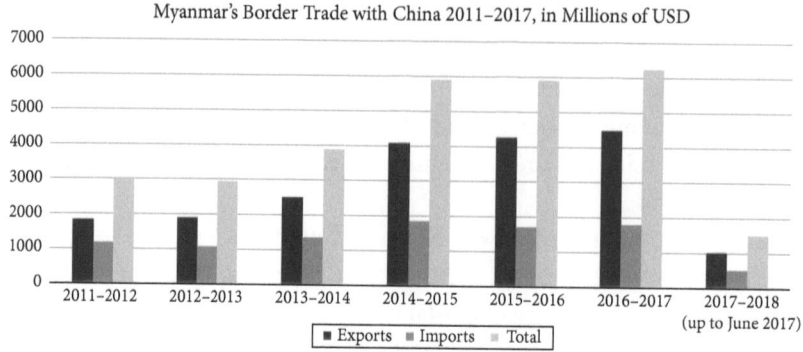

Figure 6.7 Myanmar's Border Trade with China 2011–2017, in Millions of USD

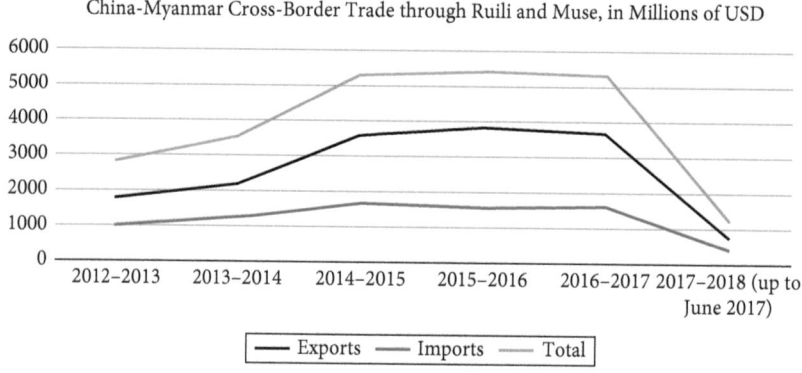

Figure 6.8 China-Myanmar Cross-Border Trade through Ruili and Muse, in Millions of USD

products, and increasingly, natural resources to China, while Chinese exports to Myanmar tend to be mainly industrial products, machinery, and electrical appliances.[70]

In terms of bilateral border trade between Myanmar and Thailand, when Ne Win's government pursued the autarkic Burmese Way to Socialism, smuggling from Thailand was the only way the Burmese urban middle class could get its hands on modern industrial products. During these periods, many ethnic rebels and militias roaming along the borderland area actively participated in black market trade. In particular, the KMT remnants discussed in earlier chapters were heavily involved in these smuggling activities; they accounted for 60–80% of Thai-Burmese

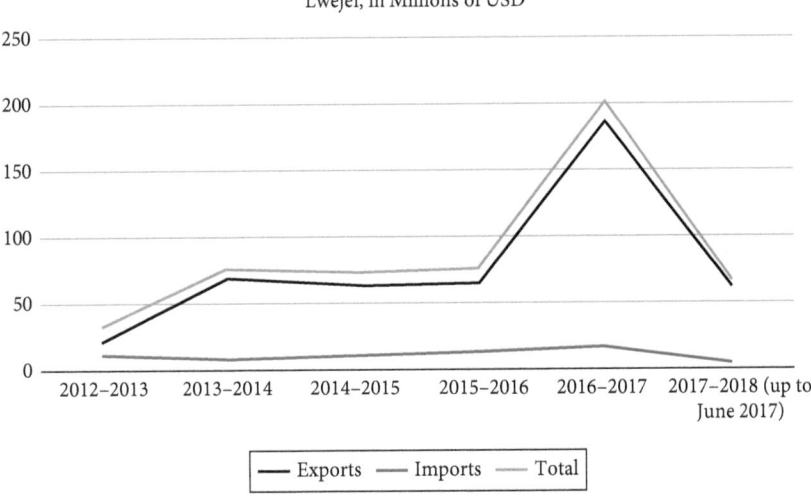

Figure 6.9 China-Myanmar Cross-Border Trade through Longchuan and Lwejel, in Millions of USD

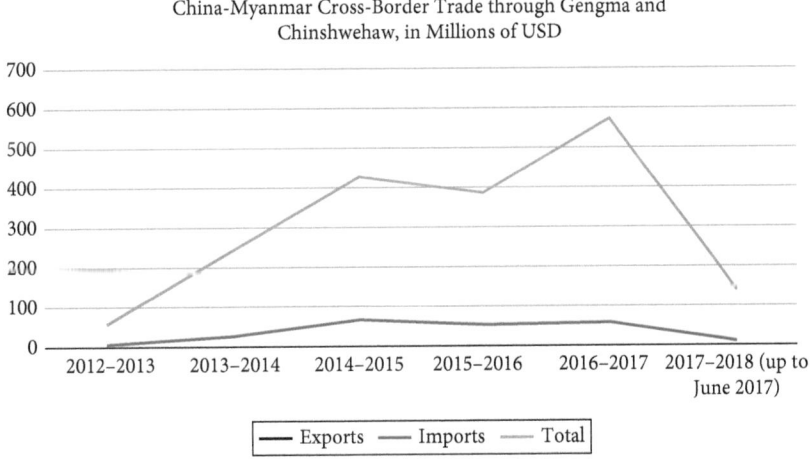

Figure 6.10 China-Myanmar Cross-Border Trade through Gengma and Chinshwehaw, in Millions of USD

border traders, taking advantage of their close network of caravans across the mountain ranges.[71]

After the SLORC took over in 1988, the military government opened up a few border cities for formal trade with Thailand: at Tachileik, Myawaddy, and Kawthaung. In addition, since Myanmar's 1997 admission to ASEAN, the regional level economic integration has accelerated with the start of the ASEAN Free Trade Area, and many of the existing tariffs between Thailand and Myanmar have been eliminated or reduced. Therefore, trade across the two countries' borders has also grown at a rapid pace during the past few years (see figs. 6.11, 6.12 and 6.13).[72] The busiest border trade route is between Myawaddy, Myanmar, and Mae Sot, Thailand; it offers a more direct transport link with Burma proper. By contrast, Tachileik is in the eastern Shan State and thus far from the population centers of Myanmar, which

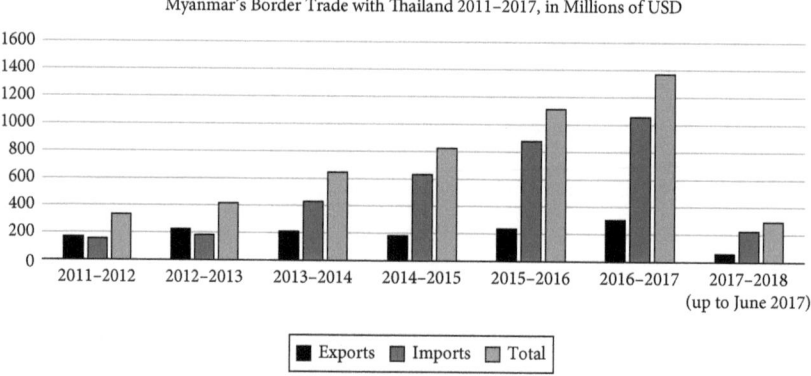

Figure 6.11 Myanmar's Border Trade with Thailand 2011–2017, in Millions of USD

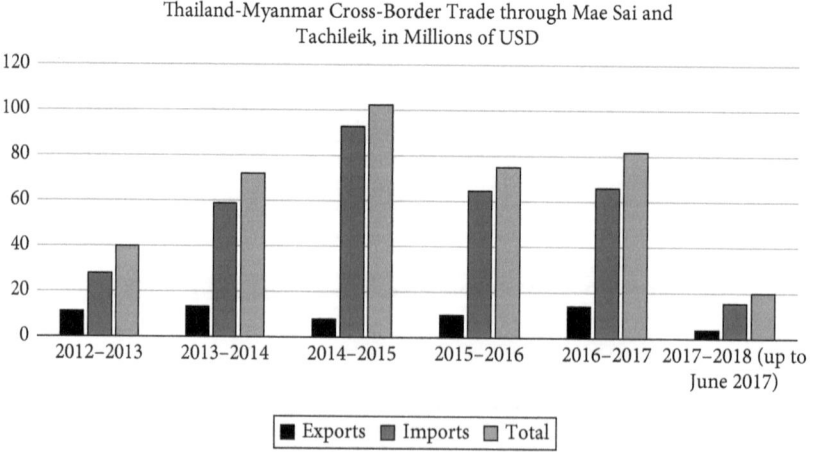

Figure 6.12 Thailand-Myanmar Cross-Border Trade through Mae Sai and Tachileik, in Millions of USD

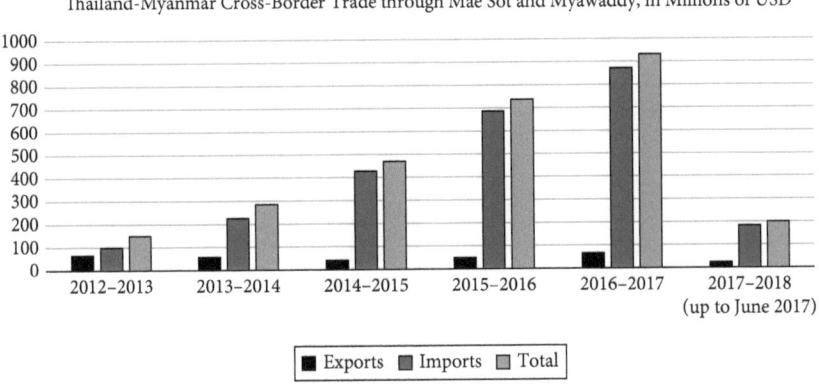

Figure 6.13 Thailand-Myanmar Cross-Border Trade through Mae Sot and Myawaddy, in Millions of USD

perhaps explains why the trade volume with Thailand via Mae Sai is smaller than that between Myawaddy and Mae Sot. Theoretically, cross-border trade at Tachileik can link with Xishuangbanna in southern Yunnan via Kengtung and Mongla. However, given the ongoing insurgency in parts of the Shan State this trade route has not realized its potential. Therefore, according to Thai statistics, the Tachileik/Mae Sai crossing only accounts for 14% of the total cross-border export value from Thailand to Myanmar.[73] The border trade pattern between Thailand and Myanmar is also similar to that between Myanmar and China, as Myanmar exports agricultural and natural resources to Thailand while importing industrial products and other appliances.

Exploitation of Myanmar's Natural Resources along the Borderland

As mentioned earlier, the ceasefire agreements between the rebel groups and the Myanmar central government have opened the door to state territorialization in the borderland areas. The consequent "ceasefire capitalism" style of development experienced there exposed Myanmar's Shan and Kachin states to the inflow of foreign investment, especially from China, but also from Singapore and Thailand. Since Thein Sein became president and implemented political reform and economic liberalization in 2011, foreign direct investment (FDI) to Myanmar has skyrocketed. As shown in

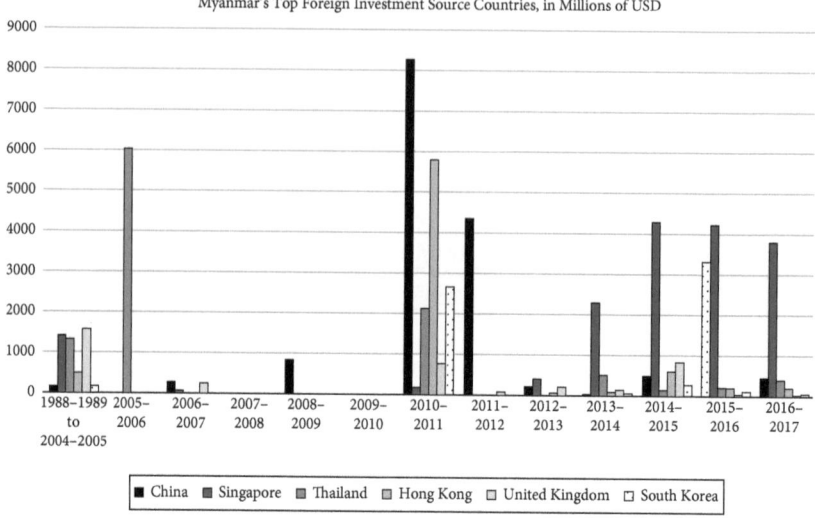

Figure 6.14 Myanmar's Top Foreign Investment Source Countries, in Millions of USD

figure 6.14, China, Singapore, and Thailand have been the top three investors in Myanmar ever since the SLORC took over power in 1988. In addition, Chinese investment flowed into Myanmar via Hong Kong and British overseas territories such as the Virgin and the Cayman Islands.[74] It is alleged that the official FDI reported by the Myanmar government underestimates the actual amount of investment from China by not counting illicit money coming across the border.

Most of the FDI that came into Myanmar went to the electric, oil, and gas sectors. These three sectors accounted for 32.7% of cumulative FDI during 1988–1989 and 33.2% during 2014–2015 (fig. 6.15).[75] Both China and Thailand have invested heavily in the oil and gas sectors and have built pipelines linking with Myanmar's coast. A gas pipeline has connected Bangkok with Myanmar's offshore gas fields, Yadana and Yetagun, in the Andaman Sea since the late 1990s. In 2009 Myanmar and China agreed to construct a US$1.5-billion crude oil pipeline and a US$1.04-billion natural gas pipeline to connect the Indian Ocean port of Kyaukphyu to Kunming, Yunnan province.[76] These two pipelines are crucial to China's energy security because they allow China to get around the Strait of Malacca for its energy supplies. The Thai and Chinese gas pipelines go through borderland territories where ethnic rebels have maintained some control. The

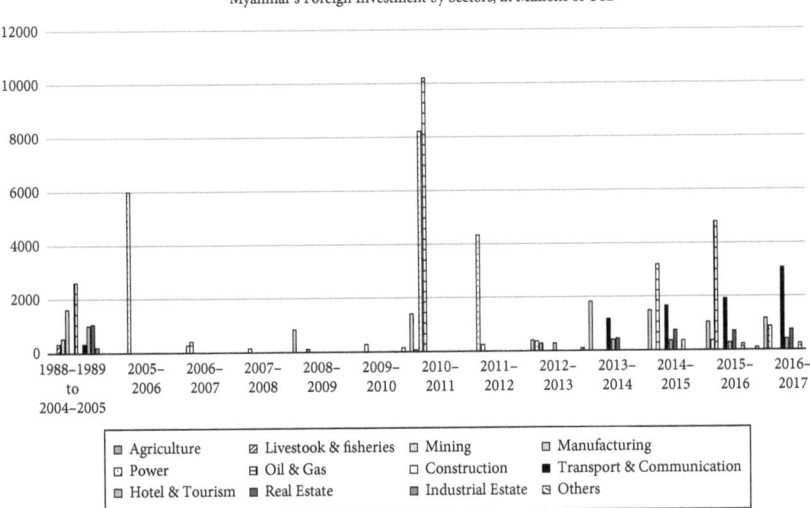

Figure 6.15 Myanmar's Foreign Investment by Sectors, in Millions of USD

security implication of China's infrastructure investment in Myanmar will be discussed more in detail in chapter 8 on prolonged conflict along the border. Thai and especially Chinese companies have also invested heavily in hydropower developments in Myanmar to feed domestic electricity needs. Chinese state-owned electricity enterprises are alleged to have been involved in every large-scale hydropower project in Myanmar.[77] Many of the dams are located in the borderland areas and on major rivers such as the Shweli, Salaween, and Irrawaddy. Construction on the most controversial Myitsone Dam in Kachin State was suspended in 2011 due to strong domestic opposition to its potentially devastating environmental impacts.[78]

Thus, Myanmar's economically more developed neighbors Thailand and China, and particularly China with its recent rapid economic growth and colossal size, have made substantial investments in Myanmar, taking advantage of its abundant natural resources to address their own domestic needs. Their large domestic markets have also resulted in craved products being "sucked out" of Myanmar, leaving behind devastating impacts.

In China, the only thing people automatically associate with Myanmar is jade, particularly the green jadeite the Chinese call feicui and have historically valued as precious. However, throughout the world jade is mostly only a Chinese item with its value determined purely by the demand from China as well as Chinese communities in Southeast Asia. Thus, with the growing

112 ASYMMETRICAL NEIGHBORS

wealth in China in recent decades, demand for Myanmar jade has soared. It is difficult to estimate the overall amount sold to the Chinese market as large quantities are smuggled across the border. In fact, controlling access to the cross-border jade trade was a source of income for the KIO for many years before the 1994 ceasefire and one of the main contested issues between it and the Myanmar government.[79] According to a report by the international non-governmental organization Global Witness, the volume of jade sold at the Myanmar Gems Emporium, which is the only official jade sale venue for the international market, has increased significantly in the 2000s (fig. 6.16).[80] The volume dropped dramatically after 2012, most likely affected by the renewed armed conflict between government troops and the KIO when the ceasefire broke down in 2011.[81]

The total value of Myanmar's jade production in 2014 was estimated at about US$31 billion, about 48% of Myanmar's official GDP.[82] The Myanmar military and its affiliated conglomerates and their cronies have direct access to much of the revenue generated by this large volume of trade in jade, in addition to the central government's official tax.[83] During the ceasefire years, granting access to the jade mines in Kachin State, where the Hpakant mine holds most of the jade deposits, was one of the main tactics used by the Myanmar military to co-opt the ceasefire groups. At the same time, the Myanmar military's increasing presence in Kachin State deprived the KIO of access to the Hpakant mines, revenues from which the KIO thought itself entitled to tax. Additionally, in catering to Chinese market demand, the government's business interests have also

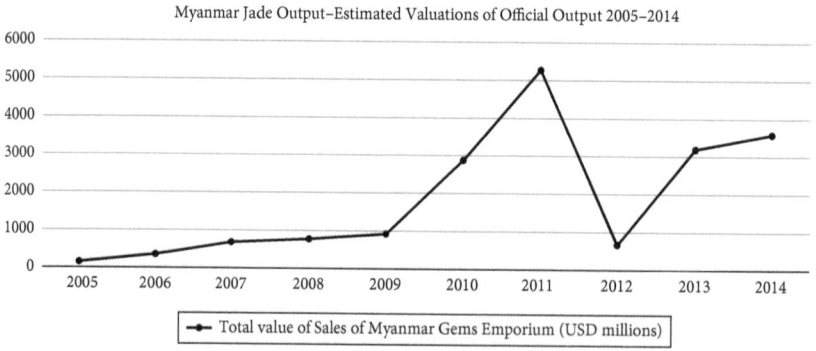

Figure 6.16 Myanmar Jade Output—Estimated Valuations of Official Output 2005–2014

created a strong sense of deprivation in Kachin State because the rapid expansion of industrialized natural resource extraction, as in the jade mines, has not yielded tangible benefits for local people.[84] Instead, harsh working conditions and the easy availability of heroin result in many Hpakant mine workers becoming addicted to drugs and contracting HIV.[85] While wealth has been accumulated by a small group of elites, most of the Kachin miners have been left destitute.

The same can also be said of China's demand for timber in Myanmar. Due to environmental destruction wrought by deforestation resulting from rapid industrialization, in 1998, Beijing banned logging in the upper Yangtze River region, which includes Yunnan and much of the Southwest. However, with the rising domestic demand for timber for manufacturing ever larger amounts of furniture thanks to the domestic real estate boom, Chinese furniture manufacturers started to turn their eyes abroad for cheap and reliable sources of timber.[86] Many began targeting the conflict-ridden Kachin and Shan states in Myanmar to secure logging rights directly from various ethnic rebels. The timber trade thus provided handsome revenues to support the KIA in its military conflict with the Myanmar government. But, since the early 2000s, the Myanmar military has become involved in the timber trade as well. In order to consolidate its own control over the northern borderland area with China, as well as to cut off revenues for the KIO, an agreement was signed between Myanmar and China in 2006 that decreed timber products can only enter China in two ways, either through Yangon and then by sea to China or through the Myanmar military-controlled border crossing with the Chinese city of Ruili.[87]

From figure 6.17, we can see that Myanmar's timber trade to China has grown exponentially since the early 1990s.[88] After the 2006 agreement between the two countries, the official timber trade dropped, but it seems there are still substantial amounts of logs and sawn wood entering China illegally across the border[89] because of close business ties between Chinese timber factories and Myanmar ethnic rebel groups like the KIO. Typically, Chinese timber businesses get logging concessions within areas under rebel control, employ Chinese labor and machinery for logging, and even build roads to transport these logs to wood processing factories on the Chinese side of the border. In April 2014, Myanmar officially banned the export of unprocessed logs so as to stimulate the domestic wood processing industry, yet logging and smuggling across the Chinese border continued. For example, in July 2015, more than one hundred Chinese timber workers were sentenced to

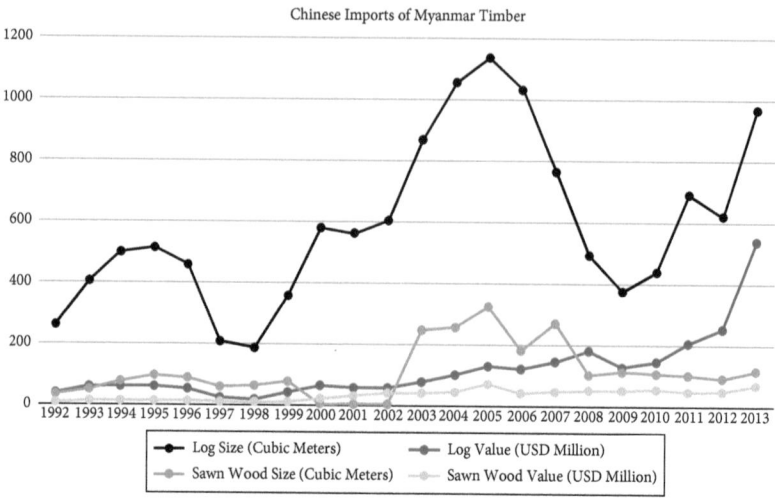

Figure 6.17 Chinese Imports on Myanmar Timber

twenty years in prison for illegal logging in Myanmar's Kachin State, but were later pardoned by Myanmar President Thein Sein.[90] So, despite the official bilateral agreement between China and the Myanmar central government, Chinese timber businesses have continued to engage in the illicit timber trade, enabled by the ongoing KIA insurgency, corrupt Chinese borderland local governments, and lack of oversight. Such rampant exploitation has led to a significant reduction of Myanmar forest reserves; the United Nation's Forest and Agriculture Organization (FAO) estimates that between 1990 and 2010, Myanmar's annual forest loss was 1.15 million acres, a total loss of nearly 20% of its forests.[91]

Narcotics continue to plague the China-Myanmar-Thailand borderland. As discussed in previous chapters, the political economy during the Cold War period made the Golden Triangle notorious for its production and trade. The remnants of the KMT army, as well as the famous drug warlord Khun Sa and his Mong Tai Army, were key suppliers of drugs for the North American and European markets. After the collapse of the CPB, several groups along the Sino-Myanmar border (party to the ceasefires discussed earlier), such as the UWSA, the MNDAA, and NDAA, have all relied upon opium and heroin production to finance their armed groups in the post ceasefire periods.[92] Although in recent decades Afghanistan has overtaken Myanmar in the production of opium and heroin, Myanmar's Shan and

Kachin states remain the East and Southeast Asian hub for narcotics, not only for heroin but also for methamphetamine and other synthetic drugs.[93] Even poppy cultivation has increased in recent years (table 6.1). The opening of the Yunnan border trade routes since the late 1980s has made China a popular transit route for drugs going through Chinese inland provinces to Hong Kong and then on to the international market. Although Thailand remains one of main market and transit countries for Golden Triangle drugs, in recent years increasingly more demand has come from the Chinese market.[94] According to a 2013 estimate, about 70% of the Golden Triangle heroin was exported to China.[95]

To tackle the drug epidemic, the Chinese government pressured the ceasefire groups across the border in Myanmar to ban opium, especially the groups that were long under China's influence (the UWSA, the MNDAA, and NDAA). During 2003 and 2006, for example, opium cultivation was banned in the Kokang and Wa areas, which led to a dramatic reduction in the amount of poppy planted in Myanmar (table 6.1). Furthermore, the Chinese government started an opium substitution program to encourage cultivation of other cash crops in the borderland area. Through an Opium Replacement Special Fund, from the mid-2000s the Chinese State Council provides financial incentives for Chinese business to invest in Myanmar agribusiness, such as rubber and bananas, to replace poppy cultivation.[96] The Chinese companies involved in these schemes receive several state-sponsored benefits, such as cash, lowering of bureaucratic hurdles for investment, and quotas for imported, tariff-free crops produced under the program.[97] Between 2005 and 2008, the Yunnan government approved schemes under this program worth a total CNY1.2 billion, covering an area in the Kachin and Shan states of about 1 million mu.[98] However, these programs have not curtailed opium production. In fact, opium production in Myanmar increased significantly after 2006 because of the relocation of poppy plantations to southern Shan states.[99] In addition, the Myanmar state also increasingly relied upon opium production to finance its military and associated militias to expand their territorial control in the borderland area in competition with the other armed rebel groups.[100] Chinese intervention in opium substitution programs has proved controversial: they have not benefited the local ethnic population but Chinese business people and have led to rampant land confiscation and displacement for local communities.[101]

Table 6.1 Estimated Poppy Cultivation in Myanmar Shan and Kachin States by Planted Hectare, 2002–2015

Year	2002	2003	2004	2005	2006	2007	2008	2009	2010	2011	2012	2013	2014	2015
Shan State	74,600	57,200	41,000	30,800	20,500	25,300	25,300	30,000	35,000	39,800	46,000	53,300	51,400	50,300
Shan State Annual change	—	−23%	28%	−25%	−33%	+23%	0%	+19%	+17%	+14%	16%	+16%	−3.6%	−2%
Kachin State	—	—	1,100	2,000	1,020	1,440	1,500	1,400	3,000	3,800	5,100	4,600	5,100	4,200
Kachin State Annual change	—	—	—	—	—	—	—	—	—	+27%	+33%	−10%	11%	−17%
Myanmar total	81,400	62,200	44,200	32,800	21,500	27,700	28,500	31,700	38,100	43,600	51,000	57,800	57,600	55,500
Myanmar Annual change	—	−24%	−29%	−26%	−34%	+29%	+3%	+11%	+20%	+14%	+17%	+13%	−0.3%	−4%

United Nations Office on Drugs and Crime (UNODC), Myanmar Opium Survey 2003, 2004, 2005; UNODC, Opium Poppy Cultivation in the Golden Triangle: Lao PDR, Myanmar, Thailand 2006; UNODC, Opium Poppy Cultivation in South East Asia 2007, 2008, 2009; UNODC, South-East Asia Opium Survey 2010, 2011, 2012, 2013, 2014, 2015. Note: Figures are estimates largely based on remote satellite sensing. These data can be accessed at https://www.unodc.org/unodc/index.html?ref=menutop. See Kramer et al., Bouncing Back, 20–23 for a critique of the UNODC data.

Concluding Remarks

The trajectories of economic development in the borderland area between China, Myanmar, and Thailand have been uneven. In fact, the pace of such asymmetrical development has only increased in recent years. Although the economic conditions in areas along the China-Myanmar-Thailand borders are subject to their respective national economic situations, the close connections across the borders have led to specific patterns of trade flows. The strong pull of China and Thailand has exerted strong centrifugal forces over the borderland area in Myanmar. With Myanmar lagging behind its two more economically powerful neighbors, trade patterns in the borderland area are dependent upon the needs of the Chinese and Thai markets and thus are quite detached from Myanmar's domestic market. This also manifests in the wider circulation of Chinese and Thai currencies on the Myanmar side of the border and the unpopularity of the kyat, Myanmar's national currency. The political economy of natural resource exploitation has further demonstrated the penetration by Chinese capital in Myanmar's borderland area.

7

Comparative Nation Building across the Borderland Area

At a barbeque stall in the night market in the center of Laiza, several Kachin youth gathered around a table over some chilled bottles of Snow, a Chinese beer. Among them were two young men, new arrivals from Myitkyina to the KIA-occupied Laiza, and in their own words, there to "join the revolution." Since the breakdown of the ceasefire agreement between the Myanmar central government and the KIA in 2011, renewed military confrontations have caused tens of thousands of Kachin people to flee their homes and seek refuge along the China-Myanmar border in the swelling IDP camps around Laiza.

The two young men had become incensed at the horrible treatment suffered by the Kachin people during attacks by Myanmar government soldiers, and the ideological goal of Kachin autonomy (or independence) in what they call Kachinland became ever more appealing. Despite its poor reputation when they were growing up in Myitkyina, more and more Kachin youth seem to support the KIA and its use of military means to achieve Kachin autonomy or independence. This perhaps reflects the fact that during the nearly two-decade ceasefire, between 1994 and 2011, many in Kachin State felt that the Kachin people became ever more marginalized, and economic changes in the name of development led only to the exploitation of natural resources for the benefit of the Myanmar state. Kachin cultural expression continues to be repressed while the Myanmar's state's push for Burmanization has only intensified. Especially for many Kachin who grew up in Myitkyina, their Burmese language skills are often much better than their Kachin (Jingpo) because Kachin-language instruction is banned in the schools, and the only place to learn Kachin is in the home or the church, or in KIA-occupied areas where it is taught in the schools. Surprisingly, many people I met in Laiza often commented on how the Chinese government has done a better job at allowing Jingpo to be taught in schools.[1] The ethnic minority autonomy system in China, which is often decried as inadequate or even fake, ironically has become the object of envy for some on the other side of the border.

Instead of taking up arms to resist the Myanmar central government, many other ethnic minorities in Myanmar simply chose the exit option. In addition to the sizable number of refugees, most came to Thailand either as legal or illegal migrant labor, like the Shan discussed in the previous chapter. Most are obviously drawn by the higher wages, despite the often harsh working conditions. Additionally, cultural and linguistic affinities between the Shan and Thai also have made adjusting to life in Thailand easier. Thailand's sympathy toward the Shan on the basis of pan-Tai sentiment has led it to offer asylum for many Shan nationalists, who have established exile organizations, particularly in Chiang Mai. In the summer of 2014, I visited in a suburb of Chiang Mai the headquarters of the Shan Herald News Agency (SHAN), one of the largest Shan nationalist news distributors in the exile community. Actively monitoring the political transitions ongoing in Myanmar and the Shan State at the time, Khunsai, the head of SHAN, was uncertain about the best strategy for the future of the Shan State. Although some Shan political parties took part in the 2015 general election, many Shan nationalists in exile were not too optimistic about the future of a federated Myanmar where the Shan could enjoy genuine autonomy. Instead, many were simply disillusioned and sought better economic opportunities in Thailand. I met Harn at one of the ubiquitous massage parlors in Chiang Mai. A young man in his late twenties originally from a village outside Taunggyi, he had been working as a foot masseur in Thailand for three years. When asked to compare life as a Shan in Myanmar and in Thailand, Harn replied that being a Shan in Myanmar was hard because of the lack of job opportunities and because Shan peoples have been pushed aside as more and more Bamar have migrated to the Shan states. On the other hand, although it's easier for him to pass in Thailand because he speaks impeccable Thai, ultimately he doesn't feel he belongs there because he will always be treated as a foreigner from Myanmar. Thus, despite the Thai government or academics' occasional homage to the common ethnic ties between the Thai and the Shan, such as calling the Shan Tai Yai (major Tai) and the Thai themselves Tai Noi (minor Tai), in reality Thai society demarcates a clear boundary between itself and its poorer ethnic kin from the Shan State.

This chapter examines the comparative nation-building processes along the borderland area between the China, Myanmar, and Thailand. It first traces the different modes of national identity construction in the three countries and discusses how the modern conceptions of being Chinese, Myanmar, and Thai have developed and transformed. The chapter analyzes a range of nation-building policies that the national governments of the three countries have or have tried to implement in their respective jurisdictions in the borderland area. Specifically, it traces how nation-building policies in each country, through the medium of cross-border ethnic ties, affect the other's abilities to implement these policies and the responses they have received from the concerned ethnic minority groups across national borders.

Three Modes of National Identity Construction

China's nation-building project can still be seen as an ongoing process. Imperial Chinese dynasties engaged in multilayered administrations incorporating both centralized rule and localized autonomy. In particular, the last dynasty, the Qing, can be characterized by the multi-ethnic nature of its political authority, since after all, the ruling elites were predominantly Manchus, an Inner Asian people.[2] Through military expeditions, the Qing managed to expand the previous Ming territory and made significant incursions into Inner and Central Asia.[3] This territorial expansion of the Qing Empire also meant the further incorporation of diverse ethnic groups. After the collapse of the Qing in 1911, ROC founding father Sun Yat-sen propagated the concept of the Chinese nation as comprising five nationalities (wuzu gonghe)—Han, Manchu, Mongol, Tibetan, and Muslim—in order to counter the disintegration of multi-ethnic China and "win" over the loyalties of the major ethnic minority groups for the purpose of maintaining its territorial integrity.[4] It is worth noting that the wuzu gonghe concept of Chinese national composition did not include the diverse ethnic minority populations of the Southwest. This shows how little political significance these groups had for the new Republican government and how little the government knew about of the exact demographics of ethnic minorities in the mountainous southwestern regions.

In contrast with the ROC government, which was weak as a result of foreign aggression and internal challenges, the CCP, when it rose to power in 1949, was able to form a significantly stronger state with the capacity to subdue any domestic dissent. Consolidating Chinese territorial integrity in the ethnic peripheral regions was treated as a top priority by the new communist government. Borrowing from the Soviet Union's model, the CCP adopted a political structure granting ethnic minority groups certain rights of autonomy and self-government, promising them rights equal to the majority Han Chinese, and allowing them to develop and use their native languages.[5] Thus, after the communist government pacified the peripheral areas, it immediately set up a list of autonomous areas. The five autonomous regions—Guangxi, Inner Mongolia, Ningxia, Tibet, and Xinjiang—were given provincial status. In Yunnan, with its more than thirty ethnic minority groups, several larger ethnic groups were granted autonomy at the prefectural level, while smaller or more scattered groups were granted autonomy at the county or even township level. For example, in the borderland area between China and Myanmar, Dehong and Xishuangbanna where most of the Chinese Tai population live, became autonomous prefectures.[6]

The Beijing government's first major nation-building project was the Ethnic Identification Project (minzu shibie), designed to count the number of ethnic groups in China and categorize their general traits, distributions, and populations. Carried out in the mid-1950s, the project provided the CCP detailed information about the ethnic composition of Chinese society, but also provided a means for the government to better regulate ethnic minority affairs.[7] The modern-day Chinese nation, according to the CCP's categorization, comprises fifty-five ethnic minority groups in addition to the majority Han Chinese. Although there were elements of arbitrariness in the classification schemes, and many separate ethnic groups were lumped together, the classification became institutionalized in the form of identity cards and gradually became internalized. The paternalistic character of the CCP and its Han Chinese leadership presented the Han Chinese as the "older brother" (laodage) of the Chinese nation and treated the ethnic minority groups as the civilizing target.[8]

Despite accommodation and co-optation of ethnic-minority elites in the early years, the communist government's ethnic minority policies turned repressive as domestic politics became radicalized. Particularly during the CR, not only was there significant violence against minorities in the ethnic regions, but the CCP's overall tolerance toward ethnic cultural differences reached its nadir. The idea that ethnic minorities were distinct from the Han Chinese was rejected, and the party came to believe that minorities should be treated in the same way as the Han, as granting ethnic minorities special treatment would hinder their assimilation into the greater Chinese society.[9] The end of the CR led the CCP to make efforts to redress the excesses committed in the ethnic minority areas. The 1982 Constitution, which is still in use today, elaborates a wide range of minority rights to be realized through national and local legislatures.[10] For example, Article 4 states that the Chinese state "protects the lawful rights and interests of the minority nationalities and upholds and develops the relationship of equality, unity and mutual assistance among all of China's nationalities."[11] The same document also states that ethnic equality is to be cherished and prohibits discrimination against and oppression of any ethnic minority groups.

The 1984 Law on Regional Autonomy (LRA, minzu quyu zizhifa), allows ethnic autonomous areas—such as the aforementioned autonomous regions, prefectures, and counties—to adapt, modify, or supplement national law according to local conditions. More power was given to autonomous areas in terms of education, culture, environment, health care, and family planning.[12] There is, for example, an emphasis on the preferential hiring and promotion of ethnic minorities in enterprises, government institutions, and public security forces. The draconian family planning policy was also loosened to allow ethnic minority couples to have two children in urban areas and more in rural areas. Bilingualism was once again permitted and promoted. Preferential treatment and quotas have also been implemented for minority students in secondary and tertiary education. Although the implementation of the LRA varies by location, and the effectiveness of the autonomy provisions has been questioned, at least on paper the Chinese nation conceptualized as multi-ethnic and with ethnic minorities granted certain cultural rights has been propagated by the CCP throughout the modern period.

In recent years, in the name of economic development, Han migration to ethnic minority areas has increased, inevitably exerting great demographic pressure on local minority populations that might dread growing assimilationist pressure and increasing competition in the job market.[13] The Chinese government has also stepped up its effort to promote the teaching of Mandarin Chinese in ethnic minority areas, and language education reform programs have been carried out to limit ethnic language education.[14] Recently, there has been debate about whether the ethnic autonomy system should be rethought altogether, with some calling for the system to be abolished, rather than improving it or moderating repressive policies. Citing the failure of the Soviet model, many argue that China should learn from the US melting-pot model, where "the absence of group-differentiated institutions, laws, or privileges encourages natural ethnic mingling and a shared sense of civic belonging."[15]

In contrast with the Chinese nation-building model, an effort to make sense of its own transition from an empire to a multi-ethnic nation-state, the Thai nation-building project has, since the early twentieth century, been determining how to incorporate into Thai society the sizable Overseas Chinese community estimated at about a quarter of its population in the nineteenth century.[16] In fact, the Thai state's dilemma of how to deal with these Overseas Chinese hinged upon domestic political changes in China as well as changes in the international politics of East Asia as a result of imperial power contestations. Centuries of tributary/trading relations brought many Chinese traders to Siam, but migration from Southern China intensified in the late-nineteenth century due to domestic political instability caused by the Taiping Rebellion.[17] By then, Overseas Chinese already filled a crucial economic role in Siam because of lucrative trading relations with China and because they were exempted from corvée labor: many became actively involved in tax farming for the Siamese court.[18] In 1909, the Qing government claimed, for the first time, that Chinese abroad were under its protection, redefining them as citizens whose loyalty should be to China rather than European colonies in Southeast Asia.[19] A new Law of Nationality set out a *jus sanguinis* principle that defined anyone born to either a Chinese father or mother as a Chinese citizen and also granted dual citizenship to all Chinese and their descendants living abroad.[20] Given their economic clout in Siam, where both Chinese business and labor contributed heavily to modernization projects, the Siamese court under Rama VI King Vajiravudh was prompted to issue its own Nationality Act of 1913, which was based on a *jus soli* basis and granted everyone born on Siamese territory citizenship.[21] This was done ostensibly because the Siamese government became "possessive of their Chinese subjects."[22]

However, the rising popularity of republicanism among Overseas Chinese alarmed the Siamese royalty. Sun Yat-sen visited Bangkok in 1910 right before the fall of the Qing Dynasty to solicit support among the Overseas Chinese community for his republican revolutionary cause. In 1912 there was an aborted assassination attempt on Rama VI.[23] King Vajiravudh began to take a harsher view of the presence of the Chinese in Siamese society and published an essay in 1914 that portrayed the Chinese as "The Jews of the Orient;" he denounced them as "vampires who steadily suck dry an unfortunate victim's life-blood," a reference to the dominant economic position of the Chinese and the fact that they sent money back to China.[24] Such a negative portrayal of the Chinese was perhaps motivated by the king's anxious desire to prevent the spread of republicanism within Thai society.[25]

The Siamese government had no intention of excluding the Chinese. Rather, such denunciation should be interpreted as applying pressure on them to assimilate and be loyal to the Siamese king. Indeed, the loyalty of the Chinese toward Siam was weak at the time, as the community was generally concerned with political changes back in China, as it was the main financer of revolutions in the homeland.[26] After the founding of the ROC, the 1929 Nationality Law continued the *jus sanguinis* principle of the Qing and granted citizenship to all ethnic Chinese around the world, including in Siam.[27] Additionally, Overseas Chinese were officially included in various official bodies such as the Overseas Chinese Affairs Committee (OCAC) (qiaowu weiyuanhui), as well as in various branches of the KMT and its affiliate organizations.[28] The KMT government actively promoted Chinese education in Southeast Asia by registering and establishing Chinese schools, with the purpose of developing the skills of the Overseas Chinese so they could better serve the homeland.[29] Heavily influenced by the Republican government's nationalist ideological mobilizations, Overseas Chinese communities were increasingly tied to the political situation within China. In Thailand, the Overseas Chinese community was actively mobilized to boycott and protest Japanese aggression in China.[30]

Thus, after the fall of the absolute monarchy in 1932, the Phibun government intensified its assimilationist pressure on the Chinese community for fear of their entanglement in the politics back in China. On the one hand, a 1939 modification to the Nationality Act demanded that those Chinese who wanted to naturalize must change their Chinese names to Thai and that they should send their children to Thai schools, speak Thai, and cut all allegiance to China.[31] A series of acts were passed during 1938–1939 to wrest the Thai economy from Chinese control. The Chinese were excluded from many professions, from trading in several popular commodities, and from certain residential areas. Chinese schools and presses were closed down;[32] later, in 1943, the Chinese were prevented from buying land.[33] This pressure was aimed at those Chinese migrants who were not Thai citizens rather than at the Chinese born in Thailand who were natural-born Thai citizens, the ultimate goal being to induce Chinese migrants to naturalize and assimilate.

From 1950 on, the Thai government also tightened immigration quotas, making new migration from China almost impossible. Thus, the Chinese population in the country became increasingly dominated by those born in Thailand, and the assimilation pressure also compelled many to become culturally and linguistically Thai.[34] Fearing communist infiltration of the Chinese community, the Thai government deported many left-leaning Chinese while explicitly branding communism as "a totally un-Thai enterprise, a negation of the livelihood, history and civilization of the Thai race."[35] Finally, at the Bandung Afro-Asian Conference in 1955, PRC Premier Zhou Enlai proclaimed that China was willing to negotiate with Southeast Asian governments on the nationality and citizenship of the Overseas Chinese.[36] Subsequently in the Sino-Indonesian Dual Nationality Treaty of 1955, the PRC officially abandoned the *jus sanguinis* principle, which effectively relinquished its claim over Overseas Chinese in Southeast Asia. Reception of this change in Thailand was positive because it essentially meant Bangkok could be confident about the loyalties of the Chinese minority in its territory.[37]

Solving the Chinese question thus consumed Thai government's nation-building efforts for almost half a century. Throughout, the Thai state's approach to the meaning of being Thai has emphasized three principles of Thainess: loyalty to the nation, religion, and the king (chat, satsana, and phra mahakasat).[38] Thus, implicitly at least, to be Thai one has to speak the Thai language, be a Buddhist, and be loyal to the monarchy.[39] Particularly since the 1960s, a series of military governments have promoted the Thai monarchy as symbolizing Thai nationalism, while at the same time encouraging loyalty and obedience toward the authoritarian military regime.[40] Thus, in contrast with the official policy recognizing a multi-ethnic Chinese nation, the Thai concept leaves much less room for alternative ethnic and cultural expression, while emphasizing assimilation.

In comparison with both the Chinese and Thai cases, the Myanmar national identity formation process has been more contentious. As we discussed in chapter 3, Burma was colonized by Britain and ruled as a province of British India. This resulted in mass migration of people from the South Asian subcontinent, and the prevalence of Indians "gave the appearance of an Indo-British occupation rather than British occupation of Burma."[41] Indians dominated the lower administrative positions of the colonial bureaucracy, and more significantly, Indian moneylenders (chettiars) came to control land in the Irrawaddy Delta area; they were heavily resented by the Bamar population and became the image associated with foreign exploitation.[42] In addition to the Indians, ethnic groups such as the Karen, Kachin, and Chin, many of whom were converted to Christianity by Western missionaries, were employed disproportionally in the police and military, while the majority Bamar were discharged from the army, leading the Bamar people to view the colonial military as a tool through which they became subjugated by these ethnic minority groups.[43] This "divide and rule" style of colonial domination thus led to a situation whereby "ethnic, religious and cultural differences became the yardstick of national identity and political power."[44]

Because of such subordination in the land that they believed was solely theirs, Bamar nationalism grew on a very strong anti-foreign, xenophobic foundation. The 1930s nationalist campaign, dobama—"our Bamar"—was a rallying cry in opposition to those thudobama—who had dominated Burma during the colonial period.[45] In such a nationalist discourse, the us versus them dynamic established the foundation for post-independence ethnic strife, because many ethnic minorities that were prominent in the colonial administration were viewed with disdain and suspected of disloyalty. Buddhism also became associated directly with Bamar nationalism as a result of the Bamar nationalists' perceived threat from Hindus and Muslims migrating from India and from increasingly large numbers of ethnic groups in Burma converting to Christianity.[46]

All these cleavages created by the colonial experience considerably influenced the post-independence Burmese state's approach to nation building. In the 1948 Burmese Citizenship Act, the Burmese government specified that to be a Burmese citizen, one has to be a descendant from one of the eight "national races (thanyintha)"—Bamar, Chin, Kachin, Karen, Karenni, Mon, Rakhine, and Shan—who were already residents of Burma in 1823, the year before British colonization.[47] Thus, all the Indians, Chinese, and other foreign nationals would have to apply for naturalization as associated citizens and applicants go through "long and sadistic legal processes."[48] After Ne Win's coup in 1962, the Burmanization of the economy resulted in the departure of many more Indians and Chinese because foreigners were forbidden to own land and barred from many professions.[49] Later, the 1982 Citizenship Act made it even more difficult for "foreigners" to acquire Burmese citizenship, targeting mainly the Rohingya in the Rakhine State, who remain stateless to this day.[50]

As discussed in chapter 3, the Panglong Agreement promised equality among major ethnic groups and administrative autonomy for ethnic regions, but these promises were never honored.[51] As the country faced one insurgency after another, since the very day of its independence, the Burmese military, on behalf of the Bamar majority, became obsessed with holding the union together at any cost. Thus, particularly since Ne Win's rise to power in 1962, it was military force that held the Union of Burma together, not a sense of common national belonging. In Joseph Steinberg's words, "Each government of the Union of Burma has attempted to create this sense of nationhood—a sharing of national values and will amongst all of its diverse people. Yet, each effort has to a major degree been unsuccessful. Although a 'Union of Burma' as a state was titularly created, a union of people as a nation was not."[52] Instead of granting ethnic groups autonomy, a unitary state was forced on the ethnic areas that were under control of the Burmese government, with a strong emphasis on unity among ethnic groups under the Bamar hegemony.[53] Burmese became the national language, and ethnic languages were banned from the school system.[54]

Officially, the Myanmar government claims the Myanmar nation is multi-ethnic in composition. Originally, it claimed there were 8 national races of Bamar, Chin, Kachin, Karen, Karenni, Mon, Rakhine, and Shan—as listed in the 1948 and 1982 citizenship acts. However, from the mid-1980s the government started to introduce a new scheme of 135 national races, although the number 135 has been criticized as random and the classification as highly problematic.[55] Overall, the concept of and membership within the Myanmar national community are ridden with contradictions and has been described as "a contrivance for political inclusion and exclusion, for political eligibility and domination."[56]

On the one hand, the Myanmar government has consistently pushed for an image of all the national races as part of a happy union or pyitaungsu, characterized by a propaganda image of the national races wearing their respective ethnic consumes at various parades, posters, and even commercial advertising.[57] However, such overt display of unity and equality among the national races is contradicted by the reality, where the majority Bamar culture is equated with Myanmar national culture, the Burmese language is the official language, and "In order to be considered truly Myanmar (a member of the nation) one must adopt the trappings of Burman culture."[58] Furthermore, given the ongoing insurgency by several ethnic groups in the country, non-Bamar ethnic groups have to prove their loyalty to the Myanmar state while the majority Bamar does not.[59] In this regard, although to varying degrees, all three countries of China, Myanmar, and Thailand have this phenomenon of graded national belonging, with minority groups relegated to lesser status in the official discourse.

One may also add that the Myanmar national identity is more repressive and exclusionary in practice compared with China and Thailand in that violence has been much more widespread and institutionalized in its counter-insurgency campaigns against ethnic groups, and its emphasis on "indigenous" national races continues to prevent certain groups from claiming citizenship.[60] In fighting various ethnic insurgencies over the years since 1948, the Myanmar military has committed numerous human rights violations against ethnic civilians, especially through the use of the "Four Cuts" strategy—cutting off insurgents' access to food, finance, communication, and recruitment—which inevitably displaced civilians and destroyed their homes and farmland.[61] The Myanmar military has also been notorious for using rape as a weapon against ethnic minority civilians.[62] Finally, the government's constant emphasis on the "indigenous" nature of the national races continues to exclude large chunks of the population from the nation. Thus, while Chinese or Indians might have naturalized as Myanmar citizens, they are nonetheless excluded from the Myanmar nation, although curiously the Kokang, who are essentially Chinese, are categorized as a subgroup of the Shan. The worst case of course is that of the Rohingya, who have never been issued any citizenship documents and continue to be considered illegal migrants from Bangladesh.[63] Years of repression by the Myanmar government and society have led to several instances of Rohingya refugees fleeing to Bangladesh, which has recently received significant international media attention.[64] It is here that the Myanmar state's arbitrary and exclusive construction of national identity shows its ugliest manifestation.

Comparative Nation Building at the Borderland

One fruitful way to understand the formative logic of each of the three states' nation-building approach to its multi-ethnic society is looking at whether the central government, and the ethnic majority it represents, perceives enough security in the ongoing nation-building projects within its territorial domain. This sense of security or the lack thereof also has to do with whether ethnic minority groups living in these countries are content with their situations. As I have argued elsewhere, for ethnic groups with transnational kin relations, external factors can play a significant role in shaping whether and how an ethnic group is going to mobilize politically against the nation-building project imposed on it by the state. Through comparison with its external kin relations, an ethnic group can evaluate how it has been treated by the national government, and this forms the foundation of its political satisfaction or grievance. In addition, the presence of substantial external support would provide the needed opportunity, structure, and resources for the group's political mobilization.[65] This theoretical framework also fits our understanding of how ethnic groups across the borderland area of China, Myanmar, and Thailand have reacted in similar ways to changes within and across the national borders.

Although China as a whole continues to face active resistance to its nation-building projects, this is mainly in Tibet and Xinjiang, not along the southwestern border.[66] Given the different dynamics at play, the Chinese state has tailored its policies toward managing the variations in different groups' political integration.[67] For many of the ethnic minority groups living in the southwest borderland area, the frequent comparison they make in terms of political rights, cultural expression, and economic welfare is with their external kin groups in Myanmar. As a result, few groups in the Yunnan borderland area perceive a better alternative in Myanmar, and overall these ethnic groups are content with their current situation as minorities in a multi-ethnic China, while negotiating their limited space for cultural autonomy.[68]

This is the case with the Jingpo and their external kin group in Myanmar, the Kachin. A small ethnic group numbering only around one hundred and fifty thousand,[69] the Jingpo nonetheless have enjoyed relative political significance, because the group titularly shares autonomous status within the Dehong Dai and Jingpo Autonomous Prefecture. In Myanmar's Kachin State, the categorization of what constitutes the Kachin is more ambiguous, but overall strong ethnic and linguistic ties exist across the current national border between the Jingpo and Kachin.[70] During the early years of the PRC, when domestic political radicalization surged during the Great Leap Forward and Cultural Revolution, large numbers of Jingpo crossed the border into Myanmar. However, since the late 1970s, for those who remained or returned, life on the Chinese side of the border has seen more stability and economic development. In particular, the past couple of decades have further demarcated the differences between the two. As we have discussed in the previous chapter, since the 1994 ceasefire between the KIO and the Myanmar government, the Kachin borderland area has been subject to rampant natural resource exploitation and environmental degradation. The end of the ceasefire in 2011 only led to renewed militarization and the displacement of tens of thousands of borderland inhabitants within Kachin State, as well as a flow of several thousand refugees into China.[71]

Furthermore, increasing control over Kachin State by the Myanmar central government meant a strong push for Burmanization and strict control of Kachin cultural expression. For example, Ho reports that "[T]he apparent grandeur of the Jingpo manau festival in Yunnan in recent years and the state support that has been given to its development is a visible marker of these different opportunities and outcomes for many Kachin people on the Myanmar side of the border."[72] This difference in cultural expression can be explained by the Chinese state's pragmatic view of promoting ethnic-minority culture for tourism in Yunnan, thus allowing certain expressions of Jingpo linguistic and cultural autonomy, in contrast with the situation in Myanmar, where the Myanmar state has banned the teaching of the Kachin language in public schools. Such perceptions of the degradation of the situation in Kachin State and the affinity between the two populations has prompted a movement among Chinese Jingpo to support the Kachin against the Myanmar government and to offer humanitarian assistance to displaced Kachin.[73] Therefore, after Myanmar government troops bombed Laiza in December 2012, thousands of Chinese Jingpo protested across the border checkpoint, holding signs saying, "Don't be upset! We are one!" and "Support our brothers and sisters!"[74] Many Chinese Jingpo also expressed their willingness to influence the Chinese government's policy toward Kachin State.[75] Although the effect these protests by the Jingpo can have on Chinese foreign policy is debatable, one can certainly argue that the Chinese state does not want to antagonize one of its loyal minority groups.

A similar case can also be made about the Wa, who likewise straddle the Sino-Myanmar border, particularly because the territorial demarcation of the Wa areas was only finalized in the 1960 border agreement.[76] Currently, there are roughly 430,000 Wa living on the Chinese side of the border, while the number in Myanmar is difficult to come by but estimated at around 600,000. As mentioned in chapter 5, the Wa were one of the main ethnic groups recruited heavily into the CPB insurgency, and after the collapse of the CPB and signing of a ceasefire with the Myanmar government, the UWSA has become the largest ethnic rebel group in the country, especially after it fought with the Myanmar government troops to take down Khun Sa's Mong Tai Army (MTA) in 1996.[77] Afterwards, the UWSA took over the territories previously occupied by the MTA along the borderland between Myanmar and Thailand, thus adding a new southern division to its area along the Chinese border.[78]

Although the Wa speak their own language, Chinese is the lingua franca in the Wa State, with street signs written in Chinese and TV broadcast in Mandarin. The Wa State government also modeled itself on China's, and in many ways it resembles a Chinese sub-provincial entity. Because of its previous ties with the CPB, the UWSA's ties with the Chinese government have strong historical roots. Since its wider adoption of the Chinese language, in contrast with the Kachin in Myanmar who rarely speak Chinese, the Wa State also enjoys close economic integration with China. Behind these close cultural and economic relations is the tacit political or even military support that the Chinese government has given to the UWSA.[79] Officially the Wa State government claims it wants high levels of autonomy within a Federated Myanmar, and it seems its ability to maintain that autonomy is substantially greater than that of other ethnic rebels in Myanmar. Given the close ties with China in every aspect, Myanmar's nation-building projects have never even reached into the Wa State.

The relations of various Tai/Shan groups with Thailand, across the borderland between China and Myanmar, are even more indicative of how crucial comparisons with external kin groups and the availability of external support are for ethnonationalist mobilizations. As discussed in chapter 3, many of the Tai principalities shared long historical links with each other. However, these groups' reactions toward their incorporation into the respective nation-building projects of China and Myanmar have varied. Such variations can be partly explained through the external dimension. For example, the Tai groups in China have not seen in Myanmar a better alternative to their present situations, nor have they received any international support. On the other hand, the Shan nationalist movements in Myanmar do view Thailand as a better alternative and have periodically received support, both materially and symbolically, from Thailand.

China's Xishuangbanna Dai Autonomous Prefecture is a case in point. Ever since its establishment in 1953, Chinese rule over the prefecture has been secured without many open challenges. The previous political elites of the Tai Lue aristocracy were stripped of their hereditary powers, but have also been co-opted into the political system with symbolic titles. Particularly since the early 1990s, Xishuangbanna has been promoted as a "tropical paradise" in the Chinese domestic tourist market, and the region has seen closer integration with the rest of country. Because of the Chinese government's economic interest in promoting ethnic tourism in Xishuangbanna (or Yunnan in general), Tai cultural expressions have been tolerated. Thus, the Tai cultural resurgence during the past decades has been partially related to the Chinese state's tactful use of it for its own governance purpose.[80] While the Tai Lue language is taught mostly in the monasteries, linguistic assimilation with the Han Chinese is also accelerating.[81] With improving economic conditions and comparatively better life prospects compared with neighboring Myanmar or Laos, the Xishuangbanna Tai people have for the most part accepted their Chinese citizenship.[82] There have been efforts to maintain or revive Tai Lue culture, but there is little if any political activity visible in Xishuangbanna that would challenge Chinese rule.

However, this is not the case with the Shan in Myanmar. As briefly touched on in chapter 3, the KMT invasion of the Shan State led directly to the emergence of Shan nationalist insurgencies and the militarization of the Thai-Burma border. However, the Shan nationalist insurgencies have been haunted by a lack of cohesion from the start, resulting in ongoing fragmentation and regrouping of various nominally Shan rebel groups,[83] all of which claimed they were fighting for independence or autonomy on behalf of the Shan people against the Myanmar government, even while many were embroiled in the illegal trafficking of goods and drugs across the border to sustain their insurgencies.[84]

Such fragmentation notwithstanding, the variety of Shan insurgent groups survived for more than half a century in large part because of their physical locations close to the porous Thai-Myanmar border, as well as the tolerance and tacit support they received from the Thai government and society. Ever since the mid-1950s, the Thai government has practiced a "buffer-zone" policy toward various ethnic rebels along the border with Burma.[85] The policy was first designed to thwart Thailand's historical enemy, Burma, but also served to prevent communist infiltration from the north. Although the Thai state did not offer open support, rebel armies "were allowed to set up camps along the frontier, their families were permitted to stay in Thailand and they could buy arms and ammunition."[86] The Shan insurgent armies were also located geographically close to the areas under the control of the former KMT troops who, due to their extensive networks linking the Shan State with Thailand, were major traffickers of goods between the two countries, including narcotics, during Ne Win's autarkic pursuit of socialism.[87] Working together, or under the KMT who were also indirectly supported by the Thai government, the Shan insurgents obtained funding and arms to continue their fight against the Burmese government.[88] Thus, from the 1960s to the 1980s, Shan insurgent groups established close-knit networks across the border in Thailand, the porous borderland facilitating the movement of migrants as well as illicit trade.[89]

The Thai government's buffer-zone policy toward the borderland with Myanmar changed in the late 1980s when the Chatichai government started to push a new policy to "turn battlefield into marketplace." Not only did the Thai government agree to solve the problems at the border caused by the ethnic rebels, but Bangkok also obtained forest concessions from the Burmese military government in 1988, which turned out to be disastrous for the Shan armed groups who gradually lost their logging industry.[90] However, the Myanmar government continues to accuse the Thai government of supporting ethnic insurgencies along the border. In the end, Thaksin Shinawatra's government announced Thailand should abolish the buffer-zone policy and officially ended support for ethnic armed groups in Myanmar in 2003.[91]

Official Thai policy changes notwithstanding, the Shan insurgencies peaked when Khun Sa consolidated several Shan armies into one, the MTA, in 1985.[92] Through income from narcotics and other trafficked goods, the MTA was able to purchase arms and expand its recruitment along the borderland area.[93] However, Khun Sa surrendered to the Myanmar government in 1995, which led to the demise of the MTA, with only parts revived a few years later as the Shan State Army-South (SSA-S).[94] Although the SSA-S signed a ceasefire agreement with the Myanmar government in 2011, insurgencies continued in the Shan State; these will be discussed in greater detail in the next chapter.

The Shan nationalist groups are sustained in part by the ethnic kin sentiment many Thais have toward the Shan. In chapter 3, we discussed the historical connections between the Shan states and northern Siam and how the pan-Tai ideology motivated Phibun's government to annex eastern Shan states in the early 1940s. Although later Thai governments no longer use the pan-Tai rhetoric, Thai public discourse still considers the Shan as ethnic kin to the Thai, or phinorngkan.[95] In particular, some Thai intellectuals romanticized the Shan as having maintained many of the old Tai traditions that the modernized Thai society has lost.[96] Thus, Thai domestic discourse has played a role in "constructing a romantic, revolutionary image of the Shan" insurgents in their resistance against the Myanmar government.[97]

After the MTA's collapse in 1995, many Shan former insurgents and civilians crossed the border into Thailand. Concentrated in northern Thailand and particularly Chiang Mai, they established Shan exile nationalist organizations,[98] which have utilized newfound resources and freer media spaces in Thailand to disseminate information on the political situation in the Shan State, both within Thailand and to the international community.[99] Shan nationalist materials printed in Chiang Mai were brought back to the Shan states through underground channels.[100] It seems that the Thai state tolerated Shan media materials that are banned in Myanmar, which allowed the exile Shan organizations to disseminate their visions of Shan nationalism.[101] Within Thailand, Thai academics and activists, who are sympathetic toward the Shan, also mobilized domestic media to promote the Shan cause.[102] Thus, books, songs, TV programing, and movies have been made to showcase Thai support for the Shan.[103]

Suffice it to say, the Shan state is still plagued by the continual militarization of various rebel groups and militias, and there is no clear sign how and when these insurgencies will end. Although much of the Shan resistance against the Myanmar government originated from Myanmar's domestic interethnic tensions and history of military repression, it is necessary to recognize the role that neighboring Thailand has played in providing permissive conditions for successive Shan insurgencies to sustain themselves.

Separately, Thailand itself still has the task of integrating into the imagined Thai nation several groups of ethnic minorities in its geopolitical peripheries. Other than the issue of assimilating the large number of Chinese that we have discussed earlier, one main challenge that the Thai state faced during the Cold War was how to deal with the itinerant hill tribes in the northern mountainous regions. Lumping several groups together into this category, the Thai state's official discourse has treated them as particularly threatening to the territorial and national integrity of Thailand.[104] This perception of a security threat was based partly on group migrations across national borders, which the Thai state deemed as evidence that they lacked concrete ties to the Thai nation (one of the three pillars of Thai nationalism discussed earlier). But more significantly, some hill tribes, particularly the Meo, were heavily involved in the CPT insurgency during the Cold War years. In the name of counter-insurgency, the Thai military reacted violently,[105] and KMT soldiers were also employed as mercenaries to clear Meo settlements in remote mountainous areas.[106] In addition to these violent means, Bangkok has employed a list of bureaucratic measures to regulate the citizenship status of these hill tribes, providing Thai-language education to generate a sense of national belonging, and using forest management and other agricultural transformation policies through the Royal Development Projects to territorialize and sedentarize the tribes.[107]

Although the hill tribes in Thailand together number less than one million,[108] they have been featured prominently in the Thai state's nation-building projects since the 1960s, particularly since the perception of a security threat of communist infiltrations from the north intensified.[109] Because the borders are porous and the groups are migratory, the Thai state designed a complicated identity card system to document the people and regulate the communities via a layered system of citizenship.[110] Indeed, since 1967, the Thai state had offered at least seventeen different kinds of identity cards to different groups of people who have entered Thailand at various times so as to certify individual identity and control people's movements across borders.[111] However, many of the criteria used to categorize people were arbitrary, and the complex nature of the system only created confusion among the subject populations the Thai state aims to regulate, while further marginalizing them from mainstream Thai society.[112]

However, in contrast with the Shan/Tai, Kachin/Jingpo, and Wa cases we discussed earlier, none of the groups that have been categorized as hill tribes, such as Karen, Meo/Hmong, Akha, Lisu, Lahu, Yao/Iu Mien, and so forth, have received any substantial external support. At the same time, living conditions in Thailand are generally much better than in Myanmar or Laos, with their chronic poverty and warfare, which explains why migration into Thailand has continued. Lacking their own ethno-nationalist aspirations, these groups became the target of the Thai state's extensive development interventions aiming to incorporate them into the Thai nation-state.[113] Framed within the discourse of counter-insurgency and forest management, the Thai state has extended administrative control over the hill tribes through a few government agencies, such as the Department of Public Welfare (DPW), the Royal Forestry Department, and the BPP. For example, under the DPW's Hill Tribes Relations Program, a "civilizing" mission started in 1965, Thai university students were sent to teach the highlanders.[114] The Royal Forestry Department has been heavily involved in both eradicating opium production and ending swidden agriculture among hill tribes; it has consistently used forest and wildlife protection as a rationale for restricting land use by hill tribes and for relocating them.[115] Furthermore, the BPP has been crucial in enacting state control over the hill tribes in the borderland area, as well as in nation building through its extensive school systems, which "constitute concrete steps toward actualizing a vision of a territorially and psychologically consolidated Thailand by ensuring the national loyalty of border populations."[116] Crucial emphasis has been put on teaching the Thai language to the hill tribes, as well as spreading the patronage of the royal family through development projects in the borderland area.[117] Indeed, although many hill tribe people remain stateless, since the end of the Cold War a few groups have overtly challenged the Thai state's nation-building projects. In fact, most BPP-built schools have recently been transferred to the Ministry of Education or local-level administration, which suggests the Thai state is less focused on perceived security threats and there has been some success in integrating these hill tribes to Thai society.[118]

Concluding Remarks

In this comparative analysis of the intricacies of nation building among the three countries, we have noted the marked differences in their respective approaches toward the conception of national identity. Each state's version of national identity has different degrees of inclusiveness versus exclusiveness, partly predetermined by the historical processes of political contestation in the post-WWII period. However, such different versions of national belonging and the international politics of cross-border relations have demonstrated how deeply interrelated the nation-building projects have been in these three countries. Although the domestic politics of nation building in each country has played a major role, it is crucial to recognize how much the external dimension across national borders has exerted different effects on similar sets of ethnic groups. Having said that, it is in Myanmar that these ethnic insurgencies are still ongoing, and how they have been in operation over time is the subject of the next chapter.

8

Continual Contestations at the China-Myanmar Border

In February 2015, ousted Kokang rebel leader Peng Jiasheng posted an open letter on the Internet pleading for support for the Kokang's fight against repression by the Myanmar government.[1] Using sensational language, the letter appealed directly to Chinese nationalism, stating that the Kokang are ethnic Chinese and used to be part of China and blaming their separation from China on imperialism, specifically British encroachment on China's territory since the Opium War, which led to Kokang being ceded to British Burma in 1897. Peng then praised the PRC government for being strong internationally, yet lamented how the plight of Kokang had been ignored, and so the Kokang had suffered at the hands of the Bamar. He then called upon all Chinese people to support the Kokang, especially at a time when the Beijing government was reclaiming China's great power status.[2]

Indeed, since 2009, the borderland area between China and Myanmar has seen renewed armed conflict—the ceasefires between the Myanmar government and various rebel groups signed in 1989 started to break down. Government troops first drove out Peng's MNDAA and brought Kokang under direct government administration. Then, beginning in 2011, clashes with the KIA led to fierce fighting that lasted for more than two years before the on-again-off-again political dialogues restarted in 2014. In 2015 conflict restarted in Kokang when Peng led his ousted MNDAA troops in an attempt to retake their former headquarters. Then, in late 2016, a coalition calling itself the Northern Alliance engaged in a series of skirmishes with Myanmar government troops in northern Shan State, which borders China, while Myanmar's political transition was ongoing. Since 2011, Thein Sein has led the formation of a civilian government, the first in more than two decades. In 2015, the electoral victory of Aung San Suu Kyi's NLD party more formally heralded a mostly democratic political system in the country. Suu Kyi herself has invested in a renewal of peace negotiations through the Twenty-first

Century Panglong Conferences, from 2016 onwards. Yet, no end seems in sight for these decades-long armed conflicts.

This chapter traces domestic politics in Myanmar in the recent past and examines how an interplay between domestic forces and regional geopolitical changes has led to the continual contestation along the borderland area between China and Myanmar. It first situates the ongoing armed conflicts within the broader context of Myanmar's recent domestic political transition. It then discusses the ongoing military clashes along the Sino-Myanmar border since 2009. Finally, it discusses how much of a role China has played in the continuation of these clashes, as well as whether or how Myanmar's northern neighbor can help facilitate a peaceful settlement in the bilateral borderland area, within the broader remit of changing bilateral relations.

Myanmar's Political Transition

Myanmar's military government developed a notorious reputation for suppressing domestic opposition, especially since the nullification of the 1990 election results and the subsequent house arrest of Aung San Suu Kyi, which lasted for almost two decades. The international sanctions levied against the country not only caused economic stagnation but also pushed the government to seek diplomatic protection from China against Western pressure for regime change. In 2005, the generals even moved the capital of the country from Yangon to Naypyidaw, fearing the US would invade, as they did in Iraq. Then in 2007, China helped shield the military government by vetoing a UN Security Council resolution condemning Myanmar's human rights abuses and political repression; the resolution was sponsored by the United States and United Kingdom in response to the 2003 Depayin incident.[3] In return for this diplomatic protection, China reaped handsome economic and strategic rewards, as discussed in chapter 6. However, deepening dependence on China had already caused a strong sense of unease within the military government, which traditionally prided itself on a neutral foreign policy.

Indeed, the generals realized the need to undertake some political reforms, given the domestic and international pressure they were under and so created a road map for drafting a new constitution and called for a national election in 2010.[4] Although the 2008 Constitution was very controversial, it paved the way for the transition from a military to a civilian government. But, the military had secured its veto power under the new constitution before undertaking political reform, allocating itself 25% of seats in both the lower and upper houses of the national parliament (Pyidaungsu Hluttaw), and so guaranteeing its power to veto any constitutional change.[5] Additionally, the constitution designated the commander-in-chief as the supreme leader of the Myanmar military, with the authority to nominate three cabinet ministers for defense, home affairs, and border area affairs.[6] After the constitution was approved by a referendum, which was widely claimed to be rigged, the military felt it was time to shed the uniform for civilian rule.

The 2010 election, although rigged and boycotted by the NLD, ushered in a government formed by former military men through the Union Solidarity and Development Party, and Thein Sein was elected president.[7] Few people were expecting the new civilian government to genuinely open up the political process, but to the surprise of many, that was what Thein Sein did. Indeed, the military government ushered in a period of solid democratization from their position of strength, as secured by the newly ratified constitution.[8] During Thein Sein's first year of office, political reforms were implemented to lift censorship, release political prisoners, and let opposition parties and civil society function relatively freely.[9] In the 2012 by-election, the NLD won a landslide victory, and Aung San Suu Kyi became optimistic that the country was on the right track for some fundamental political change.[10]

While such political transformations were gaining momentum, the area around Myanmar's northern border with China became engulfed in renewed armed conflict. The cause of the breakdown of the ceasefire agreements with various ethnic armed groups was laid out in the 2008 Constitution, Chapter VII of which demands that "All the armed forces in the Union shall be under the command of the Defence Services."[11] The military's strategy, under this chapter, was to rid the country of existing ethnic armed groups by reorganizing them into Border Guard Forces (BGF) under the control of regional military commanders. As discussed previously in chapter 6, the series of ceasefires signed between the government and various ethnic rebels since 1989 only agreed on the cessation of hostilities, while letting the armed groups retain their weapons, troops, and a substantial degree of autonomy. But the government viewed this stalemate as temporary and intended, when the time was right, to establish full control of all of Myanmar's "sovereign" territory. The armed groups, of course, saw this initiative as inimical to their interests as it would bring their autonomous existence to an end.

After the announcement of the BGF scheme in April 2009, the government set several deadlines for compliance, which were extended numerous times. Certainly, some groups that had weak military capabilities complied, but many others were determined not to go down without a fight. It was in this context that the war in Kokang flared up in 2009, and the official ceasefire that had existed with the former CPB legacy groups since 1989 broke down.

Renewed Conflicts along the Sino-Myanmar Border

Conflicts in Kokang

As an ethnic Kokang militant group and offshoot of the CPB after its collapse in 1989, the MNDAA signed a ceasefire with the Yangon government and became Special Region No. 1 of Northern Shan State. Ethnically Chinese, the Kokang armed group occupied a small piece of territory right next to the Chinese border with its capital in Laogai. Before the ceasefire was broken, the Kokang area was known for drug trafficking, as well as illegal gambling and prostitution catering to Chinese tourists across the border. Like many of the rebel groups who signed ceasefire agreements with the central government but did not lay down their arms, the MNDAA had de facto autonomy in running its own affairs under the leadership of Peng Jiasheng, and its military was not subordinate to the Myanmar military. Because of its small size relative to the KIA and UWSA, with only a thousand or so soldiers, and weaker military capabilities, Kokang was the first area targeted by the Myanmar government for implementation of its BGF scheme.

On August 8, 2009, Myanmar troops moved into Laugai and attempted to raid Peng Jiasheng's house on drug-related allegations.[12] After a two-week standoff between the two sides, the Myanmar military took advantage of an internal split between Peng Jiasheng and Bai Shoucheng, vice chairman of the Kokang Special Region. Bai came out in support of the Myanmar military and joined forces to attack the MNDAA, still under Peng's leadership.[13] Although several other ethnic armed groups, such as the UWSA and the Mongla-based NDAA joined in support of Peng, the MNDAA forces were quickly overrun by the Myanmar military. By the end of the month, the central government had captured Laugai. Ousted, Peng went into hiding; Bai's troops joined the BGF, and he was appointed leader of Kokang, now loyal to the government in Naypyidaw.

Although the conflict was relatively small in scale, 37,000 refugees reportedly crossed the border into the Yunnan province border town of Nansan.[14] Although many were Chinese citizens who had previously worked in Kokang, many were Kokang and other ethnic minorities from Myanmar. During the conflict, a bomb had landed on the Chinese side of the border and killed one civilian, but by the end of August, the Chinese government began forcing refugees who were not Chinese citizens back to Kokang.[15] Thus, after one month of turmoil, the confrontations in Kokang receded, and the situation across the border returned to normal.

Afterwards Peng went into hiding for several years at his son-in-law Lin Mingxian's stronghold in Mongla. But, fighting erupted again in Kokang when Peng returned, with his troops and supported by several other ethnic rebel armies, including the Ta'ang National Liberation Army (TNLA) and the Arakanese Army (AA).[16] On February 9, 2015, the MNDAA attacked Myanmar government posts around Laogai. Ambushed by the rebel armies, the Myanmar military suffered heavy losses, with forty-seven killed and a further seventy-three injured during four days of fighting.[17] Naypyidaw declared a state of emergency on February 17, while trying to regroup to fend off MNDAA and its allies' attacks.[18] Fighting lasted until May, when the Myanmar government seized the last MNDAA stronghold.[19] During the conflict, another refugee exodus occurred, and an estimated forty to fifty thousand civilians fled into China, where temporary shelters were provided in Nansan.[20]

Conflicts in Kachin State and Northern Shan State

In September 2010, having quelled the MNDAA, the Myanmar military declared all existing ceasefire agreements "null and void," which was essentially declaration of war on all the ethnic armed groups that resisted the BGF scheme.[21] The military's next target was the KIA, which boasted a more formidable military force than the MNDAA, with about eight thousand soldiers and more sophisticated weaponry. Fighting started in June 2011 when Myanmar government troops attacked KIA positions east of Bhamo in Kachin State and spread throughout both Kachin and the Northern Shan State. Between June 2011 and October 2012, there were more than two thousand four hundred clashes between the KIA and government troops, which reportedly led to the deaths of at least seven hundred KIA soldiers and between five and ten thousand government soldiers.[22] Fighting intensified again in December 2012 and January 2013, when the Myanmar military made heavy use of airstrikes and artillery against KIA positions around the rebels' headquarters in Laiza.[23] However, in contrast with their easy success against the MNDAA in Kokang, the Myanmar military could not take down the KIA, which maintained control around Laiza. Because of the close proximity of Laiza to the Chinese border, several bombs also landed on the Chinese side. Indeed, because several KIA strongholds are also very close to the Chinese border, the conflict has led to thousands of Kachin refugees crossing the border into China, in addition to the one hundred and fifty thousand internally displaced within Kachin and Shan states.[24] Although both the Myanmar government and the KIA agreed to hold peace talks from early 2013, nothing substantial has come out of these prolonged negotiations. Confrontations between the two continue sporadically. One of the worst casualties suffered by the KIA was in November 2014 when Myanmar government troops fired artillery shells into a KIA training ground and killed twenty-three cadets.[25]

Myanmar government troops clashed not only with the KIA but also with several other ethnic armed groups in the Shan states, including the TNLA and AA, with the latter often fighting alongside the KIA. In addition, government troops also clashed with ethnic armed groups that have nominally secured new ceasefire agreements, such as the SSA-North and SSA-South. Adding to the complexities of the ongoing military contestations are clashes among existing ethnic armed groups and with groups that have been organized into the BGF schemes, as well as with other private militias associated with the Myanmar government.[26] In late 2016, a Northern Alliance comprised of the KIA, TNLA, AA, and MNDAA attacked Muse, a major trading town right on the Chinese border, threatening cross-border trade between the two countries.[27] See table 8.1 for military clashes between ethnic armed groups and Myanmar government troops since 2011.

The Resource Curse

Although it is clear that the immediate cause for the collapse of the ceasefire was the government's BGF scheme, structural reasons prolong the ethnic groups' political grievances with Myanmar; these were discussed in the previous chapter on the political origins of Myanmar's ethnic problems. A few

Table 8.1 Clashes between Ethnic Armed Groups and the Myanmar Government Troops since mid 2011

	2011–2012	2013	2014	2015	2016
KIA	<2,400	<1,500	73	96	82
TNLA	80+	42	113	219	309
MNDAA			15	51	1
RCSS[a]	68	27	13	13	6
SSPP[b]	130	25	17	34	9
Northern Alliance					136+

Data for 2012–2014 are from Burma News International, Deciphering Myanmar's Peace Process: A Reference Guide 2015 (Chiang Mai, Thailand: Burma News International, 2015), 13–14. Data for 2015 and 2016 are from Burma News International, Deciphering Myanmar's Peace Process: A Reference Guide 2016 (Chiang Mai, Thailand: Burma News International, 2017), 4–5. There are some variations in the numbers of clashes according to different sources reported in these reference guides. I mostly used the number reported by news media. If that was not available, I used the Non State Armed Groups (NSAGs) claims.

[a] RCSS is the acronym of the Restoration Council of Shan State, which is also called the SSA-South.

[b] SSPP is the acronym of the Shan State Progressive Party, which is also called the SSA-North.

additional factors served as catalysts for contention, such as the unfair distribution of revenues from natural resource exploitation and the environmental and social implications of huge infrastructural projects with their attendant land confiscation, flooding, and forced relocation of local communities in the Kachin and Shan states.[28]

As discussed in chapter 6, the growing Chinese demand for timber and jade produced in Kachin State has encouraged the Myanmar central government to increase control over access to these commodities. But, the ability to tax such trade has been the lifeblood of the KIA, and since it considers itself the representative of the Kachin people, it also considers that it has a natural right to those revenues. Indeed, one common complaint among the Kachin people is that despite the abundant natural resources in Kachinland, revenues have been siphoned off by the Myanmar central government while the people have been left with poverty and environmental degradation.[29] Thus, fighting over key territories in Kachin State between the KIA and the Myanmar government troops are often over natural resources. For example, skirmishes between them in the Hpakant jade mine in the summer of 2012 led over six thousand miners and residents to flee.[30] In January 2017, Myanmar government troops captured three bases from the KIA in Southern Kachin State around Bhamo, alleging the bases had been used as a hub for smuggling timber into China.[31]

The two gas and oil pipelines that connect Kyaukphyu port in Myanmar's Rakhine State with Kunming, Yunnan, have also proved controversial, because their routes traverse territories under the control of various ethnic armed groups in the Shan State. In June 2011, fighting between Myanmar government troops and the SSA-North broke out in Hsipaw, through which a gas pipeline was planned.[32] This pipeline also goes through territories under the control of the KIA's Fourth Brigade in Northern Shan State, where there have also been clashes because the KIA believed the Myanmar government was attempting to remove the KIA presence in the area.[33] Indeed, the KIA perceived that the Myanmar government wanted to push it out of territories that might be used for infrastructure connectivity with China.[34] For example, in 2010 the Chinese and Myanmar governments began discussing a railway that would cut through northern Myanmar to Rakhine State, linking with the railway to the border town of Ruili, then under construction. Although the Myanmar government later canceled this project, citing lack of support among the general population,[35] one can imagine what the consequences for ongoing insurgencies would be had it proceeded. Similarly, several major hydropower investments made by China on the Irrawaddy and Salween rivers have also aroused popular anger, which has fueled ongoing conflicts.[36] Indeed, we can see that natural resources in the Kachin and Shan states have been instrumental in prolonging the ongoing insurgencies. It also seems apparent that China's role in these insurgencies is crucial. To understand the prospects for peace and stability in the borderland area, it is vital to examine recent changes in bilateral relations between China and Myanmar in the context of Myanmar's domestic political transformation and subsequent changes in international diplomatic relations.

Changing Bilateral Relations between China and Myanmar

To fully understand the dynamic of relations between China and Myanmar, we must also consider the role of the United States. In 1988, the US government introduced a series of sanctions against Myanmar to protest the military's violent suppression of the student movement that year. These sanctions were tightened and Myanmar dubbed a pariah state after the 1990 election result was nullified, and Aung San Suu Kyi, who had led the NLD to victory in that election, was put under house arrest.[37] In the ensuing years, the US government took a hard line against the country, imposing, for example, restrictions on new investment in Myanmar after 1997, together with travel bans on some top military figures. Following the Depayin incident in 2003, the US government extended its travel ban to a wider range of military figures, prohibited Myanmar imports to the United States, and also prevented US banks from dealing with the country. Furthermore, after the "Saffron Revolution" in 2007, the United States imposed a ban on gem stones and jadeite from Myanmar, along with more travel bans.[38]

However, as discussed in chapter 6, Western sanctions against Myanmar did not lead to their intended goal of regime change, but simply redirected Myanmar's trading relations to its neighbors in East and Southeast Asia, with China the biggest beneficiary. Western diplomatic isolation, and in particular the threat of regime change, as in Iraq—at least as perceived by the generals—was one reason why the military government moved its capital to the inland and newly built city of Naypyidaw in 2005.[39] Pressures from the West also pushed the country further into the embrace of China, its protector in the United Nations.[40] However, when the Obama administration started to reevaluate its strategic interests in Asia, especially in the context of China's expansion of influence and its more aggressive foreign policy orientation in the region after 2008,[41] Myanmar's strategic importance has become ever more obvious. In the meantime, there were also internal disagreements within Myanmar over the country's overdependence on China and perceived Chinese economic dominance.[42] For example, an internal Myanmar study of relations with the United States, carried out in 2004, called for the government to improve bilateral relations with the United States in order to alleviate the potential costs of Myanmar's reliance on China.[43]

US foreign policy toward Myanmar started to change in 2009. On August 14, US Senator Jim Webb of Virginia visited the country, meeting Senior General Than Shwe, as well as Aung San Suu Kyi. There is no public information about what exactly Webb discussed with Than Shwe and Suu Kyi. However, after his return to the United States, a detailed review of US policy toward Myanmar was carried out by the Obama administration.[44] Top US government officials subsequently made a flurry of visits to Myanmar to pave the way for a normalization of relations. Later that year, President Obama also met Than Shwe on the sidelines of a US-ASEAN meeting in Singapore. Thus began the whole process of re-engagement between the two nations.[45]

Thein Sein's initiation of the process of political liberalization was, then, well-received by the United States, which reciprocated with a strong diplomatic offensive initiated by top-level official government visits to Myanmar. The visit by US Secretary of State Hillary Clinton in December 2011 was the first visit by a US secretary of state since 1955.[46] Most significantly, US President Barack Obama also made a historic visit to Myanmar in mid-November 2012, the first ever visit to Myanmar by a US president.[47] The rapprochement between Myanmar and the United States thus occurred in the shadow of the US policy shift known as the "Asian Pivot," which represented a strategic vision of beefing up US presence in the Asia-Pacific region and building up a coalition of countries around China.[48]

However, warming US-Myanmar relations have caused great apprehension in Beijing over the intentions of the United States for their role in China's "backyard" and the possible security implications for Chinese interests in Myanmar. Many Chinese commentators believe that it was during the first visit by Jim Webb that the United States promised it would reciprocate positively if Myanmar was willing to distance itself from China.[49] It was subsequently noted with suspicion that in September 2011 President Thein Sein announced the suspension of construction work on the Myitsone Dam, which was being built by China Power Investment Corporation (CPI) to produce electricity for Chinese consumption. This suspension of work, for which the government cited environmental concerns, has been widely interpreted as a sign of the Myanmar government distancing itself from the Chinese "stranglehold."[50] The Chinese government also hinted that the United States played a significant part in it, because the announcement by President Thein Sein came a day after a meeting between Myanmar Foreign Minister Wunna Maung Lwin and US Envoy Derek Mitchell in Washington, DC, and naturally, suspicions were raised that this was not just a coincidence. China's suspicions that this amounted to Western efforts to sabotage Chinese projects and drive a wedge between China and Myanmar was confirmed by a Wikileaks reports about the US embassy's funding of anti-Myitsone activities both in and outside of Myanmar.[51]

After the normalization of relations between the US and Myanmar, many of the international sanctions were lifted, and foreign investment started pouring in. Japanese investment and aid came right away with a pledge of US$10 million in grant aid in September 2011 and another US$2 million promised in March 2012. After Thein Sein's visit to Tokyo, Japan pledged an additional US$2.1 million in grant aid and announced that it would forgive some US$3.7 billion of Myanmar's debt.[52] At the same time, the Myanmar government no longer faced international isolation, and its leaders were able to travel frequently to the West as invited guests. Clearly, the Myanmar government had a significantly improved hand for managing its relations with China, upon whom it was no longer so dependent diplomatically or even economically.

Thus, the geostrategic competition between the United States and China has offered Myanmar more capacity to push back against China's position in the country. At the same time, Myanmar's domestic political transition created room for interest groups opposing Chinese investment in the country to mobilize. Many also took advantage of the newly available freedom of speech to criticize the Chinese government, because of its past support for the military junta. Because of the confluence of these factors, many of China's investment projects came under significant public and official pressure. In addition to the Myitsone Dam, China's investment in the Letpadaung Copper Mine has also faced tremendous popular criticism and resistance. The plan to build rail lines linking Yunnan to the Indian Ocean has also been shelved, due to Myanmar's lack of interest, as mentioned earlier. All this pressure has made China anxious about its existing investment in Myanmar, which also underlies its dilemma about how to respond.

Myanmar's rapid political changes and foreign policy shift toward the West caught China off guard. The perception of Myanmar as a "loyal" ally and as a relatively secure strategic "backyard" no longer holds. Rather, the United States' diplomatic overtures to Myanmar have generated tremendous anxiety over the its strategic design in Myanmar and led to palpable fear of further US containment of China along its previously "safe" southwestern border. The United States has issued many reassurances that it does not intend to contain China and that its diplomatic overtures toward Myanmar are not about China, but many in China see this as merely cheap diplomatic rhetoric. Beijing has interpreted the increased US presence in Myanmar as a potential threat to China's access to the Indian Ocean, its oil and gas pipelines, and even its border security—especially after the United States tried to get involved in the Kachin peace negotiation process (more on this later).[53]

So, China has found itself in a very awkward position. On the one hand, there has been significant anger in Beijing and Yunnan about the Myanmar government's "betrayal," creating a strong impression of Myanmar as "untrustworthy."[54] In particular, China viewed the suspension of the Myitsone Dam project as a breach of contract by Myanmar, and the CPI has suffered significant financial losses as Myanmar doesn't seem to want to give it financial compensation, citing a lack of transparency in negotiations of the agreement with the previous military government.[55] However, it seems there is not much China can do to make Naypyidaw comply with its demands. Retaliation against Myanmar runs the risk of pushing it further into the embrace of the West, which obviously is not in China's interest. Furthermore, China's heavy investments in hard infrastructure, such as the two pipelines, mean it is beholden to the Myanmar government's policies and vulnerable to Myanmar's internal ethnic conflicts. The financial stakes underlying these two pipelines are extremely high. In China's own calculation they drastically outweigh the setbacks in the Myisone Dam project, for example. China's priority has shifted to maintaining as much of its existing access to Myanmar as it can without losing too much ground to Western and Japanese competitors. Deciding how to respond to the changing situation in Myanmar thus poses a significant challenge for Beijing. It requires a proactive engagement with the Myanmar government, but also communicating its resolve on issues it deems pertinent to China's national interests, which it hopes Naypyidaw would respect.

In a nutshell, there has been a large increase in the number and range of diplomatic engagements initiated by China in recent years, which reflects these concerns. Immediately after Hillary Clinton's visit to Myanmar, China State Councilor Dai Bingguo visited Naypyidaw, on December 19. At the same time, China's then-ambassador to Myanmar, Li Junhua, met Aung San Suu Kyi for the first time since she had become the democratic opposition leader.[56] In February 2012, the speaker of the Myanmar parliament, Shwe Mann, visited Beijing; a few months later, in September, Wu Bangguo, Chairman of China's National People's Congress, paid a return visit to Naypyitaw. Then, in September 2012, President Thein Sein visited Nanning for the China-ASEAN Expo and met Xi Jinping, and visited China and met Xi in April 2013. Apparently, during this meeting, Xi "deviated from earlier talking points to say that the Sino-Burmese friendship should not 'be disturbed by external forces,' an unusually direct statement that reflects China's growing concern over Western influence in Burma."[57] There have also been top-level official military visits. In July 2013, President Thein Sein received Vice Chairman of the Central Military Commission of China Fan Changlong in Naypyidaw.[58] In addition, in October 2013, Xi Jingping welcomed Min

Aung Hlaing, commander-in-chief of the Myanmar Defense Service, in Beijing.[59] China has obviously felt the challenge posed by the US diplomatic offensive in Myanmar and has tried to regain some lost ground by actively seeking meetings with top officials from Myanmar.

In March 2013, China posted a new ambassador to Myanmar, Yang Houlan, who is believed to be a more seasoned diplomat capable of dealing with the challenges China now faces in the country. After his arrival, he made several changes to how the Chinese embassy approaches the Myanmar opposition forces and civil society in general. First, he established a communication office to handle relations with the growing number of civil society groups in Myanmar and to facilitate outreach to local media. Setting up accounts on Facebook and Twitter—which ironically are banned in China—the Chinese Embassy in Myanmar started actively approaching both domestic and international media. The perception was that previously there had been a great deal of misinformation about what the Chinese government and Chinese investors do in Myanmar; setting up such communication channels were crucial for winning over the Myanmar public.[60] In response to this initiative, and as part of it, many Chinese corporations in Myanmar have started reaching out to media and talking about corporate social responsibility and other such issues, addressing previous accusations that Chinese investments took no consideration of potential environmental or social costs. The most prominent success is the Chinese government's outreach to the NLD, which culminated in Aung San Suu Kyi's visit to China in June 2015, before her party's victory in the national election.[61]

Because of the ongoing problems surrounding Chinese investment in Myanmar, including its many dams and mining projects, the Chinese government initially stopped or delayed new investments. According to Yun Sun, "Chinese investment in the nation plummeted—approximately $12 billion from 2008 to 2011 to just $407 million in the 2012/2013 fiscal year."[62] However, we have seen in chapter 6 that Chinese investment to Myanmar rebounded in the 2015/2016 fiscal year, perhaps indicating that by this time bilateral relations had stabilized, especially after Suu Kyi's visit to Beijing. During the years when the Myanmar government's intentions and relations with the West were uncertain, China's withholding of investment to Myanmar reflected its concern about the long-term feasibility and safety of its investments in the country given the ongoing changes that are taking place. On the other hand, these changes could also be interpreted as Beijing using its economic clout to demonstrate to the Myanmar government that

China can play a crucial role in the economic construction of the country. It will be extremely difficult for Myanmar to divorce from its interdependence with China, the second largest economy in the world, with which it shares a border.

China's Changing Reactions to Ongoing Insurgencies in Myanmar

We can now make sense of the changes in the Chinese government's responses to the militarized ethnic conflicts along the Sino-Myanmar border within this broader geostrategic change surrounding Myanmar's domestic political transformation and diplomatic breakthroughs. Indeed, we can observe a more assertive Chinese reaction toward Myanmar regarding the latter's management of its ethnic issues, as clearly illustrated by the drastically different responses to the 2009 and 2015 Kokang conflicts. After the Kachin conflict flared up again, the Chinese government became directly involved in peace negotiations between the KIA and the Myanmar government, which was unprecedented in Chinese diplomatic practices.

On 1 September 2009 at a Chinese Ministry of Foreign Affairs (MOFA) media briefing by spokeswoman Jiang Yu, a journalist asked whether China was worried about the border security between China and Myanmar, when the refugee camps for the Kokang conflict would be closed, and whether China would ask the refugees to leave. Yu replied that "China and Myanmar are friendly neighbors, and we want to see that Myanmar maintains peace, stability and development . . . we want to see the situation along the border quickly return to stability and for the refugees to return home soon." In response to another journalist's question about whether China provided help for the refugees, she answered,

> The Yunnan provincial government has taken active measures and settled more than 10,000 Myanmar refugees . . . However, I want to emphasize that maintaining stability along the border suits the fundamental interest of people in both countries and is both governments' mutual responsibility. We hope Myanmar properly resolves its domestic issues and takes necessary measures to return the situation on the border to normal, as well as guaranteeing the security of Chinese people and property in Myanmar.[63]

The Chinese government, in its handling of the 2009 Kokang conflict, seems to have essentially let Myanmar deal with the problem by itself, unwilling to get involved. This hands-off approach represented its belief that the Myanmar government was a friendly neighbor and could be relied upon to protect Chinese interests in the country.

In contrast, the escalation of hostilities between the KIA and Myanmar military forces since 2011 occurred when China perceived the Myanmar government as undergoing changes after the latter's foreign policy reorientation in 2011. This shift resulted in a more proactive response from China, and the Chinese government spoke out about its displeasure at how the Myanmar government was handling the Kachin conflict. On January 4, 2013, at a MOFA briefing, a reporter asked about the Chinese government's position on Myanmar's military actions against the KIA and how it would respond to the bombs that landed on the Chinese side of the border. MOFA spokeswoman Hua Chunying replied:

> During the military clash between Myanmar government forces and the KIA, three bombs landed on Chinese territory but didn't lead to casualties. China has raised its concerns with Myanmar, demanding that Myanmar take immediate measures to avoid such incidents in the future. Problems in northern Myanmar are Myanmar's internal affairs. China hopes the Myanmar government can solve its problems through peaceful dialogue with the relevant parties and maintain peace and stability in the borderland area.[64]

However, in the following weeks it seemed the Myanmar government did not heed the Chinese government's concerns, instead escalating its military conflict with the KIA, and bombs continued to fall on China's side of the border. On January 17, 2013, when asked about the ongoing conflict, MOFA spokesman Hong Lei expressed strong discontentment toward Myanmar, saying that,

> China has lodged an urgent complaint with Myanmar, expressed its severe concern and displeasure at the situation, and demanded that Myanmar carry out sincere investigations and take all necessary measures to prevent such incidents from occurring again. China calls for the conflicting parties to show the utmost restraint, reach a ceasefire immediately and resolve their differences through dialogue.[65]

It seemed that by this point, the Chinese government were sensing the need to become more actively involved in the conflict between the Myanmar government and the KIA and started to pressure both sides to negotiate. On January 21, 2013, the MOFA confirmed that that

> Recently, the Chinese government special envoy, MOFA Vice Minister Fu Ying, visited Myanmar, and both sides reaffirmed they would maintain peace and stability in the border region between China and Myanmar.... We think the only right way to solve the problem in northern Myanmar is through peace negotiations, and we hope the fighting parties can reach a ceasefire and begin talks. China will continue its constructive role to maintain peace and stability along the border."[66]

Indeed, after two weeks of Chinese pressure, the Myanmar government and the KIA agreed to sit down for peace talks, with the first round on February 4 and another on March 11 in Ruili, Yunnan province. Also, during this period, China appointed Ambassador Wang Yingfan as special envoy for Asian affairs, but his primary responsibility was to oversee the peace negotiations and other developments in Myanmar. In fact, during this round of negotiations, various parties, especially the KIA, considered China's approach overbearing.[67] The next round was relocated to Myitkyina, Kachin State capital. The Chinese government decided to become more directly involved, partly because it was concerned about the involvement of the United States and the United Kingdom in the peace negotiation process (the KIO and the Myanmar government sent invitations to both of these governments to send representatives to the negotiation table). China, however, was firmly against the "internationalization" of the Kachin conflict. The fear that the United States might get closer access to its southwestern border made China willing to act more aggressively in handling the Kachin peace negotiation process. In the end, over China's objections, a compromise was reached and the UN was invited to send a representative to the May 2013 peace negotiations.

The Kachin conflict thus became the first time that the Chinese government was actively involved in peace negotiations between the Myanmar government and an ethnic rebel group. This certainly represents a departure from the conventional emphasis the Chinese government places on "non-intervention in other countries' domestic affairs" in its foreign policy. Viewed within the context of China's general anxiety toward Myanmar's foreign relations with the West and its domestic political changes, it is understandable that Beijing would demonstrate to Naypyidaw the crucial position and power it wields in the borderland area.

Turning to the resumption of the Kokang conflict in 2015, after the publication of Peng's open letter, its effect in mobilizing the Chinese nationalist sentiment was electrifying. Angry Chinese nationalists began to berate the Chinese government for being weak and spineless and call for tougher action in response to the Myanmar government's mistreatment of the Kokang as an overseas Chinese group. Chinese domestic media followed up with interviews of Peng, and many carried long-form stories about Kokang's history and the past and present conflict between the MNDAA and the Myanmar central government. Then, in early March, reports started to emerge in China about Myanmar's bombs landing on the Chinese side of the border, which led Chinese foreign ministry spokesperson Hong Lei to request that Myanmar prevent further such occurrences.[68] On March 13, bombs from an airstrike by the Myanmar military landed on the Chinese side of the border, killing five Chinese nationals and injuring nine.[69] The killing of Chinese citizens by allegedly "stray" bombs from Myanmar fired up nationalists online. Many expressed anger that the "small country" Myanmar dared to bomb Chinese territory, leading to the deaths of Chinese citizens. Many also ridiculed the Chinese government, calling out its incompetency to protect its sovereignty despite its "self-claimed" big power status. Most called upon the Chinese government to take punitive action against Myanmar. Some even compared the Kokang situation to that in Crimea and stated that it was time for China to learn from Russia's example and be more protective of its co-ethnics abroad. That rhetoric prompted the government-affiliated *Global Times* to publish an editorial rejecting this comparison, emphasizing that the Kokang, even though they are ethnic Chinese, are not Chinese citizens.[70]

It is within this context that we observe the totally different response the Chinese government took toward the 2015 Kokang conflict compared to its response in 2009. After reports emerged that Chinese civilians died as a result of stray bombs from Myanmar, MOFA spokesman Hong Lei said in a March 16, 2015, media briefing, "China has lodged a strong complaint to Myanmar. Myanmar has expressed its sorrow for the Chinese casualties and will investigate and properly handle the issue. Myanmar has also sent a working group to the borderland area to carry out a joint investigation with its Chinese counterpart."[71] This time, Beijing acted firmly to extract an official apology from Myanmar, which initially refused to give one, claiming as an excuse that it was unclear who was responsible for the errant bombs. The Chinese ambassador to Myanmar, Yang Houlan, lodged an official protest with the Myanmar government and military. Fan Changlong, the vice chairman of the Chinese Central Military Commission, subsequently issued a strong protest to Min Aung Hlaing, commander-in-chief of the Myanmar Defense Services, calling on Myanmar to investigate the bombing, apologize, and compensate the victims.[72] Eventually, Myanmar's Foreign Minister U Wunna Maung Lwin made an official apology, telling his Chinese counterpart, Wang Yi, in a meeting in Beijing on April 2, "On behalf of the Myanmar government and military, I officially apologize to China and express my deep sympathy to the families of the victims and the injured."[73] The Myanmar side was also pressured to publish this apology in domestic media.[74]

Myanmar's 2015 Election and Twenty-First Century Panglong Conference

While China has taken a more interventionist approach toward the borderland conflicts in Myanmar, Myanmar's domestic political transition has also reached a landmark. Although the military's special status was preserved, the election in November 2015 was claimed as overall free and fair and saw a landslide victory for the NLD. Although Aung San Suu Kyi was prohibited by the constitution from becoming president, her uncontested authority within the NLD made her de facto head of government by virtue of her position as state councilor. The new government has faced tremendous challenges in revitalizing Myanmar's economy while continuing its political reform. At the same time, in order to safeguard the long-term stability of the country, Aung San Suu Kyi has made peace settlements with various ethnic armed groups one of the top priorities for her government.

Before the NLD electoral victory, the Thein Sein government had already initiated a political dialogue with some of the ethnic armed groups; this led to the signing of a National Ceasefire Agreement (NCA) in October 2015.[75] Although termed "national," only eight armed groups signed the agreement, while some of the largest ethnic armed groups, such as the UWSA, KIA, TNLA, AA, and MNDAA were excluded. The signed NCA included the government's demand on the "Three Main National Causes," which include "non-disintegration of the union, non-disintegration of national solidarity and perpetuation of national sovereignty." In return, the government conceded the establishment of a union on the basis of democracy and federalism.[76] However, the most sensitive topics, such as disarmament, demobilization, and reintegration of the ethnic armed forces as well as reform of the security sector, were not included in the NCA.

After Aung San Suu Kyi formed the new government, a Union Peace Dialogue Joint Committee (UPDJC) was established to replace the previous Myanmar Peace Center. She then declared the convening of the Twenty-First Century Panglong Conference, in response to her father's pivotal role in the 1946 Panglong Agreement; the first meeting lasted from late August to early December 2016. Participation in the conference was significantly broader than in the NCA, and an alliance of the NCA non-signatory armed groups was allowed to present a paper calling for radical changes to the governance of the country and the military, which was interpreted as "a great leap for a country that began its political transition from a military dictatorship only five years ago."[77] However, three insurgent groups—the MNDAA, TNLA, and AA—were not invited, while the UWSA walked out on the second day of the conference, alleging discrimination.[78] Despite early optimism, the first meeting of the conference did not result in any concrete agreement.

As discussed earlier, clashes erupted in late 2016 between the Northern Alliance and the Myanmar military. By February 2017, seven armed groups declared that they would not sign the NCA and would seek an alternative peace negotiation process under the leadership of the UWSA.[79] On February 21, these groups met at the Panghsang headquarters of the UWSA and issued a joint statement announcing their intention not to sign the NCA but to engage in political dialogue under the UWSA's leadership.[80] Additionally, they called for Chinese and UN mediation and voiced support for China's One Belt One Road initiative, promising "security guarantees" for Chinese projects in the areas under their control.[81]

Given the close relationship between the UWSA and China, there was speculation of deep Chinese involvement with these non-NCA signatory groups. Indeed, before the second meeting of the Twenty-First Century Panglong Conference in May 2017, the seven groups met again in Kunming, and it was reported that they were given permission to attend the meeting in Naypyidaw as specially invited guests because of pressure from China.[82] The second conference seems to have achieved some moderate progress, with participants reaching several agreements on political, economic, social, land, and environmental issues.[83] At the meeting, Aung San Suu Kyi also met with delegates from the seven non-NCA signatory groups, albeit separately and not as a bloc.⁸⁴ However, key hurdles remain. One is the issue of a federal army, which the Myanmar military insists on, while the ethnic armed groups all want to retain their own armed forces. At the same time, several of the ethnic armed groups do not wish to see language mandating "non-secession" or "non-secessionism" included in the draft of the Union Peace Accord.⁸⁵

Concluding Remarks

Although the 2017 Rohingya crisis in Rakhine State has significantly tarnished Aung San Suu Kyi's aura as a global democracy icon, Myanmar has made dramatic achievements in its domestic political transition and its international status during the past five years. At least within Myanmar proper, a mostly democratic political framework has been in place, and its society has witnessed a significant increase in freedom of speech and political organization. However, the most daunting issue that has continually haunted the Union of Burma ever since its founding is the ongoing strife in its ethnic-minority regions. Given that Rakhine State is not within the remit of this book, the ongoing humanitarian crisis among the Rohingya is not discussed here. Having said that, the active military insurgencies among several ethnic armed groups along the borderland area between Myanmar, China, and Thailand are indicative of the high degree of tension between the majority Bamar political center and the ethnic peripheries. Indeed, how to bring these ethnic armed groups into the Myanmar fold has been one of the top priorities for both the military and the civilian government under Aung San Suu Kyi. It seems that completely subduing the guerillas through military means has not been successful and is not going to be so in the foreseeable future. Yet the effort to start meaningful political dialogue to bring peace to the country has also not been easy. Myanmar's political elites still have a long way to go in order to bring about a political solution to the country's fractured ethnic borderland region. Through it all, Myanmar's giant neighbor to the north has become increasingly pivotal for the internal peace process as well.

9

Conclusion

A hilltop next to the village Sop Ruak offers a panoramic view of the meeting of three countries, Laos, Myanmar, and Thailand. Promoted by the local Thai authority as the "real" Golden Triangle to attract tourists who want to have a peek at this notorious center of opium cultivation and drug trafficking, one might come away disappointed at the lack of anything meaningful in such a theme-park treatment of the history of cross-border intrigue during the Cold War period. However, not far from this man-made tourist destination, new developments along this Mekong River border crossing have signaled an unprecedented level of movement of goods and people from China downstream to Thailand via Laos. Across the river at the Lao city of Tonpheung, a massive casino and hotel complex towers over the skyline. Part of the new Golden Triangle Special Economic Zone established by a Chinese conglomerate, the King Romans casino is the largest gambling joint in the Mekong region; with it an illicit economy of drug trafficking and money laundering has developed along with the movement of large numbers of Myanmar migrant workers and Chinese tourists across the Thai/Lao border.[1]

In the nearby Thai city of Chiang Saen, the national flags of China, Laos, Myanmar, and Thailand hang in front a huge industrial complex at the Chiang Saen Port Authority. Increasing traffic along the Mekong River has improved the prospect of further economic cooperation among these four countries. Moving slightly downstream to the city of Chiang Khong, the Fourth Thai-Lao Friendship Bridge, completed in 2013, has become the link that connects the road system in China with that of Thailand, forming part of Asian Highway No. 3. Increasing infrastructure connectivity has made this borderland region, which was a remote castaway place during the Cold War, look more like a center for increased regional economic integration.

In fact, one of the most recent initiatives on further regional economic integration, suggested by China and several Mekong region countries, is the establishment of the Lancang-Mekong Cooperation (LMC). In contrast with earlier regional indicatives such as the Great Mekong Subregion (GMS) initiative of the Asian Development Bank or the Western-funded Mekong River

Commission, the LMC has more Chinese involvement. A first LMC Foreign Minister's Meeting was held in Jinghong, in southern Yunnan province's Xishuangbanna region, in November 2015 after which a concept paper on the framework of the LMC was issued. Later, a First LMC Leaders' Meeting was held in Sanya, Hainan, from which came the Sanya Declaration of the First Lancang-Mekong Cooperation.[2] At the meeting, leaders of Cambodia, China, Laos, Myanmar, Thailand, and Vietnam agreed to strengthen dialogue and cooperation in three key fields: politics and security; economic and sustainable development; and social, cultural, and people-to-people exchanges. They also agreed to start cooperating in five priority areas: interconnectivity, production capacity, cross-border economic cooperation, water resources, and agriculture and poverty alleviation.[3] The emphasis is mostly on economic cooperation, which separates the LMC from the other two regional initiatives which emphasized environment protection and water resource management.

China's push for the LMC should also be understood in the context of its grand strategy of One Belt One Road (OBOR),[4] which aims at increasing connectivity between China and Southeast Asia. From the Chinese government's perspective, its southwestern provinces, such as Yunnan, should be an important conduit for the OBOR, and to this end the Chinese government has contributed US$40 billion to a new Silk Road Fund to support infrastructural construction and industrial cooperation among the GMS countries.[5] This represents China's intention to not only play "a more comprehensive role in sub-regional cooperation and project its initiative and rule-making power"[6] but also to diminish Western and Japanese influence in the region. Indeed, the LMC has been interpreted as Chinese assertion of its own regional initiative for cooperation in mainland Southeast Asia.[7] Since its establishment, China has hosted three LMC foreign ministers' meetings and has set up funding to support forty-five projects under the mechanism, including water resource research centers and cooperation on connectivity projects, industrial capacity, border trade, agriculture, and poverty alleviation.[8] Most recently, a second LMC leaders' summit was held in Phnom Penh in January 2018. Although details of how the LMC will eventually work out are still not yet clear, from the agreements available so far it seems the LMC mostly serves to further Chinese economic penetration in the GMS region, and the emphasis is on economic development rather than environmental protection and other livelihood issues surrounding the Mekong River.[9] In fact, the Mekong River Commission—which is primarily concerned with environmental protection along the Mekong River, is funded by the West, and whose membership does not include China—was excluded from the LMC meetings.[10]

China's push for the LMC and the overall OBOR strategies in Southeast Asia have thus demonstrated the increasingly dominant role the country has played in the region. The past decades of fast economic growth and expanding regional influence have only increased China's asymmetric power imbalance over its southern neighbors in Southeast Asia. This has manifested in the increasing reliance of both Thailand and Myanmar on Beijing for solutions to each country's domestic challenges. Because of domestic political transformations, Thailand and Myanmar have witnessed some unprecedented trends in relations between themselves and their northern neighbor.

Since the start of the twenty-first century, Thailand has faced domestic instability, with competing rallies and counter-rallies between political forces loosely defined as "yellow shirts" and "red shirts."[11] Such grassroots confrontations reflect the power struggles between the ousted Prime Minister Thaksin Shinawatra and the supporters of the royalist forces, which prompted the military to take over the government twice, in 2006 and 2014. In particular, the most recent coup by General Prayuth Chan-ocha has created a domestic political environment of deteriorating civil liberties and human rights violations, particularly in the draconian use of the *lèse majesté* law on political dissidents.[12] Thailand's domestic political regression created a problem for its relations with the United States, which is no longer as tolerant or supportive of military coups in Thailand as it was during the Cold War years.

Officially, the US government downgraded its military relations with Thailand, canceled some military aid and criticized the political situation in Thailand. However, US pressure, albeit feeble, did not matter much to the Thai government, as it actively courted Chinese support. On December 19, 2014, Chinese Premier Li Keqiang became the most high-profile foreign leader to visit Thailand since the coup that May.[13] A few days later, Thai Prime Minister Prayuth flew to Beijing, where he met with the Chinese president Xi Jinping; Xi expressed the hope that both countries should continue to show mutual understanding and support on issues concerning each other's core interests. In addition to closer political relations between Bangkok and Beijing, both countries have also stepped up military cooperation. Thailand has purchased submarines, tanks, and other military equipment from China, and both countries carried out a joint military exercise, Blue Strike, in 2016, considered "the most comprehensive exercise the two have ever had, including land and sea operations, and humanitarian relief training."[14]

By courting Chinese support, the Thai government has effectively resisted pressure from the United States. For example, after a January 2015 speech given by Daniel Russel, assistant US secretary for East Asian and Pacific Affairs, in which he criticized the military government, the Thai Foreign Ministry summoned top US diplomats to register its displeasure.[15] A protest was organized against Russel's speech in front of the Thai embassy in Bangkok.[16] In December 2015, Thai Prime Minister Prayuth criticized the new US Ambassador Glyn Davis for his concern about the abuse of the *lèse majesté* law, saying that his "opinion is biased and not impartial . . . This can lead to the deterioration of our long-term friendship."[17] The United States, because of the competitive dynamic between it and China for influence in Southeast Asia, cannot afford to alienate the current Thai government by pressuring it too much, lest it push Thailand further into the embrace of China.[18] Thus, it treads carefully in its dealings with the Thai government, and the annual military exercise Cobra Gold with Thai and US forces was held in 2016 and again in 2017, despite earlier indications that the United States might want to cancel it.[19] After President Donald Trump took office, relations between the two countries further improved, and in October 2017, Prayuth became the first Thai prime minister to have visited the White House in twelve years.[20] So, by keeping an open engagement with both China and the United States, Thailand has managed to maintain its autonomy from US pressure on its domestic politics. By courting closer relations with China, the current military government has been able to maintain its tight grip on power domestically as well as enjoying diplomatic freedom of action internationally.

On the other hand, relations between Myanmar and China have gone through some ups and downs during the recent past but have since stabilized, especially since Aung San Suu Kyi came into power in 2015. As the Rohingya crisis in the Rakhine State has plagued Suu Kyi and her government in 2017, she has expressed appreciation for Beijing's support for her government, for example by stating "China and Myanmar will be good neighbors forever with fraternal spirit" during a recent meeting with the visiting Chinese foreign minister.[21] Indeed, following recent international criticism over her government's handling of the Rohingya crisis, which has been branded as ethnic cleansing or even genocide, Myanmar's relations with China have to some extent reverted to the previous dependence that characterized the military government period, in the sense that Beijing continues to shelter Myanmar from international censure.

China clearly does not support international sanctions on Myanmar over the Rohingya issue and will use its veto power at the UN Security Council against any such proposal. In November 2017, given the clear intention from China as well as Russia that they would not support a resolution at the United Nations, the Security Council instead adopted a statement that condemned the violence in the Rakhine state, but without using the term ethnic cleansing.[22] Again in March 2018, China resisted UK efforts at the UN Security Council for a statement calling on Myanmar to try those responsible for attacks on the Rohingya, by offering a watered down amendment that dropped all mention of investigations or accountability.[23] On the other hand, China has been actively involved in efforts to facilitate a negotiated solution between Myanmar and Bangladesh. Instead of blindly supporting Myanmar, it also aims to soothe Bangladesh's concern about the burden of sheltering so many refugees. The Chinese government offered to mediate between the Myanmar and Bangladesh governments after Foreign Minister Wang Yi's visit to Dhaka in November 2017 and initiated a three-phase proposal on how to solve the impasse between the two countries. This involves first a ceasefire by the Myanmar military, then negotiation between the Myanmar and Bangladesh governments to solve the problem of repatriation of the Rohingya refugees, and finally help from the international community for rebuilding war-torn Rakhine State.[24] However, the Rohingya crisis is ongoing, and it is still premature to elaborate how much and for how long international pressure will mount on the Myanmar government, and what kind of political implications such pressure will have on Aung San Suu Kyi herself as well as the NLD party.

Still, on the issue of Myanmar's domestic peace process involving the ethnic rebel groups along its border, China has been playing an ever-larger mediating role. It is worth emphasizing once again how pivotal China's role in the whole process is and also how crucial the peace process in Myanmar is for China's overall strategic interests in its OBOR grand strategy. Indeed, in many of China's domestic discussions on the OBOR strategy in Southeast Asia, Myanmar is not only a crucial knot linking China and the Indian Ocean, it is also part of the corridor to the countries of South Asia. One of the commonly discussed trade linkages is the so-called Bangladesh-India-Myanmar-China Economic Corridor, intended to increase connectivity, culture, trade, and tourism ties and people-to-people contact among those countries, and especially in the border regions. The idea is to establish a closer trade network that could cut across land borders, despite the fact that these borderland areas are located in very difficult mountainous terrain.[25]

Although this kind of initiative sounds more like a fantasy than a realistic understanding of the difficulties of crossing borders between Myanmar, India, and Bangladesh, it nonetheless indicates the vision of a future in which barriers on national borders might be lowered. Perhaps because of the diplomatic support China has given to the Myanmar government on the Rohingya issue, in July both governments agreed on an MoU on the China-Myanmar Economic Corridor.[26] While the exact details of this corridor at ground level remain murky, this agreement does indicate that the Myanmar government has finally signed on to China's regional development strategies, despite its initial reluctance to do so. Similarly, despite some domestic opposition to and concern about the financial sustainability of the Kyaukphyu port facilities, the Myanmar government finally signed an agreement with the Chinese CITIC conglomerate to codevelop the special economic zone, with the CITIC group controlling 70 percent of the shares.[27]

For such grand schemes to succeed, good infrastructure connecting Myanmar and China is desperately needed. Yet, any discussion of further infrastructure connectivity between the two countries cannot escape the fact that such routes would have to pass through territories that are either under the control of ethnic rebel groups or are subject to dispute between them and the Myanmar central government. For this reason, the Chinese government has realized the unstable borderland with Myanmar is a major liability for its strategic interest in the country. The ongoing military insurgency has not only periodically pushed refugees into Chinese territory, it has also had a negative effect on local economies dependent on cross-border trade. If such conflicts continue, then the prospect for these infrastructure connectivity projects through Myanmar is going to be dim. This explains why Beijing has been so actively involved in the peace process in Myanmar lately.

In the previous chapter, we discussed how instrumental China has been in facilitating negotiations between various ethnic rebel groups and the Myanmar central government at the Twenty-First Century Panglong Conference. Particularly through the Northern Alliance under the leadership of the UWSA, Beijing has exerted pressure on both sides for ongoing dialogue. For example, at a meeting with the Northern Alliance leaders,

Chinese special envoy Sun Guoxiang reportedly said, "China hopes that peace prevails in Burma, and would not like to say who is right and who is wrong. China will not sit as a judge, but will only push all stakeholders in the peace process. China would like to urge stakeholders to solve the problems at the negotiation table and will provide advice as a friend in case problems arise."[28] Indeed, many concerned parties have noted how indispensable China is in Myanmar's peace process. For example, the International Crisis Group has stated that, "If China is determined to see sustainable peace on its border, it can use its considerable leverage as well as sophisticated diplomacy and mediation to push all sides to compromise."[29] However, there have also been speculations about China's real intensions in Myanmar's process. Bertil Linter, a longtime observer of Myanmar, notes that by demonstrating its crucial role in brokering such dialogues, Beijing intends to pressure Naypyidaw to reciprocate with concessions providing Chinese interests access to the Indian Ocean.[30] Thus, how the peace process will pan out seems to ultimately depend on how China's strategic interests align with the interests of Myanmar's domestic stakeholders, and Beijing's preponderant role would have to be carefully heeded.

Throughout the book, we have looked at the state and nation-building process in the borderland area between the three countries of China, Myanmar, and Thailand. By documenting the historical development of variations in these state and nation buildings, and their contemporary manifestations, the book emphasizes how asymmetrical power relations across national borders have deep consequences for how politics along the border are structured and the diverse outcome in state consolidation and national identity construction. Specifically, the book has pointed out the substantial influence the PRC has in the political dynamic of the borderland. With its growing power asymmetry over its southern neighbors, its influence is bound to increase, along with possible resistance against its influence. How the future of cross-border connectivity and regionalization will materialize is anyone's guess; there is also increasing uncertainty regarding China's future economic trajectory, given the ongoing trade disputes between Beijing and Washington, DC. But, I hope the stories told in this book will continue to shed light on how we understand the logic of political relations between China and its southern neighbors. China's great power ambitions might be stalled in the future, but its sheer economic and population size would still continue to exert a dominating effect in transforming the borderland area between itself and mainland Southeast Asia.

Notes

Chapter 1

1. In the book, I use Burma for the period before 1989 and Myanmar; Rangoon and Yangon according to the same rule. While there have been some controversies about the name change carried out by the military government in 1989, these days the new country name has overall been accepted by the international community. See Lowell Dittmer, ed., *Burma or Myanmar? The Struggle for National Identity* (Singapore; Hackensack, NJ: World Scientific Publishing Company, 2010).
2. "Burma Attack Breaks Kachin Truce Near China Border," *BBC News*, January 20, 2013.
3. "Ethnic Allies Join Kokang Fight," *Myanmar Times*, February 13, 2015.
4. "Government Troops 'Seize Last Stronghold of Kokang Rebels,'" *Mizzima*, May 16, 2015.
5. Willem van Schendel, "Geographies of Knowing, Geographies of Ignorance: Jumping Scale in Southeast Asia," *Environment and Planning D: Society & Space* 20, no. 6 (2002): 647–68.
6. James C. Scott, *The Art of Not Being Governed: An Anarchist History of Upland Southeast Asia* (New Haven, CT: Yale University Press, 2009).
7. Scott, 325.
8. James C. Scott, *Seeing like a State: How Certain Schemes to Improve the Human Condition Have Failed* (New Haven, CT: Yale University Press, 1999).
9. Daron Acemoglu and James Robinson, *Why Nations Fail: The Origins of Power, Prosperity, and Poverty* (New York: Crown Business, 2013).
10. Angus Deaton, *The Great Escape: Health, Wealth, and the Origins of Inequality* (Princeton, NJ: Princeton University Press, 2013).
11. Deaton, 4.
12. Deaton, 4.
13. Jim Glassman, "On the Borders of Southeast Asia: Cold War Geography and the Construction of the Other," *Political Geography* 24, no. 7 (September 2005): 784–807.
14. E. J. Hobsbawm, *Nations and Nationalism Since 1780: Programme, Myth, Reality* (Cambridge, UK; New York: Cambridge University Press, 1990).
15. Francis Fukuyama, *State Building: Governance and World Order in the Twenty-First Century* (London: Profile Books, 2004); Charles Tilly, ed., *The Formation of National States in Western Europe*, 1st ed. (Princeton, NJ: Princeton University Press, 1975).
16. Harris Mylonas, *The Politics of Nation Building: Making Co-Nationals, Refugees, and Minorities* (New York: Cambridge University Press, 2013).

17. Alfred W. McCoy, *The Politics of Heroin: CIA Complicity in the Global Drug Trade*, 1st ed. (Brooklyn, NY: Lawrence Hill Books, 1991); Ko-Lin Chin, *The Golden Triangle: Inside Southeast Asia's Drug Trade*, 1st ed. (Ithaca, NY: Cornell University Press, 2009); Bertil Lintner and Michael Black, *Merchants of Madness: The Methamphetamine Explosion in the Golden Triangle* (Chiang Mai, Thailand: Silkworm Books, 2009).
18. John Herman, *Amid the Clouds and Mist: China's Colonization of Guizhou, 1200–1700* (Cambridge, MA: Harvard University Asia Center, 2007); John Herman, "Collaboration and Resistance on the Southwest Frontier: Early Eighteenth-Century Qing Expansion on Two Fronts," *Late Imperial China* 35, no. 1 (2014): 77–112; C. Patterson Giersch, *Asian Borderlands: The Transformation of Qing China's Yunnan Frontier* (Cambridge, MA: Harvard University Press, 2006); Christian Daniels, "Chieftains into Ancestors: Imperial Expansion and Indigenous Society in Southwest China," *The China Journal*, no. 73 (January 2015): 232–35; David A. Bello, "To Go Where No Han Could Go for Long: Malaria and the Qing Construction of Ethnic Administrative Space in Frontier Yunnan," *Modern China* 31, no. 3 (2005): 283–317.
19. Colin Mackerras, *China's Minorities: Integration and Modernization in the Twentieth Century* (Hong Kong; New York: Oxford University Press, 1994).
20. Magnus Fiskesjö, "Mining, History, and the Anti-State Wa: The Politics of Autonomy between Burma and China," *Journal of Global History* 5, no. 2 (July 2010): 241–264; Wenyi Zhang and FKL Chit Hlaing, "The Dynamics of Kachin 'Chieftaincy' in Southwestern China and Northern Burma," *Cambridge Anthropology* 31, no. 2 (Autumn 2013): 88–103.
21. Robert H. Taylor, *The State in Myanmar* (London: C Hurst & Co Publishers Ltd, 2008); Matthew J. Walton, "Ethnicity, Conflict, and History in Burma: The Myths of Panglong," *Asian Survey* 48, no. 6 (2008): 889–910; Victor B. Lieberman, "Reinterpreting Burmese History," *Comparative Studies in Society and History* 29, no. 1 (January 1987): 162–194.
22. Martin Smith, *Burma: Insurgency and the Politics of Ethnic Conflict* (London: Zed Books, 1999); Ashley South, *Ethnic Politics in Burma: States of Conflict* (London; New York: Routledge, 2008).
23. James Ansil Ramsay, "Modernization and Centralization in Northern Thailand, 1875–1910," *Journal of Southeast Asian Studies* 7, no. 1 (March 1976): 16–32.
24. Hsiao-ting Lin, *Modern China's Ethnic Frontiers: A Journey to the West* (Abingdon, UK; New York: Routledge, 2010).
25. Janet C. Sturgeon, *Border Landscapes: The Politics of Akha Land Use in China and Thailand* (Seattle: University of Washington Press, 2005); Janet C. Sturgeon et al., "Enclosing Ethnic Minorities and Forests in the Golden Economic Quadrangle," *Development and Change* 44, no. 1 (January 1, 2013): 53–79. However, to get the actual numbers of different ethnic groups and their distributions can be tricky, in part because different states approach ethnic categorization differently.

26. Bin Yang, *Between Winds and Clouds: The Making of Yunnan* (New York: Columbia University Press, 2009).
27. Joy K. Park, "A Global Crisis Writ Large: The Effects of Being 'Stateless in Thailand' on Hill-Tribe Children," *San Diego International Law Journal* 10, no. 2 (March 22, 2009): 495.
28. Rogers Brubaker, *Nationalism Reframed: Nationhood and the National Question in the New Europe* (Cambridge, UK; New York: Cambridge University Press, 1996).
29. Enze Han, *Contestation and Adaptation: The Politics of National Identity in China* (New York and London: Oxford University Press, 2013).
30. Robert H. Taylor, *Foreign and Domestic Consequences of the KMT Intervention in Burma* (Ithaca, NY: Southeast Asia Program, Department of Asian Studies, Cornell University, 1973).
31. Mary P. Callahan, *Making Enemies: War and State Building in Burma* (Ithaca, NY: Cornell University Press, 2005).
32. Chao Tzang Yawnghwe, *The Shan of Burma: Memoirs of a Shan Exile* (Singapore: Institute of Southeast Asian Studies, 2010); Sai Aung Tun, *History of the Shan State: From Its Origins to 1962* (Chiang Mai, Thailand: Silkworm Books, 2009).
33. Wen-Chin Chang, *Beyond Borders: Stories of Yunnanese Chinese Migrants of Burma* (Ithaca, NY: Cornell University Press, 2014); Richard Michael Gibson and Wen H. Chen, *The Secret Army: Chiang Kai-Shek and the Drug Warlords of the Golden Triangle* (Singapore: Wiley, 2011).
34. Julia C. Strauss, "Paternalist Terror: The Campaign to Suppress Counterrevolutionaries and Regime Consolidation in the People's Republic of China, 1950–1953," *Comparative Studies in Society and History* 44, no. 1 (2002): 80–105.
35. Jian Chen, *Mao's China and the Cold War* (Chapel Hill: University of North Carolina Press, 2001); Jie Chen, "Shaking off an Historical Burden: China's Relations with the ASEAN-Based Communist Insurgency in Deng's Era," *Communist and Post-Communist Studies* 27, no. 4 (December 1, 1994): 443–62.
36. Maung Aung Myoe, *In the Name of Pauk-Phaw: Myanmar's China Policy since 1948* (Singapore; London: Institute of Southeast Asian Studies, 2011).
37. The CPB collapsed in 1989 after years of funding cuts from the Chinese Communist Party (CCP) following Deng Xiaoping's rise to power. Bertil Lintner, *The Rise and Fall of the Communist Party of Burma (CPB)* (Ithaca, NY: Southeast Asia Program, Department of Asian Studies, Cornell University, 1990).
38. Chris Baker, "An Internal History of the Communist Party of Thailand," *Journal of Contemporary Asia* 33, no. 4 (January 1, 2003): 510–41.
39. Glenn Ettinger, "Thailand's Defeat of Its Communist Party," *International Journal of Intelligence and CounterIntelligence* 20, no. 4 (August 20, 2007): 661–77.
40. Sinae Hyun, "Indigenizing the Cold War: Nation-Building by the Border Patrol Police in Thailand, 1945–1980" (PhD diss., University of Wisconsin-Madison, 2014).
41. Jack Fong, "Sacred Nationalism: The Thai Monarchy and Primordial Nation Construction," *Journal of Contemporary Asia* 39, no. 4 (November 1, 2009): 673–96.
42. Bin Yang, "'We Want to Go Home!' The Great Petition of the Zhiqing, Xishuangbanna, Yunnan, 1978–1979," *The China Quarterly*, no. 198 (2009): 401–21.

43. Mette Halskov Hansen, *Lessons in Being Chinese: Minority Education and Ethnic Identity in Southwest China* (Seattle: University of Washington Press, 1999).
44. Meghan L. Eberle and Ian Holliday, "Precarity and Political Immobilisation: Migrants from Burma in Chiang Mai, Thailand," *Journal of Contemporary Asia* 41, no. 3 (August 1, 2011): 378.
45. Wen-Chin Chang, "The Everyday Politics of the Underground Trade in Burma by the Yunnanese Chinese since the Burmese Socialist Era," *Journal of Southeast Asian Studies* 44, no. 2 (June 2013): 313.
46. Eberle and Holliday, "Precarity and Political Immobilisation," 378.
47. Kevin Woods, "Ceasefire Capitalism: Military–Private Partnerships, Resource Concessions and Military–State Building in the Burma–China Borderlands," *Journal of Peasant Studies* 38, no. 4 (October 1, 2011): 750.
48. Thomas Mullaney, *Coming to Terms with the Nation: Ethnic Classification in Modern China* (Berkeley: University of California Press, 2010).
49. Andrew Walker, ed., *Tai Lands and Thailand: Community and State in Southeast Asia* (Singapore: National University of Singapore, 2009).
50. Bertil Lintner, *Burma in Revolt: Opium and Insurgency since 1948*, 2nd ed. (Chiang Mai, Thailand: Silkworm Books, 1999); South, *Ethnic Politics in Burma*; Smith, *Burma*.
51. Bruce Reynolds, "Phibun Songkhram and Thai Nationalism in the Fascist Era," *European Journal of East Asian Studies* 3, no. 1 (2004): 119.
52. Amporn Jirattikorn, "'Pirated' Transnational Broadcasting: The Consumption of Thai Soap Operas among Shan Communities in Burma," *Sojourn: Journal of Social Issues in Southeast Asia* 23, no. 1 (2008): 30–62; Amporn Jirattikorn, "Aberrant Modernity: The Construction of Nationhood among Shan Prisoners in Thailand," *Asian Studies Review* 36, no. 3 (September 1, 2012): 336.
53. Jirattikorn, "Aberrant Modernity," 334.
54. Ashley South and Kim Jolliffe, "Forced Migration: Typology and Local Agency in Southeast Myanmar," *Contemporary Southeast Asia: A Journal of International & Strategic Affairs* 37, no. 2 (August 2015): 211–41.

Chapter 2

1. John L. Campbell, "The State and Fiscal Sociology," *Annual Review of Sociology* 19 (1993): 163–85; Miguel A. Centeno, *Blood and Debt: War and the Nation-State in Latin America* (University Park, PA: Pennsylvania State University Press, 2002); Christine Fauvelle-Aymar, "The Political and Tax Capacity of Government in Developing Countries," *Kyklos* 52, no. 3 (1999): 391–413; Cameron G. Thies, "National Design and State Building in Sub-Saharan Africa," *World Politics* 61, no. 4 (2009): 623–669.
2. World Bank Development Indicators. The data can be accessed at http://datatopics.worldbank.org/world-development-indicators/.
3. Multiple Indicator Cluster Survey (MICS) 2009–2010, Myanmar, UNICEF. The data can be accessed at http://mics.unicef.org/surveys.

4. Multiple Indicator Cluster Survey (MICS) 2012, Thailand, UNICEF. The data can be accessed at http://mics.unicef.org/surveys.
5. Keith Darden and Anna Grzymala-Busse, "The Great Divide: Literacy, Nationalism, and the Communist Collapse," *World Politics* 59, no. 1 (October 2006): 83–115.
6. Although such ceasefire agreements can be easily broken, as demonstrated by the Myanmar central military assault on the Kokang rebel-controlled area in 2009.
7. Mary P. Callahan, *Political Authority in Burma's Ethnic Minority States: Devolution, Occupation, and Coexistence* (Singapore; Washington, DC: East-West Center Washington, 2007).
8. Mandy Sadan, *Being and Becoming Kachin: Histories Beyond the State in the Borderworlds of Burma* (Oxford: British Academy, 2013).
9. Walton, "Ethnicity, Conflict, and History in Burma"; Matthew J. Walton, "The 'Wages of Burman-Ness': Ethnicity and Burman Privilege in Contemporary Myanmar," *Journal of Contemporary Asia* 43, no. 1 (February 1, 2013): 1–27.
10. Duncan McCargo, *Tearing Apart the Land: Islam and Legitimacy in Southern Thailand* (Ithaca, NY: Cornell University Press, 2008).
11. Hyun, "Indigenizing the Cold War."
12. Brian Downing, *The Military Revolution and Political Change: Origins of Democracy and Autocracy in Early Modern Europe* (Princeton, NJ: Princeton University Press, 1992); Thomas Ertman, *Birth of the Leviathan: Building States and Regimes in Medieval and Early Modern Europe* (Cambridge, UK; New York: Cambridge University Press, 1997); Edgar Kiser and April Linton, "Determinants of the Growth of the State: War and Taxation in Early Modern France and England," *Social Forces* 80, no. 2 (2001): 411–48; Edgar Kiser and April Linton, "The Hinges of History: State-Making and Revolt in Early Modern France," *American Sociological Review* 67, no. 6 (2002): 889–910; Tilly, *The Formation of National States in Western Europe*; Charles Tilly, "War Making and State Making as Organized Crime," in *Bringing the State Back In*, ed. Dietrich Reuschmeyer, Theda Skocpol, and Peter Evans (Cambridge: Cambridge University Press, 1985): 169–191.
13. Charles Tilly, *Coercion, Capital and European States: AD 990–1992*, rev. ed. (Cambridge, MA: Wiley-Blackwell, 1992), 20.
14. Tilly, *The Formation of National States in Western Europe*, 42.
15. Miguel Angel Centeno and Fernando López-Alves, eds., *The Other Mirror* (Princeton, NJ: Princeton University Press, 2001); Miguel A. Centeno and Agustin E. Ferraro, eds., *State and Nation Making in Latin America and Spain: Republics of the Possible*, reprint ed. (Cambridge, UK: Cambridge University Press, 2014).
16. Centeno, *Blood and Debt*, 23.
17. There is a body of literature that looks at rivalry and war preparation, rather than actual war making, in explaining state building. See Paul Diehl and Gary Goertz, *War and Peace in International Rivalry* (Ann Arbor, MI: University of Michigan Press, 2001); William R. Thompson, "Identifying Rivals and Rivalries in World Politics," *International Studies Quarterly* 45, no. 4 (December 1, 2001): 557–86; Cameron G. Thies, "State Building, Interstate and Intrastate Rivalry: A Study of Post-Colonial Developing Country Extractive Efforts, 1975–2000," *International Studies Quarterly*

48, no. 1 (March 1, 2004): 53–72; Cameron G. Thies, "War, Rivalry, and State Building in Latin America," *American Journal of Political Science* 49, no. 3 (July 1, 2005): 451–65; Cameron G. Thies, "The Political Economy of State Building in Sub-Saharan Africa," *Journal of Politics* 69, no. 3 (2007): 716–31.
18. Jeffrey Herbst, *States and Power in Africa: Comparative Lessons in Authority and Control*, 1st ed. (Princeton, NJ: Princeton University Press, 2000).
19. Jeffrey Herbst, "War and the State in Africa," *International Security* 14, no. 4 (1990): 134.
20. Donald L. Horowitz, *Ethnic Groups in Conflict*, 1st ed. (Berkeley: University of California Press, 1985), 563–680.
21. Of course, there are studies that look at the development of African states as a result of how rulers at the political centers negotiate with different local elites and institutions. See Catherine Boone, *Political Topographies of the African State: Territorial Authority and Institutional Choice* (Cambridge, UK; New York: Cambridge University Press, 2003); Catherine Boone, *Property and Political Order in Africa: Land Rights and the Structure of Politics* (New York: Cambridge University Press, 2014).
22. Some historical studies look at the effect of war on state development in the Chinese context, see Edgar Kiser and Yong Cai, "War and Bureaucratization in Qin China: Exploring an Anomalous Case," *American Sociological Review* 68, no. 4 (2003): 511–39; Victoria Tin-bor Hui, *War and State Formation in Ancient China and Early Modern Europe* (New York: Cambridge University Press, 2005).
23. Richard Stubbs, "War and Economic Development: Export-Oriented Industrialization in East and Southeast Asia," *Comparative Politics* 31, no. 3 (1999): 377.
24. Richard F. Doner, Bryan K. Ritchie, and Dan Slater, "Systemic Vulnerability and the Origins of Developmental States: Northeast and Southeast Asia in Comparative Perspective," *International Organization* 59, no. 2 (April 2005): 327.
25. Herbst, *States and Power in Africa*, 18.
26. For example, Andreas Forø Tollefsen and Halvard Buhaug, "Insurgency and Inaccessibility," *International Studies Review* 17, no. 1 (March 1, 2015): 6–25; Halvard Buhaug and Jan Ketil Rød, "Local Determinants of African Civil Wars, 1970–2001," *Political Geography* 25, no. 3 (March 2006): 315–35.
27. James D. Fearon and David D. Laitin, "Ethnicity, Insurgency, and Civil War," *American Political Science Review* 97, no. 1 (February 2003): 75–90.
28. James Raymond Vreeland, "The Effect of Political Regime on Civil War: Unpacking Anocracy," *Journal of Conflict Resolution* 52, no. 3 (2008): 401–25; Bethany Lacina, "Explaining the Severity of Civil Wars," *Journal of Conflict Resolution* 50, no. 2 (2006): 276–89.
29. John E. Mueller, "Presidential Popularity from Truman to Johnson," *The American Political Science Review* 64, no. 1 (1970): 18–34.
30. Anthony W. Marx, *Faith in Nation: Exclusionary Origins of Nationalism* (Oxford; New York: Oxford University Press, 2003).
31. Alberto Alesina et al., "Fractionalization," *Journal of Economic Growth* 8, no. 2 (2003): 155–94; Alberto Alesina and Eliana La Ferrara, "Participation in

Heterogeneous Communities," *The Quarterly Journal of Economics* 115, no. 3 (August 1, 2000): 847–904; James D. Fearon, "Ethnic and Cultural Diversity by Country," *Journal of Economic Growth* 8, no. 2 (June 2003): 195–222; Jose G. Montalvo and Marta Reynal-Querol, "Ethnic Diversity and Economic Development," *Journal of Development Economics* 76, no. 2 (April 2005): 293–323.

32. Monica Duffy Toft, *The Geography of Ethnic Violence: Identity, Interests, and the Indivisibility of Territory* (Princeton, NJ: Princeton University Press, 2005).

33. Frances Stewart, ed., *Horizontal Inequalities and Conflict: Understanding Group Violence in Multiethnic Societies* (Basingstoke, UK; New York: Palgrave Macmillan, 2008); Gudrun Østby, "Polarization, Horizontal Inequalities and Violent Civil Conflict," *Journal of Peace Research* 45, no. 2 (2008): 143–62; Lars-Erik Cederman, Nils B. Weidmann, and Kristian Skrede Gleditsch, "Horizontal Inequalities and Ethnonationalist Civil War: A Global Comparison," *American Political Science Review* 105, no. 3 (August 2011): 478–495.

34. Andreas Wimmer, Lars-Erik Cederman, and Brian Min, "Ethnic Politics and Armed Conflict: A Configurational Analysis of a New Global Data Set," *American Sociological Review* 74, no. 2 (2009): 316–37; Manuel Vogt et al., "Integrating Data on Ethnicity, Geography, and Conflict The Ethnic Power Relations Data Set Family," *Journal of Conflict Resolution* 59, no. 7 (October 1, 2015): 1327–42.

35. Myron Weiner, "Bad Neighbors, Bad Neighborhoods," *International Security* 21, no. 1 (July 1, 1996): 26.

36. Kristian Skrede Gleditsch, *All International Politics Is Local: The Diffusion of Conflict, Integration, and Democratization* (Ann Arbor: University of Michigan Press, 2002); Idean Salehyan and Kristian Skrede Gleditsch, "Refugees and the Spread of Civil War," *International Organization* 60, no. 2 (April 2006): 335–366; Kristian Skrede Gleditsch, "Transnational Dimensions of Civil War," *Journal of Peace Research* 44, no. 3 (2007): 293–309; Nicholas Sambanis, "Do Ethnic and Nonethnic Civil Wars Have the Same Causes?" *Journal of Conflict Resolution* 45, no. 3 (June 2001): 259–82.

37. Suda Perera, "Alternative Agency: Rwandan Refugee Warriors in Exclusionary States," *Conflict, Security & Development* 13, no. 5 (December 1, 2013): 569–88; Séverine Autesserre, *The Trouble with the Congo: Local Violence and the Failure of International Peacebuilding* (Cambridge, UK; New York: Cambridge University Press, 2010).

38. Idean Salehyan, "Transnational Rebels: Neighboring States as Sanctuary for Rebel Groups," *World Politics* 59, no. 2 (2007): 223.

39. Daniel Unger, "Ain't Enough Blanket: International Humanitarian Assistance and Cambodian Political Resistance," in *Refugee Manipulation: War, Politics, and the Abuse of Human Suffering*, ed. Stephen Stedman and Fred Tanner (Washington, DC: Brookings Institution Press, 2003): 17–56; Melissa Lee, "The International Politics of Incomplete Sovereignty: How Hostile Neighbors Weaken the State," *International Organization* 72, no. 2 (2018): 283–315.

40. Jacob D. Kathman, "Civil War Contagion and Neighboring Interventions," *International Studies Quarterly* 54, no. 4 (2010): 989.

41. Lee, "The International Politics of Incomplete Sovereignty," 7.

42. Here I treat power capabilities quite broadly to include military, economic, geographic, and demographic elements.
43. The caveat is that the different scenarios discussed here are by no means overly determining. In fact, such interactive dynamics can create different types of responses from neighboring states, which might be correlated with other factors, some domestic and others international.
44. Gerhard L. Weinberg, *Hitler's Foreign Policy 1933–1939: The Road to World War II* (New York: Enigma Books, 2005); Zara Steiner, *The Triumph of the Dark: European International History 1933–1939*, rep. ed. (Oxford; New York: Oxford University Press, 2013).
45. M. Coleman, "U.S. Statecraft and the U.S.–Mexico Border as Security/Economy Nexus," *Political Geography* 24, no. 2 (February 2005): 185–209; Peter Andreas, *Border Games: Policing the U.S.-Mexico Divide*, 2nd ed. (Ithaca, NY: Cornell University Press, 2009); Pablo Vila, *Crossing Borders, Reinforcing Borders: Social Categories, Metaphors and Narrative Identities on the U.S.-Mexico Frontier* (Austin: University of Texas Press, 2000).
46. Salehyan, "Transnational Rebels," 225; Dilip Hiro, *The Longest War: The Iran-Iraq Military Conflict* (London: Routledge, 1990).
47. Ruben Zaiotti, *Cultures of Border Control: Schengen and the Evolution of European Frontiers* (Chicago: University of Chicago Press, 2011).
48. Brubaker, *Nationalism Reframed*.
49. Brubaker, 6.
50. Han, *Contestation and Adaptation*.

Chapter 3

1. Kengtung is the old English spelling of the city's name, while the current spelling, Kyiangtong, is a closer approximation to its Burmese and Tai Khun pronunciation, with Kyiang being equivalent to Chiang, the transliteration used in Thai. There is tremendous complexity in the use of different spellings for place names in this borderland region, so for this chapter, I use Kengtung in contemporary contexts and Chiang Tung in the historical narrative. I do the same for Jinghong, the modern spelling of that city's name, using Chiang Rung when referring to the city in previous historical periods.
2. Sawbwa is the English spelling of the title used by traditional chiefs of the Burmese Shan states, based on Burmese pronunciation. In Tai or Thai, it's pronounced chao fa, which literally means lord of heaven. In this chapter, I use sawbwa in the context of Burmese states and chao fa for other Tai principalities.
3. The name is also spelled Sipsongpanna.
4. Ritpen Supin, *The Princesses of Mangrai-Kengtung (Chao Nang)* (Chiang Mai, Thailand: Tai Ethnic Art and Culture Center, Thakradat Temple, 2013), 38.
5. Taylor, *The State in Myanmar*, 272; Chao Tzang Yawnghwe, *The Shan of Burma: Memoirs of a Shan Exile* (Singapore: ISEAS Publishing, 2010), 120.

6. "Tai" refers a large family of ethnic groups who speak languages belonging to the Tai-Kadai language family and are spread throughout upland Southeast Asia. In Chiang Tung, the local Tai people are often referred as Tai Khun, while in Chiang Rung, they are Tai Lue and in Chiang Mai, Tai Yuan. The Burmese name for the Tai, however, is Shan. See Walker, *Tai Lands and Thailand*.
7. Susan Conway, "Shan Tribute Relations in the Nineteenth Century," *Contemporary Buddhism* 10, no. 1 (May 1, 2009): 31.
8. O. W. Wolters, *Culture, History and Region in South East Asian Perspectives* (Singapore: Institute of Southeast Asian Studies, 1982), 16.
9. Thongchai Winichakul, *Siam Mapped: A History of the Geo-Body of a Nation* (Honolulu, HI: University of Hawai'i Press, 1994), 82.
10. Foon Ming Liew-Herres, Volker Grabowsky, and Renoo Wichasin, *Chronicle of Sipsong Panna: History and Society of a Tai Lu Kingdom* (Chiang Mai, Thailand: Silkworm Books, 2012), 49.
11. Herman, "Collaboration and Resistance on the Southwest Frontier;" Herman, *Amid the Clouds and Mist*.
12. Bello, "To Go Where No Han Could Go for Long."
13. C. Patterson Giersch, "The Sipsong Panna Tai and the Limits of Qing Conquest in Yunnan," *Chinese Historians* 10, no. 1–2 (October 1, 2000): 71–92.
14. Liew-Herres, Grabowsky, and Wichasin, *Chronicle of Sipsong Panna*, 39.
15. Liew-Herres, Grabowsky, and Wichasin, 43.
16. Shi-Chung Hsieh, "Ethnic-Political Adaptation and Ethnic Change of the Sipsong Panna Dai: An Ethnohistorical Analysis" (PhD diss., University of Washington, 1989), 90.
17. D. G. E. Hall, *History of South East Asia* (London: Macmillan, 1981), 289.
18. Liew-Herres, Grabowsky, and Wichasin, *Chronicle of Sipsong Panna*, 46.
19. Giersch, "The Sipsong Panna Tai and the Limits of Qing Conquest in Yunnan."
20. Giersch, *Asian Borderlands*, 101.
21. Giersch, 110.
22. John Sterling Forssen Smith, *The Chiang Tung Wars: War and Politics in Mid-19th Century Siam and Burma* (Bangkok: Institute of Asian Studies, Chulalongkorn University, 2013), 65–67.
23. Smith, 13.
24. Liew-Herres, Grabowsky, and Wichasin, *Chronicle of Sipsong Panna*, 41.
25. Rattanaporn Setakun, "History of Chiang Tung," in *Things about Chiang Tung*, ed. Arunrat Vichiankiew and Narumon Ruangrangsi (Chiang Mai: Suriwongs Book Center, 1994), 35.
26. Susan Conway, *The Shan: Culture, Arts and Crafts* (Bangkok: River Books, 2006), 36.
27. Conway, 36–37.
28. Smith, *The Chiang Tung Wars*, 28.
29. Saimong Mangrai, *The Padaeng Chronicle and the Jengtung State Chronicle Translated* (Ann Arbor: University of Michigan, Center for South and Southeast Asian Studies, 1981), 250–52.
30. Mangrai, *The Padaeng Chronicle and the Jengtung State Chronicle Translated*, 254.

31. David K. Wyatt, *Thailand: A Short History*, 2nd rev. ed. (New Haven, CT: Yale University Press, 2003), 117.
32. Smith, *The Chiang Tung Wars*, 29.
33. Saenluang Ratchasomphan, *The Nan Chronicle*, trans. David K. Wyatt (Ithaca, NY: Southeast Asia Program, Cornell University, 1994), 85.
34. David K. Wyatt and Aroonrut Wichienkeeo, trans., *The Chiang Mai Chronicle* (Chiang Mai, Thailand: Silkworm Books, 1995), 170.
35. Smith, *The Chiang Tung War*, 51.
36. Smith, 61.
37. Smith, 68.
38. Michael Aung-Thwin and Maitrii Aung-Thwin, *A History of Myanmar Since Ancient Times: Traditions and Transformations* (London: Reaktion Books, 2013).
39. Smith, *The Chiang Tung Wars*.
40. Smith, 158.
41. Sethakul Ratanaporn, "Political, Social and Economic Changes in the Northern States of Thailand from the Chiang Mai Treaties of 1874 and 1883" (PhD diss., Northern Illinois University, 1989), 121.
42. Ratanaporn, 123.
43. Suthep Soonthornpasuch, "Socio-Cultural and Political Change in Northern Siam: The Impact of Western Colonial Expansion (1850–1932)," in *Changes in Northern Thailand and the Shan States 1886–1940*, ed. Prakai Nontawasee (Singapore: Institute of Southeast Asian Studies, 1988), 162–65.
44. Indeed, there are scholars who interpret Bangkok's centralizing control of Lan Na as resulting from cooperation between the two for the benefit of the British forest industry. See Chaiyan Rajchagool, *The Rise and Fall of the Thai Absolute Monarchy* (Bangkok, Thailand: White Lotus Press, 1994).
45. Ratanaporn, "Political, Social and Economic Changes in the Northern States of Thailand," 171.
46. Ratanaporn, 200.
47. Ratanaporn, 195.
48. Ratanaporn, 236.
49. Ratanaporn, 244.
50. Ratanaporn, 255.
51. Winichakul, *Siam Mapped*, 108.
52. Winichakul, 109.
53. Julia Lovell, *The Opium War: Drugs, Dreams and the Making of China* (London: Picador, 2012).
54. Stephen R. Platt, *Autumn in the Heavenly Kingdom: China, the West and the Epic Story of the Taiping Civil War* (New York: Vintage Books, 2012).
55. David Atwill, *The Chinese Sultanate: Islam, Ethnicity and the Panthay Rebellion in Southwest China, 1856–1873* (Stanford, CA: Stanford University Press, 2005).
56. Shuhuai Wang, *Muslim Rebellion in Yunnan during the Reigns of Xianfeng and Tongzhi (Xiantong Huimin Shibian)* (Taipei: Academic Sinica, 1980); Jiamo Huang, *Western Yunnan's Muslim Government's Diplomatic Relations with Great*

Britain (1869–1874) (Dianxi Huimin Zhengquan de Lianying Waijiao 1869–1874) (Taipei: Academic Sinica, 2015).

57. Lewis Milton Chere, *Diplomacy of the Sino-French War 1883–85: Global Complications of an Undeclared War* (Notre Dame, IN: Cross Cultural Publications, 1989).
58. Ning Zhang, "The Establishment of Zhengbian Subprefecture in Late Qing and Southwestern Borderland (Qingmo Zhengbianting de Shezhi Yu Xinan Bianjiang)" (master's thesis, Fudan University, 2013), 36.
59. Yong Yao, "The Nationalization of Border and Borderland Citizens—The Tribunal System of Yunnan-Burma Border Cases between China and Great Britain (Bianjing Yu Bianmin de Guojiahua—Jindai Zhongying Huisheng Dianmian Bianan Zhidu)," *Historical Anthropology Journal (Lishi Renleixue Xuekan)* 13, no. 1 (2015): 91.
60. http://www.chinaforeignrelations.net/node/148
61. Yao, "The Nationalization of Border and Borderland Citizens," 91.
62. Yao, 114.
63. Zhang, "The Establishment of Zhengbian Subprefecture."
64. Wei-Chen Yang, "Commercial Port, Railway and Cultural Interaction—A Case of Modern Yunnan (Shangbu, Tielu, Wenhua Jiaoliu—Yi Jindai Yunnan Wei Zhongxin de Taolun)," *Fujen History Journal (Furen Lishi Xuebao)*, no. 24 (December 2009).
65. Tun, *History of the Shan State*, 151.
66. Robert H. Taylor, "British Policy and the Shan States, 1886–1942," in *Changes in Northern Thailand and the Shan States 1886–1940*, ed. Prakai Nontawasee (Singapore: Institute of Southeast Asian Studies, 1988): 13–62.
67. Taylor, 18.
68. Taylor, 20.
69. Tun, *History of the Shan State*, 167.
70. Tun, 166–67.
71. Taylor, "British Policy and the Shan States," 20.
72. Taylor, 26.
73. Taylor, 27.
74. Tun, *History of the Shan State*, 177.
75. Ronald D. Renard, "Social Change in the Shan States under the British, 1886–1942," in *Changes in Northern Thailand and the Shan States 1886–1940*, ed. Prakai Nontawasee (Singapore: Institute of Southeast Asian Studies, 1988), 120.
76. Renard, 115.
77. Renard, 115.
78. Taylor, "British Policy and the Shan States," 45.
79. Scott, *The Art of Not Being Governed*, 100.
80. Edmund R. Leach, *Political Systems of Highland Burma: A Study Of Kachin Social Structure* (London: Bell, 1964).
81. Scott, *The Art of Not Being Governed*, 144.
82. Jianxiong Ma, "Salt and Revenue in Frontier Formation: State Mobilized Ethnic Politics in the Yunnan-Burma Borderland since the 1720s," *Modern Asian Studies* 48, no. 6 (November 2014): 1637–69; Jianxiong Ma, "'Luo Bandits' to 'Lahu Nationality': Ethnic Identity in the Process of Border Formation (Cong 'luofei'

Dao 'Lahuzu': Bianjianghua Guocheng Zhongde Zuqun Rentong)," *Historical Anthropology Journal (Lishi Renleixue Xuekan)* 2, no. 1 (2004): 1–32.
83. Sadan, *Being and Becoming Kachin*, 144.
84. Sadan, 168.
85. Sadan, 203.
86. Yachao Liu, "Gaitu Guiliu in the Yunnan Borderland during the Republican Period (Minguo Zai Dianxi Bianqu de Gaitu Guiliu)," *Journal of Yunnan Institute of the Nationalities (Yunnan Minzu Xueyuan Xuebao)* 16, no. 1 (1999): 64.
87. Qiang Zhu, "A Study of Tusi in Dehong and Frontier Governance in Republic of China (Minguo Shiqi de Dehong Tusi Yu Bianjiang Zhili Yanjiu)" (master's thesis, Yunnan University, 2015), 30.
88. Zhu, 28.
89. Zhu, 36.
90. Tingzhong Ma, "Tentative Analysis of Yunnan's Ethnic Education Policies during the Republican Period (Qianxi Yunnan Minguo Shiqi Minzu Jiaoyu Zhengce)," *Heilongjiang Ethnic Studies Journal (Heilongjiang Minzu Congkan)* 105 (2008): 178–82.
91. Zhu, "A Study of Tusi in Dehong and Frontier Governance in Republic of China," 69.
92. Kwok Yong Lim, "The Battle of Yunnan-Burma Road (Dec 1941–June 1942) (Chuguo Yuanzheng-Dianmianlu Huizhan de Jinxing Yu Yingxiang 1941 Nian 12 Yue–1942 Nian 6 Yue)," *Chung Cheng History Journal (Chung Cheng Lishi Xuekan)*, no. 19 (December 2016): 203.
93. Chun-shan Li, "Wartime Transport Administration in Southwest China and the Burma Road (1938–1942) (Kangzhan Shiqi Xinan Yunshu de Fazhan Yu Kunjing—Yi Dianmian Gonglu Weizhongxin de Tantao 1938–1942)," *Academia Historica Journal (Guoshiguan Guankan)*, no. 33 (September 2012): 65.
94. Frank McLynn, *The Burma Campaign: Disaster into Triumph 1942–45* (London: Vintage, 2011); Donovan Webster, *The Burma Road* (London: Macmillan, 2004).
95. Liu, "Gaitu Guiliu in the Yunnan Borderland during the Republican Period," 65.
96. Soonthornpasuch, "Socio-Cultural and Politcal Change in Northern Siam," 167.
97. M. R. Rujaya Abhakorn, "Changes in the Administrative Systems of Northern Siam, 1884–1933," in *Changes in Northern Thailand and the Shan States 1886–1940*, ed. Prakai Nontawasee (Singapore: Institute of Southeast Asian Studies, 1988), 85.
98. Abhakorn, 86.
99. During 1902–1904 a major Shan rebellion destabilised the northern provinces, but Bangkok maintained its momentum of administrative centralization. For details on the Shan rebellion, see Andrew Walker, "Seditious State-Making in the Mekong Borderlands: The Shan Rebellion of 1902–1904," *Sojourn* 29, no. 3 (November 1, 2014): 554–90.
100. Abhakorn, "Changes in the Administrative Systems of Northern Siam, 1884–1933," 89.
101. Abhakorn, 91.
102. Charles F. Keyes, "Buddhism and National Integration in Thailand," *Journal of Asian Studies* 30, no. 3 (1971): 551–67.

103. Thanet Charoenmuang, "When the Young Cannot Speak Their Own Mother Tongue: Explaining a Legacy of Cultural Domination in Lan Na," in *Regions and National Integration in Thailand 1892-1992*, ed. Volker Grabowsky (Wiesbaden: Harrassowitz Verlag, 1995), 86.
104. Abhakorn, "Changes in the Administrative Systems of Northern Siam, 1884-1933," 98.
105. Wyatt, *Thailand*, 120.
106. Wyatt, 131; Shane Strate, *The Lost Territories: Thailand's History of National Humiliation* (Honolulu, HI: University of Hawai'I Press, 2015).
107. Eiji Murashima, "The Commemorative Character of Thai Historiography: The 1942-43 Thai Military Campaign in the Shan States Depicted as a Story of National Salvation and the Restoration of Thai Independence," *Modern Asian Studies* 40, no. 4 (2006): 1081.
108. Murashima, 1085.
109. Thak Chaloemtiarana, *Thailand: The Politics of Despotic Paternalism*, 1st ed. (Ithaca, NY: Cornell Southeast Asia Program Publications, 2007), 26.
110. J. Silverstein, *Burmese Politics: The Dilemma of National Unity* (New Brunswick, NJ: Rutgers University Press, 1980), 35.
111. Won Zoon Yoon, "Japan's Occupation of Burma, 1941-1945" (PhD diss., New York University, 1971), chap. 3.
112. Silverstein, *Burmese Politics*, 52.
113. Taylor, *The State in Myanmar*, 228.
114. Silverstein, *Burmese Politics*, 84.
115. Silverstein, 102.
116. "Burma Frontier Conference: New Agreement Put to the Tribes," *Times*, February 9, 1947.
117. "Frontier Areas in Burma: Panglong Agreement," *Times*, February 12, 1947.

Chapter 4

1. Chang, *Beyond Borders*.
2. Chronology [of KMT Aggression in Burma], Myanmar National Archives Department, Series 12-9, Access no. 25.
3. As we discussed in chapter 3, historically there were many Shan states, which became a singular Shan State after Burma's independence.
4. Taylor, *Foreign and Domestic Consequences of the KMT Intervention in Burma*.
5. Yihui Qin, *History of Blood and Tears of the Nationalist Army in the Golden Triangle (Jinsanjiao guojun xueleishi)* (Taipei: Academic Sinica and Lianjing Press, 2009), 59.
6. KMT Agression, Translation of the Hon'ble Prime Minister's Speech in the Chamber of Deputies, on Monday, 2nd March 1953, Myanmar National Archives Department, Series 12-3, Access no. 172.
7. John Bresnan, *From Dominoes to Dynamos: The Transformation of Southeast Asia* (New York: Council on Foreign Relations, 1994); Cheng Guan Ang, "The

Domino Theory Revisited: The Southeast Asia Perspective," *War & Society* 19, no. 1 (May 1, 2001): 109–30; James Stuart Olson and Randy W. Roberts, *Where the Domino Fell: America and Vietnam 1945-2010*, 6th ed. (Chichester, UK: Wiley-Blackwell, 2013).
8. Qin, *History of Blood and Tears of the Nationalist Army in the Golden Triangle*, 72.
9. Daniel Fineman, *A Special Relationship: The United States and Military Government in Thailand, 1947-1958*, 1st ed. (Honolulu, HI: University of Hawai'I Press, 1997), 69–88; Chaloemtiarana, *Thailand*.
10. Palapan Kampan, "Standing Up to Giants: Thailand's Exit from 20th Century War Partnerships," *Asian Social Science* 10, no. 15 (August 2014): 155.
11. Gibson and Chen, *The Secret Army*; Taylor, *Foreign and Domestic Consequences of the KMT Intervention in Burma*.
12. Gibson and Chen, *The Secret Army*, 40.
13. Qin, *History of Blood and Tears of the Nationalist Army in the Golden Triangle*, 89.
14. Kenton Clymer, *A Delicate Relationship: The United States and Burma/Myanmar since 1945*, 1st ed. (Ithaca: Cornell University Press, 2015), 119.
15. Clymer, 126.
16. Qin, *History of Blood and Tears of the Nationalist Army in the Golden Triangle*, 153.
17. Clymer, *A Delicate Relationship*, 136.
18. Gibson and Chen, *The Secret Army*, 189.
19. Qin, *History of Blood and Tears of the Nationalist Army in the Golden Triangle*, 257.
20. Strauss, "Paternalist Terror," 83.
21. Kuisong Yang, "Reconsidering the Campaign to Suppress Counterrevolutionaries," *The China Quarterly*, no. 193 (2008): 120; Strauss, "Paternalist Terror," 87.
22. Yang, "Reconsidering the Campaign to Suppress Counterrevolutionaries," 105.
23. Luo Ruiqing, "Resolutely Suppress Counterrevolutionaries." Report presented at Central Government Ministries Cadres Conference (*jianjue zhengya fangeming: luo ruiqing zai zhongyang renmin zhengfu suoshu bumenjiguan dahuishang de baogao*), April 4, 1951.
24. He Long and Deng Xiaoping, "He, Deng, Zhang, Li's Comprehensive Report to Chairman Mao and the Military Commission Regarding the Situation of Elimination of Bandits in 1950 (*he deng zhang li guanyu wulingnian jiaofei qingkuang xiang maozhuxi ji junwei de zhonghe baogao*)," History of Contemporary Chinese Political Movements, database compiled by Chinese University of Hong Kong, January 6, 1951.
25. Southwest Bureau of Public Security (*xinan gong'anbu*), "Southwest Bureau of Public Security's Report about the Current Situation and Future Opinions of the Southwest Suppression of Counterrevolutionaries for the Past Eight Months since the Fourth National Public Security Conference (*xinan gong'anbu guanyu disici quanguo gong'an huiyihou bageyuelai xinan zhengfan jiben qingkuang ji jinhou yijian de baogao*)," July 21, 1952.
26. Southwest Bureau of Public Security.

27. Xinhua News Agency Internal Reference (*xinhuashe neibu cankao*), "Yunnan Province Experienced Many Sabotage Cases by Counterrevolutionaries in the Rural Areas (*yunnansheng nongcun fasheng fangeming fenzi pohuai anjian duoqi*)," May 17, 1954.
28. Xinhua News Agency Internal Reference.
29. Southwest Bureau of Public Security, "Southwest Bureau of Public Security's Report."
30. Yang, "Reconsidering the Campaign to Suppress Counterrevolutionaries," 108.
31. Yang, 121.
32. Editorial Committee for Xishuangbanna Dai Autonomous Prefecture Gazette (*xishuangbanna daizuzizhizhou difangzhi bianjiweiyuanhui*), *Xishuangbanna Dai Autonomous Prefecture Gazette (xishuangbanna daizuzizhizhou zhi)*, vol. 1 (Beijing: Xinhua Press, 2002), 437.
33. CCP Central Committee (*zhonggong zhongyang*), "Directive to Southwest Bureau and Yunnan Provincial Committee on Religious Works in the Borderland Area (*zhongyang guanyu bianjiang zongjiao gongzuo gei xinanju he yunnanshengwei de zhishi*)," November 1952.
34. Yunnan Provincial Government (*unnan shengwei*), "Report to the CCP Central Committee on Current Borderland Situation and Problems of Borderland Reforms (*unnan shengwei guanyu muqian bianjiang qingkuang he bianjiang gaige wenti xiang zhongyang de baogao*)," November 16, 1954.
35. Han, *Contestation and Adaptation*, 111.
36. Liu Shaoqi, "CCP Central Committee Decree on Issues of Land Reform in Yunnan (*zhongyang guanyu Yunnan tugai wenti de zhishi*)," June 16, 1952.
37. Shaoqi.
38. Xiaolin Guo, *State and Ethnicity in China's Southwest* (Leiden; Boston: Brill, 2008), 43.
39. Elizabeth J. Perry, "Rural Violence in Socialist China," *The China Quarterly*, no. 103 (1985): 414–40.
40. CCP Central Committee (*zhonggong zhongyang*), "Directive to Southwest Bureau on Yunnan Province's Report on Guidance and Steps for Borderland Ethnic Works (*zhongyang dui xinanju guanyu 'yunnanshengwei bao bianjiang minzu gongzuo fangzheng yu buzhou de yijian yijian de pishi'*)," December 6, 1952.
41. CCP Central Committee, "Directive to Southwest Bureau on Yunnan Province's Report on Guidance and Steps for Borderland Ethnic Works."
42. Editorial Committee for Dehong Prefecture Gazette (*dehongzhou shizhi bianwei bangongshi*), *Select Materials of the CCP Party History in Dehong Prefecture (zhonggong dehongzhou dangshi ziliao xuanbian)*, vol. 4 (Mangshi: Dehong Ethnic Press (*dehong minzu chubanshe*) 1989), 269.
43. Later the name "region" was changed to "prefecture" in both Xishuangbanna and Dehong.
44. Susan McCarthy, *Communist Multiculturalism: Ethnic Revival in Southwest China* (Seattle: University of Washington Press, 2009), 53.
45. Editorial Committee for Dehong Prefecture Gazette, *Select Materials of the CCP Party History in Dehong Prefecture*, vol. 1, 1989, 33.
46. Editorial Committee for Dehong Prefecture Gazette, *Select Materials of the CCP Party History in Dehong Prefecture*, vol. 2, 1989, 20.

47. Editorial Committee for Xishuangbanna Dai Autonomous Prefecture Gazette, *Xishuangbanna Dai Autonomous Prefecture Gazette*, vol. 1, 433.
48. Editorial Committee for Dehong Prefecture Gazette, *Select Materials of the CCP Party History in Dehong Prefecture*, vol. 1, 1989, 44.
49. Editorial Committee for Dehong Prefecture Gazette, 43–50.
50. Editorial Committee for Dehong Prefecture Gazette, vol. 2, 40.
51. Yan Hongyan, "Speech by Yunnan Province CCP First Secretary Yan Hongyan at Yunnan Province Borderland Works Conference (*zai yunnansheng bianjiang gongzuo huiyishang de jianghua: unnan shengwei diyishuji yan hongyan*)," 21 December 1965.
52. Yan Hongyan.
53. Editorial Committee for Dehong Prefecture Gazette, *Select Materials of the CCP Party History in Dehong Prefecture*, vol. 2, 293.
54. Lintner, *Burma in Revolt*, 12.
55. Lintner, 20–22.
56. US Rangoon Embassy to Department of State, no. 220, 26 April 1950, "Status of Various Burmese Insurrections," 790B.00/4-2650, RG 59, CDF 1950-1954, Box 4135, US NAII.
57. US London Embassy to Department of State, no. 2489, 22 May 1950, "End of Burma War Near," 790B.00/5-2250, RG 59, CDF 1950-1954, Box 4135, US NAII.
58. "Drive towards Peace," *Burma*, November 1950, 74.
59. "Drive towards Peace," 78.
60. US Rangoon Embassy to Department of State, no. 298, 18 February 1954, "Political Pressures in Burma, 1948–1954," 790B.00/2-1854, RG 59, CDF 1950-1954, Box 4138, US NAII.
61. Lintner, *Burma in Revolt*, 133.
62. US Rangoon Embassy to Department of State, telegram 694, 15 January 1954, 790B.00/1-1554, RG 59, CDF 1950-1954, Box 4138, US NAII.
63. Lintner, *Burma in Revolt*, 134–36; Gibson and Chen, *The Secret Army*, 121–29.
64. Lintner, *Burma in Revolt*, 119.
65. Maung Maung, *Grim War Aganist KMT*, 2nd ed. (Yangon, Myanmar: Seikku Cho Cho Publishing House, 2013), 29.
66. Callahan, *Making Enemies*, 158.
67. US Rangoon Embassy to Department of State, no. 668, 23 June 1959, "Political Conditions and Prospects in the Shan State," 790B.00/6-2359, RG 59, CDF 1955-1959, Box 3852, US NAII.
68. Lintner, *Burma in Revolt*, 183.
69. US Rangoon Embassy to Department of State, no. 552, 29 April 1959, "Ceremonial Renunciation of Powers by Shan Sawbwas," 790B.00/4-2959, RG 59, CDF 1955-1959, Box 3852, US NAII.
70. US Consulate Chiengmai to Department of State, no. 10, 4 December 1959, "Another 'Shan State Independence Army' News Report," 790B.00/12-1559, RG 59, CDF 1955-1959, Box 3852, US NAII.

71. Amporn Vijirakorn, *History of 55 Years of Helping the Shan Nation* (Chiang Mai, Thailand: Chiang Mai University Regional Center for Social Science and Sustainable Development, 2015).
72. Lintner, *Burma in Revolt*, 190.
73. Lintner, 143.
74. Callahan, *Making Enemies*.
75. Lintner, *Burma in Revolt*, 153.
76. Desmond Ball, *Tor Chor Dor: Thailand's Border Patrol Police: History, Organisation, Equipment and Personnel*, vol. 1 (Bangkok, Thailand: White Lotus Press, 2013), 59.
77. Chaloemtiarana, *Thailand*.
78. "Brutal Anti-Chinese Oppression by the Luang Phibun's Government in Thailand (*taiguo luanpiwen zhengfu de paihua zuixing*)," *People's Daily (renmin ribao)*, January 27, 1950.
79. "Luang Phibun is Increasingly Leaning toward the American Imperialists, and His Government is Full of American Consultants (*luanpiwen riyi toukao meidi, zhengfunei chongchi meiguo guwen*)," *People's Daily (renmin ribao)*, January 12, 1950.
80. Qin, *History of Blood and Tears of the Nationalist Army in the Golden Triangle*, 73.
81. "American Imperialists are Colluding with the Counterrevolutionary Government of Luang Phibun to Carry out Plans to Support the KMT Bandits in Burma (*meidiguozhuyi goujie luanpiwen fandong zhengfu, jinxing zhengbian taomian canfei yinmou jihua*)," *People's Daily (renmin ribao)*, June 22, 1951.
82. Fineman, *A Special Relationship*, 69–88; Chaloemtiarana, *Thailand*.
83. Correspondence from Bangkok to Foreign Office, FO 371/84363, BNA.
84. Fineman, *A Special Relationship*, 114–15.
85. Kampan, "Standing Up to Giants," 155.
86. Fineman, *A Special Relationship*, 118.
87. British Embassy Bangkok correspondence, 26 May 1952, FO 371/101192.
88. Kasian Tejapira, *Commodifying Marxism: The Formation of Modern Thai Radical Culture, 1927–1958* (Kyoto, Japan : Melbourne, Australia: Portland, OR: Trans Pacific Press, 2001), 129.
89. Chatri Ritharom, "The Making of the Thai—US Military Alliance and the SEATO Treaty of 1954: A Study in Thai Decision-Making" (PhD diss., Claremont Graduate School, 1976).
90. Ball, *Tor Chor Dor*, 64.
91. Hyun, "Indigenizing the Cold War," 79.
92. Ball, *Tor Chor Dor*, 73–74.
93. Hyun, "Indigenizing the Cold War," 79.
94. Hyun, 87.
95. McCoy, *The Politics of Heroin*, 138.
96. McCoy, 139.
97. McCoy, 143.
98. Correspondence from D. C. Rivett-Carnac to D. J. Gibson, British Consulate, Chiang Mai, 30 August 1968. FCO 15/338, BNA.

99. Gibson and Chen, *The Secret Army*, 243.
100. "Freedom Forces in Thailand," *China News*, January 9, 1968.
101. Correspondence from R. S. Scrivener, British Embassy, Bangkok, 19 June 1968. FCO 15/338, BNA.
102. Correspondence from R. S. Scrivener.

Chapter 5

1. Dorothy J. Solinger, "Politics in Yunnan Province in the Decade of Disorder: Elite Factional Strategies and Central-Local Relations, 1967–1980," *The China Quarterly*, no. 92 (1982): 628–62.
2. Roderick Macfarquhar and Michael Schoenhals, *Mao's Last Revolution* (Cambridge, MA: Harvard University Press, 2006); Patricia M. Thornton, Peidong Sun, and Chris Berry, eds., *Red Shadows*, vol. 12, *Memories and Legacies of the Chinese Cultural Revolution* (Cambridge, UK: Cambridge University Press, 2017); Frank Dikötter, *The Cultural Revolution: A People's History, 1962–1976* (Bloomsbury Paperbacks, 2017).
3. Arthur M. Bernstein, *Up to the Mountains and Down to the Villages: Transfer of Youth from Urban to Rural China* (New Haven, CT: Yale University Press, 1977).
4. Dorothy J. Solinger, *Regional Government and Political Integration in Southwest China 1949–1954: A Case Study* (Berkeley: University of California Press, 1977).
5. Solinger, "Politics in Yunnan Province in the Decade of Disorder," 633.
6. CCP Yunnan Province Party History Research Office (*zhonggong Yunnan shengwei dangshi yanjiushi*), "Yunnan 'Cultural Revolution' Movement Events Chronicle (*Yunnan 'wenhua dageming' yundong dashi jishi*)," May 18, 2005.
7. Michael Schoenhals, "Cultural Revolution on the Border: Yunnan's 'Political Frontier Defence,'" *The Copenhagen Journal of Asian Studies*, no. 19 (2004): 30.
8. Schoenhals.
9. Schoenhals, 32–36.
10. Schoenhals, 37.
11. Schoenhals, 38.
12. Schoenhals, 39.
13. Editorial Committee for Dehong Prefecture Gazette (*dehongzhou shizhi bianwei bangongshi*), *Select Materials of the CCP Party History in Dehong Prefecture* (*zhonggong dehongzhou dangshi ziliao xuanbian*), Mangshi: Dehong Ethnic Press (*dehong minzu chubanshe*), vol 5, 1989, 19.
14. CCP Yunnan Province Party History Research Office, "Yunnan 'Cultural Revolution' Movement Events Chronicle."
15. Raphael Israeli, *Islam in China: Religion, Ethnicity, Culture, and Politics* (Lanham, MD: Lexington Books, 2002).
16. Schoenhals, "Cultural Revolution on the Border," 40.
17. CCP Yunnan Province Party History Research, "Yunnan 'Cultural Revolution' Movement Events Chronicle."
18. Schoenhals, "Cultural Revolution on the Border," 31.

19. Editorial Committee for Dehong Prefecture Gazette, *Select Materials of the CCP Party History in Dehong Prefecture*, vol. 5, 1989, 19.
20. CCP Yunnan Province Party History Research Office, "Yunnan 'Cultural Revolution' Movement Events Chronicle."
21. CCP Yunnan Province Party History Research Office.
22. Yang, "'We Want to Go Home!'"
23. Editorial Committee for Xishuangbanna Dai Autonomous Prefecture Gazette (*xishuangbanna daizuzizhizhou difangzhi bianjiweiyuanhui*), Xishuangbanna Dai Autonomous Prefecture Gazette (*xishuangbanna daizuzizhizhou zhi*), vol. 2 (Beijing: Xinhua Press, 2002), 350.
24. E. C. Chapman, "The Expansion of Rubber in Southern Yunnan, China," *The Geographical Journal* 157, no. 1 (1991): 36–44.
25. Janet C. Sturgeon and Nicholas Menzies, "Ideological Landscapes: Rubber in Xishuangbanna, Yunnan, 1950 to 2007," *Asian Geographer* 25, no. 1–2 (January 1, 2006): 26.
26. Han, *Contestation and Adaptation*, 110.
27. Dru C. Gladney, "Representing Nationality in China: Refiguring Majority/Minority Identities," *Journal of Asian Studies* 53, no. 1 (1994): 105.
28. Hansen, *Lessons in Being Chinese*, 107.
29. Hansen, 107.
30. Hansen, 108.
31. McCarthy, *Communist Multiculturalism*.
32. Dobama Asiayone was the most important political organization demanding independence from British colonial rule before World War II.
33. Lintner, *The Rise and Fall of the Communist Party of Burma*, 3.
34. Lintner, 7.
35. Thakin is an honorific title, meaning "master."
36. Lintner, *The Rise and Fall of the Communist Party of Burma*, 8.
37. Klaus Fleischmann, *Documents on Communism in Burma, 1945–1977* (Hamburg: Institut für Asienkunde, 1989), 1.
38. Lintner, *The Rise and Fall of the Communist Party of Burma*, 9.
39. Hugh Tinker, *The Union of Burma: A Study of The First Years of Independence* (London: Oxford University Press, 1967), 20.
40. Lintner, *The Rise and Fall of the Communist Party of Burma*, 11.
41. Taylor, *The State in Myanmar*, 24.
42. Tinker, *The Union of Burma*, 35.
43. Lintner, *The Rise and Fall of the Communist Party of Burma*, 15.
44. "Communism in Burma: Lull in a Jungle Insurrection," *Times*, June 25, 1949.
45. Lintner, *The Rise and Fall of the Communist Party of Burma*, 17.
46. "Communist Revolt in Burma Dying Down: U Nu's Satisfaction," *Times*, November 28, 1952.
47. Lintner, *The Rise and Fall of the Communist Party of Burma*, 21.
48. S. Bhattacharya, "Burma: Neutralism Introverted," *The Australian Quarterly* 37, no. 1 (1965): 50–61.

49. Lintner, *The Rise and Fall of the Communist Party of Burma*, 21.
50. Kalyani Bandyopadhyaya, *Burma and Indonesia: Comparative Political Economy and Foreign Policy* (New Delhi: South Asian Publishers, 1983), 170–71.
51. MLM Revolutionary Study Group in the US, "Chinese Foreign Policy during the Maoist Era and Its Lessons for Today," January 2007.
52. https://www.marxists.org/history/international/comintern/sino-soviet-split/cpc/proposal.htm
53. Lintner, *The Rise and Fall of the Communist Party of Burma*, 22.
54. Hongwei Fan, "The 1967 Anti-Chinese Riots in Burma and Sino-Burmese Relations," *Journal of Southeast Asian Studies* 43, no. 2 (June 2012): 234–56.
55. Fan, 245–46.
56. Stephen Fitzgerald, *China and the Overseas Chinese: A Study of Peking's Changing Policy: 1949–1970* (Cambridge, UK: Cambridge University Press, 1972), 169–70.
57. Fan, "The 1967 Anti-Chinese Riots in Burma and Sino-Burmese Relations," 238.
58. Fan, 249.
59. Fan, 238.
60. "Red Guards in Beijing Angrily Denounce the Counter-Revolutionary Government of Ne Win (*shoudu hongweibing fennu shengtao naiwen fandong zhengfu*)," *People's Daily* (*renmin ribao*), July 2, 1967.
61. Jianzhang Zhang, *Experiences at the Communist Party of Burma (bama-pyi kunmunit party kayeekyan)* (Yangon, Myanmar: Journalist Publishing, 2016), 65.
62. Lintner, *The Rise and Fall of the Communist Party of Burma*, 25.
63. Zhang, *Experiences at the Communist Party of Burma*.
64. http://www.people.com.cn/GB/198221/198819/198859/12706724.html
65. Zhang, *Experiences at the Communist Party of Burma*, 189–90.
66. "Dare to Sacrifice, Dare to Fight, and Dare to Succeed (*ganyu xisheng ganyu douzheng ganyu shengli*)," *People's Daily* (*renmin ribao*), March 21, 1969.
67. Maung Aung Myoe, *In the Name of Pauk-Phaw*, 80–82.
68. Zin Htet et al., *That's Why It Happened: The Communist Party of Burma on the Northeast Mountain Ranges (htokchiang yithok: ashekmiaok taungtang myabauga bamabyi gummyonit pati)* (Yangon, Myanmar: Lwin Oo Book Publishing House, 2015), 152.
69. Lintner, *The Rise and Fall of the Communist Party of Burma*, 26.
70. Htet et al., *That's Why It Happened*, 102.
71. Lintner, *The Rise and Fall of the Communist Party of Burma*, 29.
72. Lintner, 30.
73. Lintner, 39.
74. Htet et al., *That's Why It Happened*, chap. 44.
75. http://www.people.com.cn/GB/198221/198819/198859/12706724.html
76. Lintner, *The Rise and Fall of the Communist Party of Burma*, 41.
77. Lintner, 46.
78. Htet et al., *That's Why It Happened*, 548.
79. Sarasin Viraphol, *Tribute and Profit: Sino-Siamese Trade, 1652–1853* (Cambridge, MA: Harvard University Asia Center, 1977); G. William Skinner, *Chinese Society in Thailand. An Analytical History* (Ithaca, NY: Cornell University Press, 1962).

80. Peng Chin, *Alias Chin Peng—My Side of History* (Singapore: Media Masters, 2003).
81. Narumit Sodsuk, *History of the People's Republic of China until the Four Modernisations: Effects on the Thai Communist Party (Prawattisat Satharanarat Prachachon Jeen jontheung Yuk Si Thansamai: Phonkrathop tor Phorkhorthor)* (Bangkok: Odeon Store, 1994), 4.
82. Daniel Dudley Lovelace, *China and "People's War" in Thailand, 1964–1969*, No. 8, China Research Monographs (Berkeley: Center for Chinese Studies, University of California, 1971), 15.
83. Kanok Wongtrangan, "Communist Revolutionary Process: A Study of the Communist Party of Thailand" (PhD diss., Johns Hopkins University, 1981), 51.
84. Tejapira, *Commodifying Marxism*, 53–56.
85. Communist Party of Thailand, *The Road to Victory: Documents from the Communist Party of Thailand* (Chicago: Liberator Press, n.d.), 10.
86. Lovelace, *China and "People's War" in Thailand*, 17.
87. Sean Turnell, *Fiery Dragons: Banks, Moneylenders and Microfinance in Burma* (Copenhagen: NIAS Press, 2009), chap. 2.
88. R. S. Randolph and W. Scott Thompson, *Thai Insurgency: Contemporary Developments* (Beverly Hills, CA; London: Sage Publications, 1981), 10.
89. I will not go into the details about the situation among the Malay in Southern Thailand in this book, even though the insurgency there now remains one of the most violent in Southeast Asia. For more information, please see McCargo, *Tearing Apart the Land*.
90. Lovelace, *China and "People's War" in Thailand*, 23.
91. Surachai Sirikrai, "Thai-American Relations in the Laotian Crisis of 1960–1962" (PhD diss., State University of New York, 1979); Dhanasarit Satawedin, "Thai-American Alliance during the Laotian Crisis, 1959–1962: A Case Study of the Bargaining Power of A Small State" (PhD diss., Northern Illinois University, 1984).
92. Lovelace, *China and "People's War" in Thailand*, 28.
93. Frank Clayton Darling, *Thailand and the United States* (Washington, DC: Public Affairs Press, 1965), chap. 6.
94. Lovelace, *China and "People's War" in Thailand*, 43.
95. Lovelace, 78.
96. "Drive U.S. Aggressors out of Southeast Asia," People's Daily, May 19, 1962; R. K. Jain, ed., *China and Thailand, 1949–83* (New Delhi: Radiant Publishers, 1984), 76.
97. Randolph and Thompson, *Thai Insurgency*, 14.
98. "Commentary," Peking Review, January 31, 1964; Jain, *China and Thailand*, 87.
99. Jain, 91.
100. Lovelace, *China and "People's War" in Thailand*, 48.
101. Lovelace, 49.
102. Lovelace, 54.
103. Lovelace, 57.
104. "Thai People's Armed Struggle Develops Swiftly and Vigorously," Peking Review, February 21, 1969; Jain, *China and Thailand*, 155.
105. Jain, *China and Thailand*, 154.
106. Randolph and Thompson, *Thai Insurgency*, 35.

107. R. Sittan, S. Boonplook, and S. Warit, *The Communist Party of Thailand Today (Phak Communist Haeng Prathet Thai Wannee)* (Bangkok: Krung Siam Publishing, 1980), 200–202.
108. Randolph and Thompson, *Thai Insurgency*, 41.
109. Sittan, Boonplook, and Warit, *The Communist Party of Thailand Today*, 146–47.
110. Gawin Chutima, "The Rise and the Fall of the Communist Party of Thailand (1973–1987)," Occasional Paper No. 12 (Center of South-east Asian Studies, University of Kent at Canterbury, 1990), 20.
111. Sittan, Boonplook, and Warit, *The Communist Party of Thailand Toda*, 22.
112. Chutima, "The Rise and the Fall of the Communist Party of Thailand," 25.
113. Marian Mallet, "Causes and Consequences of the October '76 Coup," *Journal of Contemporary Asia* 8, no. 1 (January 1, 1978): 80–103.
114. Chutima, "The Rise and the Fall of the Communist Party of Thailand," 26.
115. Randolph and Thompson, *Thai Insurgency*, 36.
116. M. Ladd Thomas, "Communist Insurgency in Thailand: Factors Contributing to Its Decline," *Asian Affairs* 13, no. 1 (1986): 17.
117. Randolph and Thompson, *Thai Insurgency*, 53.
118. Chutima, "The Rise and the Fall of the Communist Party of Thailand," x.
119. Ann Marie Murphy, "Beyond Balancing and Bandwagoning: Thailand's Response to China's Rise," *Asian Security* 6, no. 1 (January 22, 2010): 10.
120. Murphy, 10.
121. "The USSR-Vietnam Treaty Threatens World Peace and Security, Pointed out by Vice Premier Deng at Press Conference," *Xinhua*, November 9, 1978.
122. Randolph and Thompson, *Thai Insurgency*, 63.
123. Chutima, "The Rise and the Fall of the Communist Party of Thailand," 38.
124. Ettinger, "Thailand's Defeat of Its Communist Party."
125. Chutima, "The Rise and the Fall of the Communist Party of Thailand," 42.

Chapter 6

1. Recently there have been quite a few reports about the situation in Mongla, for example see "Burma's 'Wild East' Is a Debauched Land of Drugs and Vice That Reforms Forgot," *Time*, March 9, 2014.
2. "Getting Higher," *The Economist*, April 12, 2014.
3. Patrick Meehan, "Fortifying or Fragmenting the State? The Political Economy of the Opium/Heroin Trade in Shan State, Myanmar, 1988–2013," *Critical Asian Studies* 47, no. 2 (April 3, 2015): 253–82.
4. Karin Dean, "Spaces and Territorialities on the Sino–Burmese Boundary: China, Burma and the Kachin," *Political Geography* 24, no. 7 (September 2005): 808–30.
5. Data on the three countries' economic development are from World Bank Development Indicators.
6. Qunjian Tian, "China Develops Its West: Motivation, Strategy and Prospect," *Journal of Contemporary China* 13, no. 41 (November 1, 2004): 611–36.

7. Hongchang Yang, *Yunnan Province and Mekong River Regional Cooperation: China's Locally Initiated Development (Yunnansheng Yu Meigonghe Quyu Hezuo: Zhongguo Difang Zizhuxing de Fazhan)* (Hong Kong: Hong Kong Asia Pacific Research Institute: Chinese University of Hong Kong, 2001).
8. Asian Development Bank, *Assessing Impact in the Greater Mekong Subregion: An Analysis of Regional Cooperation Projects* (Mandaluyong City, Philippines: Asian Development Bank, 2014). Later, the Chinese province of Guangxi was also added to the list of areas covered by the GMS.
9. For more details about the GMS cooperation programs at ADB, see https://www.adb.org/publications/greater-mekong-subregion-economic-cooperation-program-overview.
10. Currently the construction of the section in Laos has commenced, while negotiations with Thai government are still ongoing. For example, see https://asia.nikkei.com/Politics-Economy/International-Relations/Land-locked-Laos-on-track-for-controversial-China-rail-link.
11. For information on the Chiang Saen port, see http://www.csp.port.co.th/eng/dataset1/data2.html.
12. Shengda He, "About Scientific Development and Several Problems Facing Yunnan's Opening Up in the New Period (Guanyu Kexue Fazhanguan He Xinshiqi Yunnan Duiwai Kaifang de Jige Wenti)," *Social Sciences in Yunnan (Yunnan Shehui Kexue)*, no. 2 (2007): 117.
13. Enze Han and Christopher Paik, "Ethnic Integration and Development in China," *World Development* 93 (May 1, 2017): 34; David S. G. Goodman, "The Campaign to 'Open up the West': National, Provincial-Level and Local Perspectives," *The China Quarterly*, no. 178 (2004): 317–34.
14. http://finance.people.com.cn/GB/8215/174398/10627441.html
15. *Yunnan Statistical Yearbook, 2015*, which can be accessed at www.chinadataonline.com.
16. Czeslaw Tubilewicz and Kanishka Jayasuriya, "Internationalisation of the Chinese Subnational State and Capital: The Case of Yunnan and the Greater Mekong Subregion," *Australian Journal of International Affairs* 69, no. 2 (March 4, 2015). 192.
17. Xiaobo Su, "From Frontier to Bridgehead: Cross-Border Regions and the Experience of Yunnan, China," *International Journal of Urban and Regional Research* 37, no. 4 (July 1, 2013): 1213–32.
18. Robert J. Muscat, *The Fifth Tiger: Study of Thai Development Policy* (Armonk, NY: M. E. Sharpe, 1994), 88; Michael T. Rock, *Dictators, Democrats, and Development in Southeast Asia: Implications for the Rest* (New York, NY: Oxford University Press, 2016), 53.
19. Benedict Anderson, "Murder and Progress in Modern Siam," *New Left Review*, I, no. 181 (1990): 38–39.
20. Jasper Goss and David Burch, "From Agricultural Modernisation to Agri-Food Globalisation: The Waning of National Development in Thailand," *Third World Quarterly* 22, no. 6 (December 1, 2001): 974.

21. Richard F. Doner, *The Politics of Uneven Development: Thailand's Economic Growth in Comparative Perspective* (Cambridge, UK; New York: Cambridge University Press, 2009), 96.
22. Doner, 117.
23. Amalia Rossi, "Turning Red Rural Landscapes Yellow? Sufficiency Economy and Royal Projects in the Hills of Nan Province, Northern Thailand," *Austrian Journal of South-East Asian Studies* 5, no. 2 (December 30, 2012): 278; Tom Marks, *Making Revolution: The Insurgency of the Communist Party of Thailand in Structural Perspective* (Bangkok, Thailand: White Lotus Press, 1994), 196.
24. Andrew Walker, *Thailand's Political Peasants: Power in the Modern Rural Economy* (Madison: University of Wisconsin Press, 2012), 54.
25. http://www.tsdf.or.th/en/royally-initiated-projects/10757-the-royal-project-foundation/
26. Chanida Chitbundid, *The Royal Projects: The Making of King Bhumibol's Royal Hegemony (Khrongkan an Nueang Chak Phra Rathcadamri: Karn Sathaphana Phraratcha Amnartnam Nai Phrabatsomdet Phrachaoyuhua)* (Bangkok: The Foundation of the Promotion of Social Science and Humanities Textbooks Project, 2007); Sai S. W. Latt, "More Than Culture, Gender, and Class: Erasing Shan Labor in the 'Success' of Thailand's Royal Development Project," *Critical Asian Studies* 43, no. 4 (December 1, 2011): 531–50.
27. Rossi, "Turning Red Rural Landscapes Yellow?" 281.
28. For data, see *Thailand Statistical Yearbooks* (National Statistical Office, Ministry of Information and Communication Technology, The Kingdom of Thailand).
29. Jim Glassman, *Thailand at the Margins: Internationalization of the State and the Transformation of Labour* (London and New York: Oxford University Press, 2004), 138.
30. Eberle and Holliday, "Precarity and Political Immobilisation," 378.
31. Siriluk Masviriyakul, "Sino-Thai Strategic Economic Development in the Greater Mekong Subregion (1992–2003)," *Contemporary Southeast Asia* 26, no. 2 (2004): 308.
32. Takao Tsuneishi, "The Regional Development Policy of Thailand Its Economic Cooperation with Neighbouring Countries," Discussion Papers 32 (Institute of Developing Economies, Japan External Trade Organization, 2005); Takao Tsuneishi, "Development of Border Economic Zones in Thailand:Expansion of Border Trade and Formation of Border Economic Zones," Discussion Papers 153 (Institute of Developing Economies, Japan External Trade Organization, 2008).
33. Although the Thai government seems to have changed its mind on SEZs recently. See https://asia.nikkei.com/Economy/Thailand-scraps-new-economic-zones-and-plans-regional-linkups.
34. Takao Tsuneishi, "Border Trade and Economic Zones on the North-South Economic Corridor: Focusing on the Connecting Points between the Four Countries," Discussion Papers 205 (Institute of Developing Economies, Japan External Trade Organization, 2009).
35. Jim Glassman, "Recovering from Crisis: The Case of Thailand's Spatial Fix," *Economic Geography* 83, no. 4 (2007): 364.
36. Ibid..

37. Stephen D. Krasner, *Structural Conflict: Third World Against Global Liberalism* (Berkeley: University of California Press, 1985), 295.
38. David I. Steinberg, *Burma: The State of Myanmar* (Washington, DC: Georgetown University Press, 2001), 20.
39. Martin Smith, *State of Strife: The Dynamics of Ethnic Conflict in Burma* (Washington, DC: East-West Center Press, 2007), 19.
40. Tin Maung Maung Than, *State Dominance in Myanmar: The Political Economy of Industrialization* (Singapore: ISEAS Publishing, 2007), 292.
41. Taylor, *The State in Myanmar*, 377.
42. Taylor, 378.
43. Steinberg, *Burma: The State of Myanmar*, 131.
44. South, *Ethnic Politics in Burma*, 122.
45. South, 119.
46. Martin Smith, "Reflections on the Kachin Ceasefire: A Cycle of Hope and Disappointment," in *War and Peace in the Borderlands of Myanmar: The Kachin Ceasefire, 1994–2011*, ed. Mandy Sadan (Copenhagen: NIAS Press, 2016), 85.
47. Lee Jones, "Understanding Myanmar's Ceasefires: Geopolitics, Political Economy and State-Building," in *War and Peace in the Borderlands of Myanmar: The Kachin Ceasefire, 1994–2011*, ed. Mandy Sadan (Copenhagen: NIAS Press, 2016), 100.
48. Woods, "Ceasefire Capitalism."
49. State Law and Order Restoration Council (SLORC) and State Peace and Development Council (SPDC), Development and Prosperity for Myanmar (*Tine Kyo Pyi Pyu*), vol. I, 1988–1991, 45.
50. State Law and Order Restoration Council (SLORC) and State Peace and Development Council (SPDC), Development and Prosperity for Myanmar (*Tine Kyo Pyi Pyu*), vol. II, 1991–1995, 361–365.
51. Jones, "Understanding Myanmar's Ceasefires," 101.
52. John Buchanan, Tom Kramer, and Kevin Woods, *Developing Disparity: Regional Investment in Burma's Borderlands* (Amsterdam: Transnational Institute (TNI), 2013); Kevin Woods, *Commercial Agriculture Expansion in Myanmar: Links to Deforestation, Conversion Timber, and Land Conflicts* (Washington, DC: Forest Trends, 2015).
53. *Key Indicators for Asia and the Pacific 2017* (Asian Development Bank, 2017).
54. Please note that trade data from different sources often do not add up as different governments and agencies use different ways of calculating them. So the statistics presented here are for illustrative purposes only.
55. Kevin Woods, "Ceasefire Capitalism: Military-Private Partnerships, Resource Concessions and Military-State Building in the Burma–China Borderlands," *Journal of Peasant Studies* 38, no. 4 (October 1, 2011): 747–70.
56. Lee Jones, "The Political Economy of Myanmar's Transition," *Journal of Contemporary Asia* 44, no. 1 (February 1, 2014): 144.
57. Enze Han, "Borderland Ethnic Politics and Changing Sino-Myanmar Relations," in *War and Peace in the Borderlands of Myanmar: The Kachin Ceasefire, 1994–2011*, ed. Mandy Sadan (Copenhagen: NIAS Press, 2016), 156.

58. Helen James, "Myanmar's International Relations Strategy: The Search for Security," *Contemporary Southeast Asia* 26, no. 3 (2004): 533.
59. Winston Set Aung, *The Role of Informal Cross-Border Trade in Myanmar*, Asia Paper Series (Singapore: Institute for Security & Development Policy, 2009).
60. Mya Than, "Myanmar's Cross-Border Economic Relations and Cooperation with the People's Republic of China and Thailand in the Great Mekong Subregion," *Journal of GMS Development Studies* 2 (2005): 45.
61. Mya Than, 38.
62. Min Zin, "Burmese Attitude toward Chinese: Portrayal of the Chinese in Contemporary Cultural and Media Works," *Journal of Current Southeast Asian Affairs* 31, no. 1 (January 1, 2012): 115–31.
63. Kuah Khun Eng, "Negotiating Central, Provincial, and County Policies: Border Trading in South China," in *Where China Meets Southeast Asia: Social & Cultural Change in the Border Regions*, ed. Grant Evans, Christopher Hutton, and Kuah Khun Eng (Singapore: Institute of Southeast Asian Studies, 2000), 74.
64. Eng, 77; Tim Summers, *Yunnan—A Chinese Bridgehead to Asia: A Case Study of China's Political and Economic Relations with Its Neighbours* (Oxford: Chandos Publishing, 2013), 57.
65. Eng, "Negotiating Central, Provincial, and County Policies: Border Trading in South China," 77.
66. Toshihiro Kudo, "Myanmar's Economic Relations with China: Can China Support the Myanmar Economy," Discussion Papers 066 (Institute of Developing Economies, Japan External Trade Organization, 2006), 23.
67. Ministry of Commerce, The Republic of the Union of Myanmar, http://www.commerce.gov.mm/en/dobt/border-trade-data.
68. Ingrid d'Hooghe, "Regional Economic Integration in Yunnan," in *China Deconstructs: Politics, Trade and Regionalism*, ed. David S. G. Goodman and Gerald Segal (London ; New York: Routledge, 1994), 307.
69. Koji Kubo, "Myanmar's Cross-Border Trade with China: Beyond Informal Trade," Discussion Papers 625 (Institute of Developing Economies, Japan External Trade Organization, 2016), 1.
70. Mya Than, "Myanmar's Cross-Border Economic Relations and Cooperation with the People's Republic of China and Thailand in the Great Mekong Subregion," 44.
71. Wen-Chin Chang, "Venturing into 'Barbarous' Regions: Transborder Trade among Migrant Yunnanese between Thailand and Burma, 1960s–1980s," *Journal of Asian Studies* 68, no. 2 (2009): 550.
72. Ministry of Commerce, The Republic of the Union of Myanmar, http://www.commerce.gov.mm/en/dobt/border-trade-data.
73. Choen Krainara and Jayant K. Routray, "Cross-Border Trades and Commerce between Thailand and Neighboring Countries: Policy Implications for Establishing Special Border Economic Zones," *Journal of Borderlands Studies* 30, no. 3 (July 3, 2015): 356.
74. OECD, *OECD Investment Policy Reviews: Myanmar 2014* (Paris: OECD Publishing, 2014), 56.

75. Stephen Gelb, Linda Calabrese, and Xiaoyang Tang, *Foreign Direct Investment and Economic Transformation in Myanmar* (London: Supporting Economic Transformation, Overseas Development Institute, 2017), 31, https://www.odi.org/publications/10774-foreign-direct-investment-and-economic-transformation-myanmar.
76. Maung Aung Myoe, *In the Name of Pauk-Phaw*, 152–53.
77. David Doran, Matthew Christensen, and Thida Aye, "Hydropower in Myanmar: Sector Analysis and Related Legal Reforms," *The International Journal of Hydropower & Dams* 21, no. 3 (2014): 87–91.
78. For example, see Laur Kiik, "Nationalism and Anti-Ethno-Politics: Why 'Chinese Development' Failed at Myanmar's Myitsone Dam," *Eurasian Geography and Economics* 57, no. 3 (May 3, 2016): 374–402.
79. Author's interview with KIO officer, Laiza, Kachin State, 2014.
80. Global Witness, "Jade: Myanmar's 'Big State Secret,'" 2015, 101. https://www.globalwitness.org/en/campaigns/oil-gas-and-mining/myanmarjade/.
81. Mandy Sadan, ed., *The War and Peace in the Borderlands of Myanmar: The Kachin Ceasefire, 1994–2011* (Copenhagen: NIAS Press, 2016).
82. Global Witness, "Jade," 26.
83. Global Witness, 27.
84. Laur Kiik, "Conspiracy, God's Plan and National Emergency: Kachin Popular Analyses of the Ceasefire Era and Its Resource Grabs," in *War and Peace in the Borderlands of Myanmar: The Kachin Ceasefire, 1994–2011*, ed. Mandy Sadan (Copenhagen: NIAS Press, 2016), 218.
85. Aye Win Myint, "Instead of Jade, Myanmar's Gem Scavengers Find Heroin and Destitution," *Reuters*, December 15, 2015.
86. Ts'ui-p'ing Ho, "People's Diplomacy and Borderland History through the Chinese Jingpo Manau Zumko Festival," in *War and Peace in the Borderlands of Myanmar: The Kachin Ceasefire, 1994–2011*, ed. Mandy Sadan (Copenhagen: NIAS Press, 2016), 176.
87. Woods, "Ceasefire Capitalism," 757.
88. Min Dong et al., "Exploring Sino-Burma Timber Trade (Zhongmian Mucai Maoyi Tanjiu)," *Issues of Forestry Economics (Linye Jinji Wenti)* 36, no. 2 (2016): 146.
89. Forest Trends, *Analysis of Sino-Myanmar Timber Trade (Zhongmian Mucai Maoyi Fenxi)*, Policy Brief (Forest Trends, 2014), 1.
90. Wang Xu, "155 Chinese Workers Pardoned," *China Daily*, July 31, 2015.
91. Woods, *Commercial Agriculture Expansion in Myanmar*, 3.
92. Lintner, *Burma in Revolt*.
93. Chin, *The Golden Triangle*; Martin Jelsma, Tom Kramer, and Pietje Vervest, eds., *Trouble in the Triangle: Opium and the Conflict in Burma* (Chiang Mai, Thailand: Silkworm Books, 2005).
94. Ko-lin Chin and Sheldon X. Zhang, *The Chinese Heroin Trade: Cross-Border Drug Trafficking in Southeast Asia and Beyond* (New York; London: New York University Press, 2015), 4.

95. Tom Kramer et al., *Bouncing Back: Relapse in the Golden Triangle* (Amsterdam: Transnational Institute (TNI), 2014), 17.
96. Xiaobo Su, "Nontraditional Security and China's Transnational Narcotics Control in Northern Laos and Myanmar," *Political Geography* 48 (September 2015): 72–82; Xiaobo Su, "Development Intervention and Transnational Narcotics Control in Northern Myanmar," *Geoforum* 68, Supplement C (January 1, 2016): 10–20.
97. Woods, "Ceasefire Capitalism," 764.
98. 1 mu = 0.1647 acre.
99. Kramer et al., *Bouncing Back*.
100. Meehan, "Fortifying or Fragmenting the State?"
101. Woods, "Ceasefire Capitalism;" Woods, *Commercial Agriculture Expansion in Myanmar*.

Chapter 7

1. Teaching of ethnic languages in China varies tremendously across different provinces. In Yunnan, Jingpo language teaching is actually limited in its locations and levels and only available at select primary schools in Dehong.
2. Pamela Kyle Crossley, *A Translucent Mirror: History and Identity in Qing Imperial Ideology* (Berkeley: University of California Press, 2000); Mark C. Elliott, *The Manchu Way: The Eight Banners and Ethnic Identity in Late Imperial China* (Stanford, CA: Stanford University Press, 2001).
3. Peter C. Perdue, *China Marches West: The Qing Conquest of Central Eurasia* (Cambridge, MA: Harvard University Press, 2005).
4. James Leibold, "Positioning 'Minzu' within Sun Yat-Sen's Discourse of Minzuzhuyi," *Journal of Asian History* 38, no. 2 (2004): 163–213.
5. Han, *Contestation and Adaptation*; Hansen, *Lessons in Being Chinese*.
6. Hsieh, "Ethnic-Political Adaptation and Ethnic Change of the Sipsong Panna Dai;" Yos Santasombat, *Lak Chang: A Reconstruction of Tai Identity in Daikong* (Canberra: Australian National University Press, 2011).
7. Mullaney, *Coming to Terms with the Nation*.
8. Stevan Harrell, "Introduction: Civilizing Projects and the Reaction to Them," in *Cultural Encounters on China's Ethnic Frontiers*, ed. Stevan Harrell (Seattle: University of Washington Press, 1995): 3–36.
9. Thomas Heberer, *China and Its National Minorities: Autonomy or Assimilation* (Armonk, NY: Routledge, 1989); Mackerras, *China's Minorities*.
10. Barry Sautman, "Ethnic Law and Minority Rights in China: Progress and Constraints," *Law & Policy* 21, no. 3 (July 1, 1999): 288.
11. http://english.peopledaily.com.cn/constitution/constitution.html
12. Barry Sautman, "Preferential Policies for Ethnic Minorities in China: The Case of Xinjiang," *Nationalism and Ethnic Politics* 4, no. 1–2 (March 1, 1998): 86–118.
13. Han, *Contestation and Adaptation*, 38.

14. Gerard A. Postiglione, ed., *China's National Minority Education: Culture, Schooling, and Development*, vol. 1090, *Garland Reference Library of Social Science*, vol. 42 *Reference Books in International Education* (New York: Falmer Press, 1999).
15. James Leibold, *Ethnic Policy in China: Is Reform Inevitable?* (Washington, DC: East-West Center, 2013), 21.
16. Disaphol Chansiri, *The Chinese Émigrés of Thailand in the Twentieth Century* (Youngstown, NY: Cambria Press, 2008), 48.
17. George William Skinner, *Chinese Society in Thailand: An Analytical History* (Ithaca, NY: Cornell University Press, 1957); Gungwu Wang, *The Chinese Overseas: From Earthbound China to the Quest for Autonomy* (Cambridge, MA: Harvard University Press, 2002).
18. Wasana Wongsurawat, "Beyond Jews of the Orient: A New Interpretation of the Problematic Relationship between the Thai State and Its Ethnic Chinese Community," *Positions* 24, no. 2 (May 1, 2016): 566.
19. Enze Han, "Bifurcated Homeland and Diaspora Politics in China and Taiwan towards the Overseas Chinese in Southeast Asia," *Journal of Ethnic and Migration Studies* 45, no. 4 (2019): 577–94.
20. James Jiann Hua To, *Qiaowu: Extra-Territorial Policies for the Overseas Chinese* (Leiden: Brill Academic Publishers, 2014), 54..
21. Jeffery Sng and Pimpraphai Bisalputra, *A History of the Thai-Chinese* (Singapore: Editions Didier Millet, 2015), 270.
22. Sng and Bisalputra, 244.
23. Wongsurawat, "Beyond Jews of the Orient," 560.
24. Walter F. Vella, *Chaiyo!: King Vajiravadh and the Development of Thai Nationalism* (Honolulu, HI: University of Hawai'i Press, 1986), 194.
25. Wongsurawat, "Beyond Jews of the Orient," 561.
26. Milton Esman, "The Chinese Diaspora in Southeast Asia," in *Modern Diasporas in International Politics*, ed. Gabriel Shaffer (Kent, UK: Croom Helm Ltd, 1986).
27. Shelley Rigger, "Nationalism versus Citizenship in the Republic of China on Taiwan," in *Changing Meanings of Citizenship in Modern China*, ed. Merie Goldman and Elizabeth Perry (Cambridge, MA: Harvard University Press, 2002): 353–374; Dan Shao, "Chinese by Definition: Nationality Law, Jus Sanguinis, and State Succession," *Twentieth-Century China* 35, no. 1 (2009): 4–28.
28. Pál Nyíri, "Reorientation: Notes on the Rise of the PRC and Chinese Identities in Southeast Asia," *Southeast Asian Journal of Social Science* 25, no. 2 (1997): 163.
29. Fitzgerald, *China and the Overseas Chinese*, 8.
30. Eiji Murashima, "The Thai-Japanese Alliance and the Overseas Chinese in Thailand," in *Southeast Asian Minorities in the Wartime Japanese Empire*, ed. Paul H. Kratoska (Oxford: RoutledgeCurzon, 2005), 192–223.
31. Chansiri, *The Chinese Émigrés of Thailand in the Twentieth Century*, 71.
32. Skinner, *Chinese Society in Thailand*, 262–67.
33. Skinner, 276.
34. Skinner, 381.

35. Chai-anan Samudavanija, "State-Identity Creation, State-Building and Civil Society, 1939–1989," in *National Identity and Its Defenders: Thailand Today*, ed. Craig J. Reynolds (Chiang Mai, Thailand: Silkworm Books, 2002), 61.
36. Fitzgerald, *China and the Overseas Chinese*.
37. Skinner, *Chinese Society in Thailand*, 379.
38. Pinkaew Laungaramsri, "Ethnicity and the Politics of Ethnic Classification in Thailand," in *Ethnicity in Asia*, ed. Colin Mackerras (London: RoutledgeCurzon, 2003), 155.
39. Pavin Chachavalpongpun, *A Plastic Nation: The Curse of Thainess in Thai-Burmese Relations* (Lanham, MD: University Press of America, 2005).
40. Michael Kelly Connors, *Democracy and National Identity in Thailand*, rev. ed. (Copenhagen: NIAS Press, 2006), 48–49.
41. Nalini Ranjan Chakravarti, *Indian Minority in Burma: Rise and Decline of an Immigrant Community* (London; New York: Oxford University Press, 1971), 97.
42. Mikael Gravers, *Nationalism as Political Paranoia in Burma: An Essay on the Historical Practice of Power* (London: Routledge, 1999), 27; Renaud Egreteau, "Burmese Indians in Contemporary Burma: Heritage, Influence, and Perceptions since 1988," *Asian Ethnicity* 12, no. 1 (February 1, 2011): 38.
43. Walton, "The 'Wages of Burman-Ness,'" 8.
44. Gravers, *Nationalism as Political Paranoia in Burma*, 30.
45. Kei Nemoto, "The Concepts of Dobama ('Our Burma') and Thudo-Bama ('Their Burma') in Burmese Nationalism, 1930–1948," *Journal of Burma Studies* 5, no. 1 (March 30, 2011): 3.
46. Gravers, *Nationalism as Political Paranoia in Burma*, 31; Alicia Turner, *Saving Buddhism: The Impermanence of Religion in Colonial Burma* (Honolulu, HI: University of Hawai'i Press, 2017).
47. The revised 1982 Citizenship Act maintained this distinction of citizens, associated citizens, and naturalized citizens.
48. Egreteau, "Burmese Indians in Contemporary Burma," 40.
49. Robert A. Holmes, "Burmese Domestic Policy: The Politics of Burmanization," *Asian Survey* 7, no. 3 (1967): 188–97.
50. Egreteau, "Burmese Indians in Contemporary Burma," 41.
51. Walton, "Ethnicity, Conflict, and History in Burma."
52. Steinberg, *Burma: The State of Myanmar*, 182.
53. Matthew J. Walton, "The Disciplining Discourse of Unity in Burmese Politics," *Journal of Burma Studies* 19, no. 1 (June 17, 2015): 1–26.
54. Mikael Gravers, "Introduction: Ethnicity against State—State against Ethnic Diversity?" in *Exploring Ethnic Diversity in Burma*, ed. Mikael Gravers (Copenhagen: NIAS Press, 2007), 21.
55. Jane M. Ferguson, "Who's Counting? Ethnicity, Belonging, and the National Census in Burma/Myanmar," *Bijdragen Tot de Taal-, Land- En Volkenkunde* 171, no. 1 (2015): 15.
56. Nick Cheesman, "How in Myanmar 'National Races' Came to Surpass Citizenship and Exclude Rohingya," *Journal of Contemporary Asia* 47, no. 3 (May 27, 2017): 462.

57. Jane M. Ferguson, "Ethno-Nationalism and Participation in Myanmar: Views from Shan State and Beyond," in *Metamorphosis: Studies in Social and Political Change in Myanmar*, ed. Renaud Egreteau and Francois Robinne (Singapore: NUS Press, 2016), 132.
58. Walton, "The "Wages of Burman-Ness," 12.
59. Walton, 13.
60. Ian Holliday, "Addressing Myanmar's Citizenship Crisis," *Journal of Contemporary Asia* 44, no. 3 (July 3, 2014): 404–21.
61. Carl Grundy-Warr and Elaine Wong Siew Yin, "Geographies of Displacement: The Karenni and the Shan across the Myanmar-Thailand Border," *Singapore Journal of Tropical Geography* 23, no. 1 (March 1, 2002): 93–122; Amnesty International *"All the Civilians Suffer": Conflict, Displacement, and Abuse in Northern Myanmar* (London: Amnesty International, 2017).
62. Shan Women's Action Network and Shan Human Rights Foundation, *License to Rape: The Burmese Military Regime's Use of Sexual Violence in the Ongoing War in Shan State* (Chiang Mai, Thailand: Shan Human Rights Foundation, 2002); Jane M. Ferguson, "Is the Pen Mightier than the AK-47? Tracking Shan Women's Militancy within and beyond," *Intersections: Gender and Sexuality in Asia and the Pacific*, no. 33 (2013).
63. Syeda Naushin Parnini, "The Crisis of the Rohingya as a Muslim Minority in Myanmar and Bilateral Relations with Bangladesh," *Journal of Muslim Minority Affairs* 33, no. 2 (June 1, 2013): 281–97.
64. Lindsey N. Kingston, "Protecting the World's Most Persecuted: The Responsibility to Protect and Burma's Rohingya Minority," *The International Journal of Human Rights* 19, no. 8 (November 17, 2015): 1163–75.
65. Han, *Contestation and Adaptation*.
66. Enze Han and Christopher Paik, "Dynamics of Political Resistance in Tibet: Religious Repression and Controversies of Demographic Change," *The China Quarterly*, no. 217 (2014): 69–98; Enze Han, "From Domestic to International: The Politics of Ethnic Identity in Xinjiang and Inner Mongolia," *Nationalities Papers* 39, no. 6 (November 1, 2011): 941–62.
67. Han and Paik, "Ethnic Integration and Development in China."
68. Han, *Contestation and Adaptation*, 109.
69. According to the 2010 Chinese National Census, the total Jingpo population was 147,828.
70. Sadan, *Being and Becoming Kachin*, 7.
71. Seng Maw Lahpai, "State Terrorism and International Compliance: The Kachin Armed Struggle for Political Self-Determination," in *Debating Democratization in Myanmar*, ed. Nick Cheesman, Nicholas Farrelly, and Trevor Wilson (Singapore: ISEAS Publishing, 2014): 285–304.
72. Ho, "People's Diplomacy and Borderland History through the Chinese Jingpo Manau Zumko Festival," 181.

73. Elaine Lynn-Ee Ho, "Mobilising Affinity Ties: Kachin Internal Displacement and the Geographies of Humanitarianism at the China–Myanmar Border," *Transactions of the Institute of British Geographers* 42, no. 1 (March 1, 2017): 84–97.
74. Echo Hui, "Chinese Kachin Protest Against Burma's Kachin War," *The Irrawaddy*, January 11, 2013, https://www.irrawaddy.com/news/burma/chinese-kachin-protest-against-burmas-kachin-war.html.
75. Ho, "People's Diplomacy and Borderland History through the Chinese Jingpo Manau Zumko Festival," 171.
76. Magnus Fiskesjö, "People First: The Wa World of Spirits and Other Enemies," *Anthropological Forum* 27, no. 4 (April 19, 2017), 340–64.
77. Xuan Liu, "United Wa State Army in Myanmar: Origin, Development and Influence (Miandian Wabang Liangejun: Qiyuan, Fazhan Ji Yingxiang)," *Indian Ocean Economic and Political Review (Yingduyang Jingjiti Yanjiu)* 3 (2014): 78.
78. The UWSA also moved tens of thousands of people from the northern division to settle in the south. See, *Unsettling Moves: The Wa Forced Resettlement Program in Eastern Shan State (1999–2001)* (The Lahu National Development Organization, April 2002), http://www.burmalibrary.org/docs23/Unsettling_Moves-tpo.pdf.
79. There have been allegations that the Chinese government has supplied the UWSA with helicopters, for example reported by the IHS Jane's Defense Weekly in 2013, but these rumors have never been verified.
80. Enze Han, "Transnational Ties, HIV/AIDS Prevention and State-Minority Relations in Xishuangbanna, Southwest China," *Journal of Contemporary China* 22, no. 82 (2013): 594–611.
81. Thomas Borchert, "Worry for the Dai Nation: Sipsongpannā, Chinese Modernity, and the Problems of Buddhist Modernism," *Journal of Asian Studies* 67, no. 1 (2008): 107–42; Thomas Borchert, "The Abbot's New House: Thinking about How Religion Works among Buddhists and Ethnic Minorities in Southwest China," *Journal of Church and State* 52, no. 1 (2010): 112–37; Hansen, *Lessons in Being Chinese*.
82. Han, *Contestation and Adaptation*, 113; Antonella Diana, "Re-Configuring Belonging in Post-Socialist Xishuangbanna, China," in *Tai Lands and Thailand: Community and State in Southeast Asia*, ed. Andrew Walker (Honolulu, HI: University of Hawai'i Press, 2009): 192–213; Janet C. Sturgeon, "Cross-Border Rubber Cultivation between China and Laos: Regionalization by Akha and Tai Rubber Farmers," *Singapore Journal of Tropical Geography* 34, no. 1 (March 1, 2013): 70–85.
83. Pinkaew Laungaramsri, "Women, Nation, and the Ambivalence of Subversive Identification along the Thai-Burmese Border," *Sojourn: Journal of Social Issues in Southeast Asia* 21, no. 1 (April 1, 2006): 72.
84. Yawnghwe, *The Shan of Burma*, 123.
85. Bertil Lintner, "Recent Developments on the Thai-Burma Border," *IBRU Boundary and Security Bulletin* 3, no. 1 (April 1995): 72. Pornpimol Trichot, Thai Policy on Repatriation of Displaced Persons from Myanmar *(Nayobai Song Glub Phoophladthin chark Phama khong Thai)* (Bangkok: Institute of Asian Studies, Chulalongkorn University, 2004).
86. Lintner, "Recent Developments on the Thai-Burma Border," 74.

87. Chang, "The Everyday Politics of the Underground Trade in Burma by the Yunnanese Chinese since the Burmese Socialist Era."
88. Yawnghwe, *The Shan of Burma*, 126.
89. Yos Santasombat, *Power, Space, and Ethnic Identities: Political Culture of Nation-State in the Thai Society (Amnart Phuenthee lae Attalak thang Chartphan: Karnmuaeng Watthanatham khong Ratchart nai Sangkhom Thai)* (Bangkok: Princess Maha Chakri Sirindhorn Anthropology Centre, 2008).
90. Pornpimol Trichot, *The Myanmar Foreign Policy in Ethnic Minority Context and Impact on Thai-Myanmar Relationship (Karndamnoen Nayobai Tangprathet khong Phama nai Suan Samphan kab Chonklumnoi lae Pholkrathop tor Kwamsamphan Thai-Phama)* (Bangkok: Institute of Asian Studies, Chulalongkorn University: 2006), 169.
91. Trichot, 195.
92. Akni Mulamek, *Shan State: History and Revolution (Rat Shan: Prawattisat lae karn Patiwat)* (Bangkok: Matichon Book, 2005), 82.
93. Mulamek, 83.
94. Smith, *State of Strife*, 40.
95. Jirattikorn, "Aberrant Modernity," 333.
96. Thongchai Winichakul, "Nationalism and the Radical Intelligentsia in Thailand," *Third World Quarterly* 29, no. 3 (April 1, 2008): 575–91.
97. Jirattikorn, "Aberrant Modernity," 334.
98. Amporn Jirattikorn, "Shan Virtual Insurgency and the Spectatorship of the Nation," *Journal of Southeast Asian Studies* 42, no. 1 (2011): 19.
99. Ferguson, "Is the Pen Mightier than the AK-47?"
100. Jane M. Ferguson, "Revolutionary Scripts: Shan Insurgent Media Practice at the Thai-Burma Border," in *Political Regimes and the Media in Asia*, ed. Krishna Sen and Terence Lee (London; New York: Routledge, 2008):106–121.
101. Ferguson.
102. Jirattikorn, "Shan Virtual Insurgency and the Spectatorship of the Nation," 31–32.
103. Jirattikorn, 31.
104. Laungaramsri, "Ethnicity and the Politics of Ethnic Classification in Thailand," 164.
105. Robert George Cooper, *Resource Scarcity and the Hmong Response: Patterns of Settlement and Economy in Transition* (Singapore: Singapore University Press, National University of Singapore, 1984).
106. Gibson and Chen, *The Secret Army*.
107. Laungaramsri, "Ethnicity and the Politics of Ethnic Classification in Thailand," 165–67.
108. It is difficult to calculate precisely the hill tribe population in Thailand, and many in fact remain stateless. However, a major census of hill tribes conducted in 1985–1988 documented the population as 554,172. Chayan Vaddhanaphuti, "The Thai State and Ethnic Minorities: From Assimilation to Selective Integration," in *Ethnic Conflict in Southeast Asia*, ed. Kusuma Snitwngse and W. Scott Thompson (Singapore: Institute of Southeast Asian Studies, 2005), 156.
109. Rachel M. Safman, "Minorities and State-Building in Mainland Southeast Asia," in *Myanmar: State, Society and Ethnicity*, ed. N. Ganesan and Kyaw Yin Klaing (Singapore: Institute of Southeast Asian Studies, 2007), 35.

110. Duncan McCargo, "Informal Citizens: Graduated Citizenship in Southern Thailand," *Ethnic and Racial Studies* 34, no. 5 (May 1, 2011): 833–49.
111. Pinkaew Laungaramsri, "Contested Citizenship: Cards, Colors, and the Culture of Identification," in *Ethnicity, Borders, and the Grassroots Interface with the State: Studies on Southeast Asia in Honor of Charles F. Keyes*, ed. John A. Marston (Chiang Mai, Thailand: Silkworm Books, 2014), 150.
112. Laungaramsri, 158.
113. Kathleen Gillogly, "Developing the 'Hill Tribes' of Northern Thailand," in *Civilizing the Margins: Southeast Asian Government Poicies for the Development of Minorities*, ed. Christopher R. Duncan (Ithaca, NY : Cornell University Press, 2004), 116.
114. Gillogly, 122.
115. Gillogly, 130.
116. Sinae Hyun, "Building a Human Border: The Thai Border Patrol Police School Project in the Post–Cold War Era," *Sojourn: Journal of Social Issues in Southeast Asia* 29, no. 2 (July 17, 2014): 342.
117. Sinae Hyun, "Mae Fah Luang: Thailand's Princess Mother and the Border Patrol Police during the Cold War," *Journal of Southeast Asian Studies* 48, no. 2 (June 2017): 262–82; Hyun, "Indigenizing the Cold War."
118. Ball, *Tor Chor Dor*, 116.

Chapter 8

1. Peng's open letter in Chinese can be accessed at http://www.backchina.com/forum/20150212/info-1270789-1-1.html.
2. Part of this chapter appeared in Enze Han, "Geopolitics, Ethnic Conflicts along the Border, and Chinese Foreign Policy Changes toward Myanmar," *Asian Security* 13, no. 1 (January 2, 2017): 59–73; See also Han, "Borderland Ethnic Politics and Changing Sino-Myanmar Relations."
3. On May 30, 2003, scores of NLD members died following an attack by military-backed thugs on a convoy traveling with Suu Kyi near Depayin in Central Burma Zarni Mann, "A Decade Later, Victims Still Seeking Depayin Massacre Justice," *The Irrawaddy*, May 31, 2013.
4. Kyaw Yin Klaing, "Understanding Recent Political Changes in Myanmar," *Contemporary Southeast Asia: A Journal of International & Strategic Affairs* 34, no. 2 (2012): 203.
5. Maung Aung Myoe, "The Soldier and the State: The Tatmadaw and Political Liberalization in Myanmar since 2011," *South East Asia Research* 22, no. 2 (June 1, 2014): 238.
6. Myoe, 238.
7. Aurel Croissant and Jil Kamerling, "Why Do Military Regimes Institutionalize? Constitution-Making and Elections as Political Survival Strategy in Myanmar," *Asian Journal of Political Science* 21, no. 2 (August 1, 2013): 119.
8. Dan Slater, "The Elements of Surprise: Assessing Burma's Double-Edged Détente," *South East Asia Research* 22, no. 2 (June 1, 2014): 171–82.
9. Marco Bünte, "Myanmar's Protracted Transition: Arenas, Actors, and Outcomes," *Asian Survey* 56, no. 2 (April 1, 2016): 369.

10. Bünte, 369.
11. Ian Holliday, "Ethnicity and Democratization in Myanmar," *Asian Journal of Political Science* 18, no. 2 (August 1, 2010): 118.
12. Lawi Weng, "Kokang Thwart Burma Army Drug Raid," *The Irrawaddy*, August 10, 2009.
13. Chin and Zhang, *The Chinese Heroin Trade*, 49.
14. Chris Buckley, "Myanmar Refugees Begin Warily Returning from China," *Reuters*, August 31, 2009.
15. Buckley.
16. Yee Mon and Lun Min Mang, "Ethnic Allies Join Kokang Fight," *Myanmar Times*, February 13, 2015.
17. Mon and Mang.
18. "Myanmar Announces Extension of State of Emergency in Kokang Region," *China Daily*, May 19, 2015.
19. "Government Troops 'Seize Last Stronghold of Kokang Rebels,'" *Mizzima*, May 16, 2015.
20. Echo Hui, "Tens of Thousands Flee War, Airstrikes in Kokang Region," *Democratic Voice of Burma*, February 12, 2015. For a documentary of the refugee exodus into China during the 2015 conflict, see Bing Wang, *Ta'ang*, Documentary, Chinese Shadows, 2016.
21. Burma News International, *Deciphering Myanmar's Peace Process: A Reference Guide 2013* (Chiang Mai, Thailand: Burma News International, 2013), 33.
22. Burma News International, 7.
23. "Burma Attack Breaks Kachin Truce Near China Border," *BBC News*, January 20, 2013.
24. "China 'Forcing Kachin Refugees Back to Burma,'" *BBC News*, August 24, 2012; Burma News International, *Deciphering Myanmar's Peace Process*, 7.
25. Jared Ferrie, "Myanmar Kachin Rebels Say 23 Cadets Killed by Army Shell," *Reuters*, November 20, 2014.
26. Burma News International, *Deciphering Myanmar's Peace Process*, 33.
27. Chan Mya Htwe, "Conflict Fears Leave Muse Trade Stilted," *Myanmar Times*, December 1, 2016.
28. Burma News International, *Deciphering Myanmar's Peace Process*, 21.
29. Interviews in Laiza, summer 2013.
30. "Kachin War a Battle for Resources," *Radio Free Asia*, August 31, 2012.
31. Naw Noreen, "Burmese Army Captures 3 Bases from Kachin Rebels," *Democratic Voice of Burma*, January 19, 2017.
32. "Work Resumes on China-Backed Pipelines," *Democratic Voice of Burma*, June 29, 2011.
33. "Experts Warns against Turning Shwe Pipeline on While Kachin Conflict Continues," *Kachin News*, April 1, 2013.
34. Brang Hkangda, "Motives Behind Offensive Operations in Mansi," *Kachinland News*, December 16, 2013.

35. "China-Backed Railway Expansion Stalls in Myanmar," *Voice of America*, August 1, 2014.
36. Libby Hogan, "Shan Groups Warn Salween Dam Could Fuel Conflict," *Democratic Voice of Burma*, August 24, 2016. On the suspended Myitsone dam, see Kiik, "Nationalism and Anti-Ethno-Politics."
37. Bertil Lintner, "The Ex-Pariah," *Politico Magazine*, March/April 2014.
38. David I. Steinberg and Hongwei Fan, *Modern China-Myanmar Relations: Dilemmas of Mutual Dependence* (Copenhagen: NIAS Press, 2012), 331–32.
39. On the other hand, moving the capital to Naypyidaw fits with Myanmar's historical tradition of having its capital in the central plains of the country's dry zone.
40. "Russia, China Veto UN Resolution on Burma," *Voice of America*, 1 November 2009.
41. Thomas Christensen, "Obama and Asia: Confronting the China Challenge," *Foreign Affairs* 94, no. 5 (September/October 2015): 28–36.
42. Min Zin, "Burmese Attitude toward Chinese."
43. Jürgen Haacke, *Myanmar: Now A Site for Sino-US Geopolitical Competition?* SR015 *LSE IDEAS* (London: London School of Economics and Political Science, 2012).
44. Scot Marciel, "Burma: Policy Review," *Diplomacy in Action*, US Department of State, 2009, https://2009-2017.state.gov/p/eap/rls/rm/2009/11/131536.htm.
45. Nehginpao Kipgen, "US–Burma Relations: Change of Politics under the Bush and Obama Administrations," *Strategic Analysis* 37, no. 2 (March 1, 2013): 203–16.
46. "Hilary Clinton in Historical Myanmar Visit," *The Telegraph*, November 30, 2011.
47. Andrew Buncombe, "Barack Obama Becomes First US President to Visit Burma, Meeting Aung San Suu Kyi and President Thein Sein," *Independent*, November 10, 2012.
48. Kurt Campbell and Brian Andrews, *Explaining the US "Pivot" to Asia* (London: Chatham House, The Royal Institute of International Affairs, 2013).
49. Personal interview, Kunming and Yangon, summer 2013.
50. Stephanie Shannon and Nicholas Farrelly, "Whither China's Myanmar Stranglehold?" in *ISEAS Perspective: Selections 2012–2013*, ed., Kee Beng Ooi (Singapore: ISEAS-Yusof Ishak Institute, 2014); Yun Sun, "China, Myanmar Face Myitsone Dam Truths," *Asia Times Online*, February 19, 2014.
51. Yun Sun, "China's Strategic Misjudgement on Myanmar," *Journal of Current Southeast Asian Affairs* 31, no. 1 (2012): 86.
52. Sun, "China's Strategic Misjudgement on Myanmar."
53. Yun Sun, "China, the United States and the Kachin Conflict," *Great Powers and The Changing Myanmar Issue Brief* (Washington, DC: Stimson Center, 2014).
54. Interviews with officials at the Chinese Embassy in Yangon, Myanmar, summer 2014. Previously the Chinese government handled part of its foreign policy consultation toward Myanmar at the provincial level, through Yunnan, especially regarding trade and other economic relations. After the perceived debacle in bilateral relations, Beijing reassumed direct control over diplomacy.
55. Sun, "China, Myanmar Face Myitsone Dam Truths."
56. Aung Hla Tun and Ben Blanchard, "China Reaches out to Myanmar's Suu Kyi," *Reuters*, December 15, 2011.

57. Patrick Boehler, "Thein Sein Talks Investment, Kachin Conflict during China Visit," *The Irrawaddy*, April 8, 2013.
58. "Myanmar President Meets Chinese Senior Military Official," *Xinhua*, July 24, 2013.
59. "Chinese President Meets Myanmar Defense Chief," *Xinhua*, October 17, 2013.
60. "Chinese Ambassador to Myanmar: Myanmar's Transition Won't Affect Overall Bilateral Relations with China (zhongguo zhumian dashi: miandian zhuanxing wuai zhongmian guanxi daju)," *China Youth Daily (zhongguo qingnian bao)*, January 28, 2014.
61. "Aung San Suu Kyi Arrives in China for First Visit," *BBC News*, June 10, 2015.
62. Sun Yun, *Chinese Investment in Myanmar: What Lies Ahead?* Issue Brief No. 1, Great Powers and the Changing Myanmar (Washington, DC: Stimson Center, 2013).
63. For the text in Chinese, see http://ec.chineseembassy.org/chn/fyrth/t581720.htm.
64. For the text in Chinese, see http://ir.china-embassy.org/chn/fyrth/t1002817.htm.
65. For the text in Chinese, see http://www.fmprc.gov.cn/ce/cedk/chn/fyrth/t1005817.htm.
66. For the text in Chinese, see http://www.fmprc.gov.cn/ce/cedk/chn/fyrth/t1006882.htm.
67. According to my interviews in Laiza and Yangon, Wang adopted a very demanding style at the negotiation table that put off the KIA representatives who felt he was lecturing them.
68. "MOFA: Stray Bombs from Myanmar's Conflict Landed in Chinese Territory, China Expressed Concern to Myanmar (waijiaobu: miandian chongtu liudan luoru zhongguo jingnei yixiang mianfang biaoda guanqie," *People's Daily Online (renminwang)*, March 10, 2015.
69. "Fan Changlong Demands Myanmar Strictly Control Its Troops, Otherwise China Will Take Action (Fan Changlong yaoqiu mianfang yange yuesu budui foze jiangcaiqu cuoshi)," *People's Daily Online (renmingwang)*, March 15, 2015.
70. "North Myanmar Peace Imperative for China," *Global Times*, February 16, 2015. *Global Times* had to clarify the difference between Kokang and Crimea because ultimately, the Chinese government does not want to be pressured into doing what Russia did to Crimea, thus risking being called "soft" by the more hardline nationalists.
71. For the text in Chinese, see http://lb.chineseembassy.org/chn/fyrth/t1245956.htm.
72. "Myanmar Cross-Border Bombing Kills Four, Draws Protest from China," *Radio Free Asia*, March 13, 2015.
73. "Myanmar Apologizes to China over Warplane Bombing," *Xinhuanet*, April 2, 2015.
74. "Myanmar Apologizes to China over Cross-Border Bombing," *Myanmar Times*, April 3, 2015.
75. Antoni Slodkowski, "Myanmar Signs Ceasefire with Eight Armed Groups," *Reuters*, October 15, 2015.
76. Burma News International, *Deciphering Myanmar's Peace Process: A Reference Guide 2016* (Chiang Mai, Thailand: Burma News International, 2017), 29–30.
77. Jens Wardenaer, "Myanmar: Progress at Panglong despite Obstacles," *IISS Voices*, September 6, 2016.

78. "State Councilor Says Not to Put Blame on Anyone over Wa Departure," *Mizzima*, September 2, 2016.
79. "NCA Non-Signatories Disavow Peace Accord, Seek Alternative Talks," *Democratic Voice of Burma*, February 27, 2017.
80. "NCA Non-Signatories Disavow Peace Accord, Seek Alternative Talks."
81. International Crisis Group, *Building Critical Mass for Peace in Myanmar* (Yangon, Myanmar; Brussels: International Crisis Group, June 29, 2017), 4.
82. "Northern Alliance Members Arrive in Naypyidaw for Peace Conference," *The Irrawaddy*, May 23, 2017.
83. "Union Peace Conference Achieves Agreement on the Majority of Points in Five Sectors," *Mizzima*, May 26, 2017.
84. International Crisis Group, *Building Critical Mass for Peace in Myanmar*, 10.
85. "Post-Panglong, Peace Challenges Remain," *Democratic Voice of Burma*, June 5, 2017.

Chapter 9

1. Pinkaew Laungaramsri, "Commodifying Sovereignty: Special Economic Zones and the Neoliberalization of the Lao Frontier," in *Impact of China's Rise on the Mekong Region*, ed. Yos Santasombat (New York: Palgrave Macmillan, 2015), 117–46.
2. The full text of the declaration can be accessed at the Chinese Ministry of Foreign Affairs website here http://www.fmprc.gov.cn/mfa_eng/wjdt_665385/2649_665393/t1350039.shtml.
3. Carl Middleton and Jeremy Allouche, "Watershed or Powershed? Critical Hydropolitics, China and the 'Lancang-Mekong Cooperation Framework,'" *The International Spectator* 51, no. 3 (2016): 111.
4. This has also been translated as Belt and Road Initiatives.
5. Guangsheng Lu, *China Seeks to Improve Mekong Sub-Regional Cooperation: Causes and Policies*, Policy Report (Singapore: S. Rajaratnam School of International Studies, Nanyang Technological University, 2016), 8.
6. Lu, 15.
7. Middleton and Allouche, "Watershed or Powershed?" 111.
8. Laura Zhu, "Five Things to Know about the Lancang-Mekong Cooperation Summit," *South China Morning Post*, January 9, 2018.
9. David Hutt, "China Flexes Its Control on the Mekong," *Asia Times*, January 11, 2018.
10. Hutt.
11. Pavin Chachavalpongpun, "The Necessity of Enemies in Thailand's Troubled Politics," *Asian Survey* 51, no. 6 (2011): 1019–41; Marc Askew, ed., *Legitimacy Crisis in Thailand*, no. 5 *King Prajadhipok's Institute Yearbook* (Nonthaburi; Chiang Mai, Thailand: King Prajadhipok's Institute, 2010).
12. Andrew MacGregor Marshall, *A Kingdom in Crisis: Thailand's Struggle for Democracy in the Twenty-First Century* (London: Zed Books, 2014); Pavin Chachavalpongpun, ed., *Good Coup Gone Bad: Thailand's Political Development Since Thaksin's Downfall*

(Singapore: Institute of Southeast Asian Studies, 2014); Federico Ferrara, *The Political Development of Modern Thailand* (Cambridge University Press, 2015).
13. "Thailand Welcomes China's Li as US Ties Cool over Coup," *Reuters*, December 18, 2014.
14. Pongphisoot Busbarat, "Thai–US Relations in the Post-Cold War Era: Untying the Special Relationship," *Asian Security* 13, no. 3 (September 2, 2017): 270.
15. Shawn W. Crispin, "Thai Coup Alienates US Giving China New Opening," Yale Global Online, March 5, 2015, https://yaleglobal.yale.edu/content/thai-coup-alienates-us-giving-china-new-opening.
16. Busbarat, "Thai–US Relations in the Post-Cold War Era," 265.
17. Busbarat, 269.
18. An opinion piece on the American Interest website does compare the United States getting Myanmar out of China's grasp with China getting Thailand out of United States' orbit. See "Is Thailand's Coup an Opening for China?" The American Interest (blog), May 23, 2014. https://www.the-american-interest.com/2014/05/23/is-thailands-coup-an-opening-for-china/.
19. Prashanth Parameswaran, "US, Thailand Launch 2016 Cobra Gold Military Exercises Amid Democracy Concerns," *The Diplomat*, September 2, 2016. https://thediplomat.com/2016/02/us-thailand-launch-2016-cobra-gold-military-exercises-amid-democracy-concerns/.
20. Rattaphol Onsanit, "Thailand's Prime Minister Finds Common Ground with Trump," VOA News, October 7, 2017.
21. Htet Naing Zaw, "Chinese Foreign Minister Promises Continued Support for Myanmar," *The Irrawaddy*, November 20, 2017.
22. The statement can be accessed here: https://www.un.org/press/en/2017/sc13055.doc.htm.
23. "China Resists Britain's Push for UN Statement in Probe on Myanmar's Rohingya Crisis," *The Guardian*, March 9, 2018.
24. K. S. Venkatachalam, "Can China Solve the Rohingya Crisis?" *The Diplomat*, December 2, 2017.
25. Mohd Aminul Karim and Faria Islam, "Bangladesh-China-India-Myanmar (BCIM) Economic Corridor: Challenges and Prospects," *The Korean Journal of Defense Analysis* 30, no. 2 (2018): 283–392.
26. Nan Lwin, "China, Myanmar Agree 15-Point MoU on Economic Corridor," *The Irrawaddy*, July 6, 2018.
27. "Gov't Inks Agreement with Chinese Firm to Develop Kyaukphyu SEZ," *The Irrawaddy*, November 8, 2018.
28. "China Plays Its Hand in Burma," *The Irrawaddy*, 23 May 2017.
29. International Crisis Group, *Building Critical Mass for Peace in Myanmar*, ii.
30. Bertil Lintner, "China Captures Myanmar's Peace Process," *Asia Times*, June 3, 2017.

Chinese Bibliography

Chinese Books and Journal Articles

Dong, Min, Huang Yingjie, Luo Mingcan, Liu Deqin. "Exploring the Sino-Burma Timber Trade (Zhongmian Mucai Maoyi Tanjiu)." *Issues of Forestry Economics* 36, no. 2 (2016): 143–7. / 董敏, 黄颖洁, 罗明灿, 刘德钦. "中缅木材贸易探究." 林业经济问题 36卷2期 (2016): 143–7.

Editorial Committee for Dehong Prefecture Gazette. *Select Materials of the CCP Party History in Dehong Prefecture*. Mangshi: Dehong Ethnic Press, 1989. / 德宏州史志编委办公室. 中共德宏州党史资料选编. 芒市:德宏民族出版社, 1989.

Editorial Committee for Xishuangbanna Dai Autonomous Prefecture Gazette. *Xishuangbanna Dai Autonomous Prefecture Gazette*. Beijing: Xinhua Press, 2002. / 西双版纳傣族自治州地方志编辑委员会. 西双版纳傣族自治州志. 北京:新华出版社, 2002.

European Forest Institute. *Summary Report on the Research Program of Sino-Myanmar Border Timber Trade* (中缅边境木材研究项目总结报告). European Forest Institute, n.d.

He, Shengda. "About Scientific Development and Several Problems Facing Yunnan's Opening Up in the New Period." *Social Sciences in Yunnan*, no. 2 (2007): 115–20. / 贺圣达."关于科学发展观和新时期云南对外开放的几个问题." 云南社会科学2期 (2007): 115–20.

Huang, Jiamo. *Western Yunnan's Muslim Government's Diplomatic Relations with Great Britain (1869–1874)*. Taipei: Academic Sinica, 2015. / 黄嘉谟, 滇西回民政权的联英外交(1869–1874). 台北:中央研究院近代史研究所, 2015.

Li, Chun-shan. "Wartime Transport Administration in Southwest China and the Burma Road (1938–1942)." *Academia Historica Journal*, no. 33 (2012): 57–88. / 李君山. "抗战时期西南运输的发展与困境-以滇缅公路为中心的探讨 (1938–1942)." 国史馆馆刊33期 (2012): 57–88.

Lim, Kwok Yong. "The Battle of Yunnan-Burma Road (Dec 1941–June 1942)." *Chung Cheng History Journal*, no. 19 (2016): 203–50. / 林国荣. "出国远征-滇缅路会战的进行与影响." 中正历史学刊19期 (2016): 203–50.

Liu, Xuan. "United Wa State Army in Myanmar: Origin, Development and Influence." *Indian Ocean Economic and Political Review*, no. 3 (2014): 71–93. / 刘璇, "缅甸瓦邦联合军：起源，发展及影响." 印度洋经济体研究3期 (2014): 71–93.

Liu, Yachao. "Gaitu Guiliu in the Yunnan Borderland during the Republican Period." *Journal of Yunnan Institute of the Nationalities*, no. 1 (1999): 63–69. / 刘亚朝, "民国在滇西边区的改土归流." 云南民族学院学报1期 (1999): 63–69.

Ma, Jianxiong. "'Luo Bandits' to 'Lahu Nationality': Ethnic Identity in the Process of Border Formation." *Historical Anthropology Journal* 2, no. 1 (2004): 1–32. / 马剑雄. "从'倮匪'到'拉祜族'-边疆化过程中的族群认同." 历史人类学学刊 2卷1期 (2004): 1–32.

Ma, Tingzhong. "Tentative Analysis of Yunnan's Ethnic Education Policies during the Republican Period." *Heilongjiang Ethnic Studies Journal*, no. 105 (2008): 178-82 / 马廷中. "浅析云南明国时期民族教育政策." 黑龙江民族丛刊105期 (2008): 178-82.

Qin, Yihui. *History of Blood and Tears of the Nationalist Army in the Golden Triangle*. Taipei: Academic Sinica and Lianjing Press, 2009. / 覃怡辉. 金三角国军血泪史. 台湾中央研究院和联经出版实业股份有限公司, 2009.

Wang, Shuhuai. *Muslim Rebellion in Yunnan during the Reigns of Xianfeng and Tongzhi*. Taipei: Academic Sinica, 1980. / 王树槐. 咸同云南回民事变. 台北:中央研究院近代史研究所, 1980.

Yang, Hongchang. *Yunnan Province and Mekong River Regional Cooperation: China's Locally Initiated Development*. Hong Kong: Hong Kong Asia Pacific Research Institute, Chinese University of Hong Kong, 2001. / 杨洪常. 云南省于湄公河区域合作:中国地方自主性的发展.香港:香港中文大学香港亚太研究所, 2001.

Yang, Wei-Chen. "Commercial Port, Railway and Cultural Interaction—A Case of Modern Yunnan." *Fujen History Journal*, no. 24 (2009): 93–115. / 杨维真. "商埠, 铁路, 文化交流-以近代云南为中心的探讨." 辅仁历史学报24期 (2009): 93–115.

Yao, Yong. "The Nationalization of Border and Borderland Citizens—The Tribunal System of Yunnan-Burma Border Cases between China and Great Britain." *Historical Anthropology Journal* 13, no. 1 (2015): 87–130. / 姚勇. "边境与边民的国家化-近代中英会审滇缅边案制度." 历史人类学学刊13卷1期 (2015): 87–130.

Zhang, Ning. "The Establishment of Zhengbian Subprefecture in Late Qing and Southwestern Borderland." Master's thesis, Fudan University, 2013. / 张宁, "清末镇边厅的设置与西南边疆." 复旦大学硕士论文, 2013.

Zhu, Qiang. "A Study of Tusi in Dehong and Frontier Governance in Republic of China." Master's thesis, Yunnan University, 2015. / 朱强. "民国时期的德宏土司与边疆治理研究." 云南大学硕士论文, 2015.

PRC Leaders' Speeches and Political Directives

The following selected speeches and political directives are from the "The History of Contemporary Chinese Political Movements" database compiled by the Chinese University of Hong Kong.

CCP Central Committee. "Directive to Southwest Bureau and Yunnan Provincial Committee on Religious Works in the Borderland Area." November 1952. / 中共中央. "中央关于边疆宗教工作给西南局和云南省委的指示." 1952年11月.

CCP Central Committee. "Directive to Southwest Bureau on Yunnan Province's Report on Guidance and Steps for Borderland Ethnic Works." December 6, 1952. 中共中央. "中央对西南局关于云南省委所报边疆民族工作方针与步骤的意见的批示." 1952年12月6日.

CCP Yunnan Province Party History Research Office. "Yunnan 'Cultural Revolution' Movement Events Chronicle." May 18, 2005. / 中共云南省委党史研究室. "云南'文化大革命'运动大事记实." 2005年5月18日.

He, Long, and Deng Xiaoping. "He, Deng, Zhang, Li's Comprehensive Report to Chairman Mao and the Military Commission regarding the Situation of Elimination of Bandits in 1950." January 6, 1951. 贺龙与邓小平. "贺邓张李关于50年剿匪情况向毛主席及军委的综合报告." 1951年1月6日.

Liu, Shaoqi. "CCP Central Committee Decree on Issues of Land Reform in Yunnan." June 16, 1952. / 刘少奇. "中央关于云南土改问题的指示." 1952年6月16日.

Luo, Ruiqing. "Resolutely Suppress Counterrevolutionaries: Report by Luo Ruiqing at Central Government Ministries Cadres Conference." April 4, 1951. / 罗瑞卿. "坚决镇压反革命：罗瑞卿在中央人民政府所属部门机关大会上的报告." 1951年4月4日。

Southwest Bureau of Public Security. "Southwest Bureau of Public Security's Report about the Current Situation and Future Opinions of the Southwest Suppression of Counterrevolutionaries for the Past Eight Months since the Fourth National Public Security Conference." July 21, 1952. / 西南公安部. "西南公安部关于第四次全国公安会议后八个月来西南镇反基本情况及今后意见的报告." 1952年7月21日.

Yan Hongyan. "Speech by Yunnan Province CCP First Secretary Yan Hongyan at Yunnan Province Borderland Works Conference." December 21, 1965. / 阎红彦. "在云南省边疆工作会议上的讲话：云南省委第一书记阎红彦." 1965年12月21日.

Yunnan Provincial Government. "Report to the CCP Central Committee on Current Borderland Situation and Problems of Borderland Reforms." November 16, 1954. 云南省委. "云南省委关于目前边疆情况和边疆改革问题向中央的报告." 1954年11月16日.

Chinese Newspapers

"American Imperialists are Colluding with the Counterrevolutionary Government of Luang Phibun to Carry out Plans to Support the KMT Bandits in Burma." *People's Daily*. June 22, 1951. / "美帝国主义勾结銮披汶反动政府，进行整编逃缅残匪阴谋计划." 人民日报. 1951年6月22日.

"Brutal Anti-Chinese Oppression by Luang Phibun's Government in Thailand." *People's Daily*. January 27, 1950. / "泰国銮披汶政府的排华罪行." 人民日报. 1950年1月27日.

"Chinese Ambassador to Myanmar: Myanmar's Transition Won't Affect Overall Bilateral Relations with China." *China Youth Daily*. January 28, 2014. / "中国驻缅大使：缅甸转型无碍中缅关系大格局." 中国青年报. 2014年1月28日.

"Dare to Sacrifice, Dare to Fight, and Dare to Succeed." *People's Daily*. March 21, 1969. / "敢于牺牲敢于斗争敢于胜利." 人民日报. 1969年3月21日.

"Fan Changlong Demands Myanmar Strictly Control Its Troops, Otherwise China Will Take Action." *People's Daily Online*. March 15, 2015. / "范长龙要求缅方严格约束部队否则将采取措施." 人民网. 2015年3月15日.

"Luang Phibun Is Increasingly Leaning toward the American Imperialists, and His Government Is Full of American Consultants." *People's Daily*. January 12, 1950. / "銮披汶日益投靠美帝，政府内充斥美国顾问." 人民日报. 1950年1月12日.

"MOFA: Stray Bombs from Myanmar's Conflict Landed in Chinese Territory, China Expressed Concern to Myanmar." *People's Daily Online*. March 10, 2015. / "外交部：缅甸冲突流弹落入中国境内 已向缅方表达关切." 人民网. 2015年3月10日.

"Red Guards in Beijing Angrily Denounce the Counter-Revolutionary Government of Ne Win." *People's Daily*. July 2, 1967. / "首都红卫兵愤怒声讨奈温反动政府." 人民日报. 1967年7月2日.

"Yunnan Province Experienced Many Sabotage Cases by Counterrevolutionaries in the Rural Areas." *Xinhua News Agency Internal Reference*. May 17, 1954. / "云南省农村发生反革命分子破坏案件多起." 新华社内部参考. 1954年5月17日.

Thai Bibliography

Chitbundid, Chanida. *The Royal Projects: The Making of King Bhumibol's Royal Hegemony*. Bangkok: The Foundation of the Promotion of Social Science and Humanities Textbooks Project, 2007. / ชนิดา ชิตบัณฑิตย์, **โครงการอันเนื่องมาจากพระราชดำริ: การสถาปนาพระราชอำนาจนำในพระบาทสมเด็จพระเจ้าอยู่หัว** (กรุงเทพฯ: มูลนิธิโครงการตำราสังคมศาสตร์และมนุษยศาสตร์, 2550).

Mulamek, Akni. *Shan State: History and Revolution*. Bangkok: Matichon Book, 2005. / อัคนี มูลเมฆ, **รัฐฉาน: ประวัติศาสตร์และการปฏิวัติ**, (กรุงเทพฯ: สำนักพิมพ์มติชน, 2548).

Santasombat, Yos. *Power, Space, and Ethnic Identities: Political Culture of the Nation-State in Thai Society*. Bangkok: Princess Maha Chakri Sirindhorn Anthropology Center, 2008. / ยศ สันตสมบัติ, **อำนาจ พื้นที่ และอัตลักษณ์ทางชาติพันธุ์: การเมืองวัฒนธรรมของรัฐชาติในสังคมไทย** (กรุงเทพฯ: ศูนย์มานุษยวิทยาสิรินธร, 2551).

Sittan, R., S. Boonplook, and S. Warit. *The Communist Party of Thailand Today*. Bangkok: Krung Siam Publishing, 1980. / สิทธานต์ รักษ์ประเทศ, บุญปลูก ส่วนพงษ์ และ วฤทธิ์ ชินสาย, **พรรคคอมมิวนิสต์แห่งประเทศไทยวันนี้** (กรุงเทพฯ: สำนักพิมพ์กรุงสยาม, 2523).

Sodsuk, Narumit. *History of the People's Republic of China until the Four Modernizations: Effects on the Thai Communist Party*. Bangkok: Odeon Store, 1994. / นฤมิตร สอดสุข, **ประวัติศาสตร์สาธารณรัฐประชาชนจีนจนถึงยุคสี่ทันสมัย: ผลกระทบต่อ พคท.** (กรุงเทพฯ: โอเดียนสโตร์, 2537).

Trichot, Pornpimol. *Thai Policy on Repatriation of Displaced Persons from Myanmar*. Bangkok: Institute of Asian Studies, Chulalongkorn University, 2004. / พรพิมล ตรีโชติ, **นโยบายส่งกลับผู้พลัดถิ่นจากพม่าของไทย** (กรุงเทพฯ: สถาบันเอเชียศึกษา จุฬาลงกรณ์มหาวิทยาลัย, 2547).

Trichot, Pornpimol. *Myanmar Foreign Policy in the Ethnic Minority Context and its Impact on the Thai-Myanmar Relationship*. Bangkok: Institute of Asian Studies, Chulalongkorn University, 2006. / พรพิมล ตรีโชติ, **การดำเนินนโยบายต่างประเทศของพม่าในส่วนสัมพันธ์กับชนกลุ่มน้อยและผลกระทบต่อความสัมพันธ์ไทย-พม่า** (กรุงเทพฯ: สถาบันเอเชียศึกษา จุฬาลงกรณ์มหาวิทยาลัย, 2549).

Vijirakorn, Amporn. *History beyond the Nation State: 55 Years of the Shan Resistance Movement*. Chiang Mai, Thailand: Chiang Mai University Regional Center for Social Science and Sustainable Development, 2015. / อัมพร จิรัฐติกร, **ประวัติศาสตร์นอกกรอบรัฐชาติ: 55 ปี ขบวนการกู้ชาติไทใหญ่** (เชียงใหม่: ศูนย์ศึกษาชาติพันธุ์และการพัฒนา คณะสังคมศาสตร์ มหาวิทยาลัยเชียงใหม่, 2558).

Burmese Bibliography

State Law and Order Restoration Council (SLORC) and State Peace and Development Council (SPDC). *Development and Prosperity for Myanmar*. Vols. I–IV. / နိုင်ငံတော်ငြိမ်ဝပ်ပိပြားမှု တည်ဆောက်ရေးအဖွဲ့ ။ နိုင်ငံတော်အေးချမ်းသာယာရေးနှင့် ဖွံ့ဖြိုးရေးကောင်စီ။ တိုင်းကျိုးပြည်ပြု (အတွဲ ၁-၄)။

Zhang, Jianzhang. *Experiences at the Communist Party of Burma*. Translated by Wakema Mann Phoe Aye. Yangon, Myanmar: Journalist Publishing, 2016. / ကျမ်းကျိန်ကျန်း (ဘာသာပြန်ဆိုသူ - မန်းဖိုးအေး၊ ဂါးခယ်မ)။ ဗမာပြည်ကွန်မြူနစ်ပါတီ ခရီးကြမ်း ။ ရန်ကုန်၊ မြန်မာ - ဂျာနယ်လစ် စာပေ။ ၂၀၁၆။

Zin Htet et al. *That's Why It Happened: The Communist Party of Burma on the Northeast Mountain Ranges*. Yangon, Myanmar: Lwin Oo Book Publishing House, 2015. / ရဲဘော်ဇင်ထက်၊ ထွန်းသိန်း၊ အောင်မင်း၊ ဗိုလ်မှူးကြီးဟောင်း စန်းပွင့် ။ ထို့ကြောင့် ဤသို့ (အရှေ့မြောက်တောင်တန်းများပေါ်က ဗမာပြည်ကွန်မြူနစ်ပါတီ) ။ ရန်ကုန်၊ မြန်မာ - လွင်ဦးစာပေ။ ၂၀၁၅။

English Bibliography

Abhakorn, M. R. Rujaya. "Changes in the Administrative Systems of Northern Siam, 1884–1933." In *Changes in Northern Thailand and the Shan States 1886–1940*, edited by Prakai Nontawasee, 63–108. Singapore: Institute of Southeast Asian Studies, 1988.

Acemoglu, Daron, and James Robinson. *Why Nations Fail: The Origins of Power, Prosperity, and Poverty*. New York: Crown Business, 2013.

Alesina, Alberto, Arnaud Devleeschauwer, William Easterly, Sergio Kurlat, and Romain Wacziarg. "Fractionalization." *Journal of Economic Growth* 8, no. 2 (2003): 155–94.

Alesina, Alberto, and Eliana La Ferrara. "Participation in Heterogeneous Communities." *The Quarterly Journal of Economics* 115, no. 3 (August 1, 2000): 847–904.

Amnesty International. "'All the Civilians Suffer': Conflict, Displacement, and Abuse in Northern Myanmar." London: Amnesty International, 2017.

Anderson, Benedict. "Murder and Progress in Modern Siam." *New Left Review*, I, no. 181 (1990): 33–48.

Andreas, Peter. *Border Games: Policing the U.S.-Mexico Divide*. 2nd ed. Ithaca, NY: Cornell University Press, 2009.

Ang, Cheng Guan. "The Domino Theory Revisited: The Southeast Asia Perspective." *War & Society* 19, no. 1 (May 1, 2001): 109–30.

Asian Development Bank. *Assessing Impact in the Greater Mekong Subregion: An Analysis of Regional Cooperation Projects*. Mandaluyong City, Philippines: Asian Development Bank, 2014.

Askew, Marc, ed. *Legitimacy Crisis in Thailand*. No. 5. King Prajadhipok's Institute Yearbook. Chiang Mai, Thailand, 2010.

Atwill, David. *The Chinese Sultanate: Islam, Ethnicity, and the Panthay Rebellion in Southwest China, 1856–1873*. Stanford, CA: Stanford University Press, 2005.

Aung, Winston Set. *The Role of Informal Cross-Border Trade in Myanmar*. Asia Papers Series. Singapore: Institute for Security & Development Policy, 2009.

Aung-Thwin, Michael, and Maitrii Aung-Thwin. *A History of Myanmar since Ancient Times: Traditions and Transformations*. London: Reaktion Books, 2013.

Autesserre, Séverine. *The Trouble with the Congo: Local Violence and the Failure of International Peacebuilding*. Cambridge, UK; New York: Cambridge University Press, 2010.

Baker, Chris. "An Internal History of the Communist Party of Thailand." *Journal of Contemporary Asia* 33, no. 4 (January 1, 2003): 510–41.

Ball, Desmond. *Tor Chor Dor: Thailand's Border Patrol Police*. Vol. 1. *History, Organisation, Equipment and Personnel*. 2 vols. Bangkok, Thailand: White Lotus Press, 2013.

Bandyopadhyaya, Kalyani. *Burma and Indonesia: Comparative Political Economy and Foreign Policy*. New Delhi: South Asian Publishers, 1983.

Bello, David A. "To Go Where No Han Could Go for Long: Malaria and the Qing Construction of Ethnic Administrative Space in Frontier Yunnan." *Modern China* 31, no. 3 (2005): 283–317.

Bernstein, Arthur M. *Up to the Mountains and Down to the Villages: Transfer of Youth from Urban to Rural China*. New Haven, CT: Yale University Press, 1977.

Bhattacharya, S. "Burma: Neutralism Introverted." *The Australian Quarterly* 37, no. 1 (1965): 50–61.

Boone, Catherine. *Political Topographies of the African State: Territorial Authority and Institutional Choice*. Cambridge, UK; New York: Cambridge University Press, 2003.

———. *Property and Political Order in Africa: Land Rights and the Structure of Politics*. New York: Cambridge University Press, 2014.

Borchert, Thomas. "The Abbot's New House: Thinking about How Religion Works among Buddhists and Ethnic Minorities in Southwest China." *Journal of Church and State* 52, no. 1 (2010): 112–37.

———. "Worry for the Dai Nation: Sipsongpannā, Chinese Modernity, and the Problems of Buddhist Modernism." *Journal of Asian Studies* 67, no. 1 (2008): 107–42.

Bresnan, John. *From Dominoes to Dynamos: The Transformation of Southeast Asia*. New York: Council on Foreign Relations, 1994.

Brubaker, Rogers. *Nationalism Reframed: Nationhood and the National Question in the New Europe*. Cambridge, UK; New York: Cambridge University Press, 1996.

Buchanan, John, Tom Kramer, and Kevin Woods. "Developing Disparity: Regional Investment in Burma's Borderlands." Amsterdam: Transnational Institute (TNI), 2013.

Buhaug, Halvard, and Jan Ketil Rød. "Local Determinants of African Civil Wars, 1970–2001." *Political Geography* 25, no. 3 (March 2006): 315–35.

Bünte, Marco. "Myanmar's Protracted Transition: Arenas, Actors, and Outcomes." *Asian Survey* 56, no. 2 (April 1, 2016): 369–91.

Burma News International. *Deciphering Myanmar's Peace Process: A Reference Guide 2013*. Chiang Mai, Thailand: Burma News International, 2013.

———. *Deciphering Myanmar's Peace Process: A Reference Guide 2015*. Chiang Mai, Thailand: Burma News International, 2015.

———. *Deciphering Myanmar's Peace Process: A Reference Guide 2016*. Chiang Mai, Thailand: Burma News International, 2017.

Busbarat, Pongphisoot. "Thai–US Relations in the Post-Cold War Era: Untying the Special Relationship." *Asian Security* 13, no. 3 (September 2, 2017): 256–74.

Callahan, Mary P. *Making Enemies: War and State Building in Burma*. Ithaca, NY: Cornell University Press, 2005.

———. *Political Authority in Burma's Ethnic Minority States: Devolution, Occupation, and Coexistence*. Singapore: Institute of Southeast Asian Studies; Washington, DC: East-West Center Washington, 2007.

Campbell, Kurt, and Brian Andrews. *Explaining the US "Pivot" to Asia*. London: Chatham House, The Royal Institute of International Affairs, 2013.

Cederman, Lars-Erik, Nils B. Weidmann, and Kristian Skrede Gleditsch. "Horizontal Inequalities and Ethnonationalist Civil War: A Global Comparison." *American Political Science Review* 105, no. 3 (August 2011): 478–95.

Centeno, Miguel A., and Agustin E. Ferraro, eds. *State and Nation Making in Latin America and Spain: Republics of the Possible*. Reprint. Cambridge, UK: Cambridge University Press, 2014.

Centeno, Miguel Angel. *Blood and Debt: War and the Nation-State in Latin America*. University Park, PA: Penn State University Press, 2002.

Centeno, Miguel Angel, and Fernando López-Alves, eds. *The Other Mirror*. Princeton, NJ: Princeton University Press, 2001.

Chachavalpongpun, Pavin. *A Plastic Nation: The Curse of Thainess in Thai-Burmese Relations.* Lanham, MD: University Press of America, 2005.

———, ed. *Good Coup Gone Bad: Thailand's Political Development Since Thaksin's Downfall.* Singapore: Institute of Southeast Asian Studies, 2014.

———. "The Necessity of Enemies in Thailand's Troubled Politics." *Asian Survey* 51, no. 6 (2011): 1019–41.

Chakravarti, Nalini Ranjan. *Indian Minority in Burma: Rise and Decline of an Immigrant Community.* London; New York: Oxford University Press, 1971.

Chaloemtiarana, Thak. *Thailand: The Politics of Despotic Paternalism.* 1st ed. Ithaca, NY: Cornell Southeast Asia Program Publications, 2007.

Chang, Wen-Chin. *Beyond Borders: Stories of Yunnanese Chinese Migrants of Burma.* Ithaca, NY: Cornell University Press, 2014.

———. "The Everyday Politics of the Underground Trade in Burma by the Yunnanese Chinese since the Burmese Socialist Era." *Journal of Southeast Asian Studies* 44, no. 2 (June 2013): 292–314.

———. "Venturing into 'Barbarous' Regions: Transborder Trade among Migrant Yunnanese between Thailand and Burma, 1960s–1980s." *Journal of Asian Studies* 68, no. 2 (2009): 543–72.

Chansiri, Disaphol. *The Chinese Émigrés of Thailand in the Twentieth Century.* Youngstown, NY: Cambria Press, 2008.

Chapman, E. C. "The Expansion of Rubber in Southern Yunnan, China." *The Geographical Journal* 157, no. 1 (1991): 36–44.

Charoenmuang, Thanet. "When the Young Cannot Speak Their Own Mother Tongue: Explaining A Legacy of Cultural Domination in Lan Na." In *Regions and National Integration in Thailand 1892-1992*, edited by Volker Grabowsky, 82–93. Wiesbaden: Harrassowitz Verlag, 1995.

Cheesman, Nick. "How in Myanmar 'National Races' Came to Surpass Citizenship and Exclude Rohingya." *Journal of Contemporary Asia* 47, no. 3 (May 27, 2017): 461–83.

Chen, Jian. *Mao's China and the Cold War.* Chapel Hill: University of North Carolina Press, 2001.

Chen, Jie. "Shaking off an Historical Burden: China's Relations with the ASEAN-Based Communist Insurgency in Deng's Era." *Communist and Post-Communist Studies* 27, no. 4 (December 1, 1994): 443–62.

Chere, Lewis Milton. *Diplomacy of the Sino-French War 1883-85: Global Complications of an Undeclared War.* Notre Dame, IN: Cross Cultural Publications, 1989.

Chin, Ko-Lin. *The Golden Triangle: Inside Southeast Asia's Drug Trade.* 1st ed. Ithaca, NY: Cornell University Press, 2009.

Chin, Ko-lin, and Sheldon X. Zhang. *The Chinese Heroin Trade: Cross-Border Drug Trafficking in Southeast Asia and Beyond.* New York; London: New York University Press, 2015.

Chin, Peng. *Alias Chin Peng—My Side of History.* Singapore: Media Masters, 2003.

Christensen, Thomas. "Obama and Asia: Confronting the China Challenge." *Foreign Affairs* 94, no. 5 (September/October, 2015): 28–36.

Chutima, Gawin. "The Rise and the Fall of the Communist Party of Thailand (1973-1987)." Occasional Paper No. 12. Center of South-East Asian Studies, University of Kent at Canterbury, 1990.

Clymer, Kenton. *A Delicate Relationship: The United States and Burma/Myanmar since 1945.* 1st ed. Ithaca, NY: Cornell University Press, 2015.

Coleman, M. "U.S. Statecraft and the U.S.–Mexico Border as Security/Economy Nexus." *Political Geography* 24, no. 2 (February 2005): 185–209.
Communist Party of Thailand. *The Road to Victory: Documents from the Communist Party of Thailand.* Chicago: Liberator Press, n.d.
Connors, Michael Kelly. *Democracy and National Identity in Thailand.* Rev. ed. Copenhagen: NIAS Press, 2006.
Conway, Susan. "Shan Tribute Relations in the Nineteenth Century." *Contemporary Buddhism* 10, no. 1 (May 1, 2009): 31–37.
———. *The Shan: Culture, Arts and Crafts.* Bangkok: River Books, 2006.
Cooper, Robert George. *Resource Scarcity and the Hmong Response: Patterns of Settlement and Economy in Transition.* Singapore: Singapore University Press, National University of Singapore, 1984.
Croissant, Aurel, and Jil Kamerling. "Why Do Military Regimes Institutionalize? Constitution-Making and Elections as Political Survival Strategy in Myanmar." *Asian Journal of Political Science* 21, no. 2 (August 1, 2013): 105–25.
Crossley, Pamela Kyle. *A Translucent Mirror: History and Identity in Qing Imperial Ideology.* Berkeley: University of California Press, 2000.
Daniels, Christian. "Chieftains into Ancestors: Imperial Expansion and Indigenous Society in Southwest China." *The China Journal*, no. 73 (January 2015): 232–35.
Darden, Keith, and Anna Grzymala-Busse. "The Great Divide: Literacy, Nationalism, and the Communist Collapse." *World Politics* 59, no. 1 (October 2006): 83–115.
Darling, Frank Clayton. *Thailand and the United States.* Washington, DC: Public Affairs Press, 1965.
Dean, Karin. "Spaces and Territorialities on the Sino–Burmese Boundary: China, Burma and the Kachin." *Political Geography* 24, no. 7 (September 2005): 808–30.
Deaton, Angus. *The Great Escape: Health, Wealth, and the Origins of Inequality.* Princeton, NJ: Princeton University Press, 2013.
Diana, Antonella. "Re-Configuring Belonging in Post-Socialist Xishuangbanna, China." In *Tai Lands and Thailand: Community and State in Southeast Asia*, edited by Andrew Walker, 163–80. Honolulu, HI: University of Hawai'i Press, 2009.
Diehl, Paul, and Gary Goertz. *War and Peace in International Rivalry.* Ann Arbor, MI: University of Michigan Press, 2001.
Dikötter, Frank. *The Cultural Revolution: A People's History, 1962–1976.* London: Bloomsbury Paperbacks, 2017.
Dittmer, Lowell, ed. *Burma or Myanmar? The Struggle for National Identity.* Singapore; Hackensack, NJ: World Scientific Publishing Company, 2010.
Doner, Richard F. *The Politics of Uneven Development: Thailand's Economic Growth in Comparative Perspective.* Cambridge, UK; New York: Cambridge University Press, 2009.
Doner, Richard F., Bryan K. Ritchie, and Dan Slater. "Systemic Vulnerability and the Origins of Developmental States: Northeast and Southeast Asia in Comparative Perspective." *International Organization* 59, no. 2 (April 2005): 327–61.
Doran, David, Matthew Christensen, and Thida Aye. "Hydropower in Myanmar: Sector Analysis and Related Legal Reforms." *The International Journal of Hydropower & Dams* 21, no. 3 (2014): 87–91.
Downing, Brian. *The Military Revolution and Political Change: Origins of Democracy and Autocracy in Early Modern Europe.* Princeton, NJ: Princeton University Press, 1992.

Eberle, Meghan L., and Ian Holliday. "Precarity and Political Immobilisation: Migrants from Burma in Chiang Mai, Thailand." *Journal of Contemporary Asia* 41, no. 3 (August 1, 2011): 371–92.
Egreteau, Renaud. "Burmese Indians in Contemporary Burma: Heritage, Influence, and Perceptions since 1988." *Asian Ethnicity* 12, no. 1 (February 1, 2011): 33–54.
Elliott, Mark C. *The Manchu Way: The Eight Banners and Ethnic Identity in Late Imperial China*. Stanford, CA: Stanford University Press, 2001.
Ertman, Thomas. *Birth of the Leviathan: Building States and Regimes in Medieval and Early Modern Europe*. Cambridge, UK; New York: Cambridge University Press, 1997.
Ettinger, Glenn. "Thailand's Defeat of Its Communist Party." *International Journal of Intelligence and CounterIntelligence* 20, no. 4 (August 20, 2007): 661–77.
Fan, Hongwei. "The 1967 Anti-Chinese Riots in Burma and Sino-Burmese Relations." *Journal of Southeast Asian Studies* 43, no. 2 (June 2012): 234–56.
Fearon, James D. "Ethnic and Cultural Diversity by Country." *Journal of Economic Growth* 8, no. 2 (June 2003): 195–222.
Fearon, James D., and David D. Laitin. "Ethnicity, Insurgency, and Civil War." *American Political Science Review* 97, no. 1 (February 2003): 75–90.
Ferguson, Jane M. "Ethno-Nationalism and Participation in Myanmar: Views from Shan State and Beyond." In *Metamorphosis: Studies in Social and Political Change in Myanmar*, edited by Renaud Egreteau and Francois Robinne, 127–50. Singapore: NUS Press, 2016.
———. "Is the Pen Mightier than the AK-47? Tracking Shan Women's Militancy Within and Beyond." *Intersections: Gender and Sexuality in Asia and the Pacific*, no. 33 (2013). http://intersections.anu.edu.au/issue33/ferguson.htm.
———. "Revolutionary Scripts: Shan Insurgent Media Practice at the Thai-Burma Border." In *Political Regimes and the Media in Asia*, edited by Krishna Sen and Terence Lee, 106–21. London: New York: Routledge, 2008.
———. "Who's Counting? Ethnicity, Belonging, and the National Census in Burma/Myanmar." *Bijdragen Tot de Taal-, Land- En Volkenkunde* 171, no. 1 (2015): 1–28.
Ferrara, Federico. *The Political Development of Modern Thailand*. Cambridge, UK: Cambridge University Press, 2015.
Fineman, Daniel. *A Special Relationship: The United States and Military Government in Thailand, 1947–1958*. 1st ed. Honolulu, HI: University of Hawai'i Press, 1997.
Fiskesjö, Magnus. "Mining, History, and the Anti-State Wa: The Politics of Autonomy between Burma and China." *Journal of Global History* 5, no. 2 (July 2010): 241–64.
———. "People First: The Wa World of Spirits and Other Enemies." *Anthropological Forum* 27, no. 4 (April 19, 2017): 340–64.
Fitzgerald, Stephen. *China and the Overseas Chinese: A Study of Peking's Changing Policy: 1949–1970*. Cambridge, UK: Cambridge University Press, 1972.
Fleischmann, Klaus. *Documents on Communism in Burma, 1945–1977*. Hamburg: Institut für Asienkunde, 1989.
Fong, Jack. "Sacred Nationalism: The Thai Monarchy and Primordial Nation Construction." *Journal of Contemporary Asia* 39, no. 4 (November 1, 2009): 673–96.
Forest Trends. *Analysis of Sino-Myanmar Timber Trade (Zhongmian Mucai Maoyi Fenxi)*. Policy Brief. Forest Trends, 2014.
Fukuyama, Francis. *State Building: Governance and World Order in the Twenty-First Century*. London: Profile Books, 2004.

Gelb, Stephen, Linda Calabrese, and Xiaoyang Tang. *Foreign Direct Investment and Economic Transformation in Myanmar*. London: Supporting Economic Transformation, Overseas Development Institute, 2017. https://www.odi.org/publications/10774-foreign-direct-investment-and-economic-transformation-myanmar.

Gibson, Richard Michael, and Wen H. Chen. *The Secret Army: Chiang Kai-Shek and the Drug Warlords of the Golden Triangle*. Singapore: Wiley, 2011.

Giersch, C. Patterson. *Asian Borderlands: The Transformation of Qing China's Yunnan Frontier*. Cambridge, MA: Harvard University Press, 2006.

———. "The Sipsong Panna Tai and the Limits of Qing Conquest in Yunnan." *Chinese Historians* 10, no. 1–2 (October 1, 2000): 71–92.

Gillogly, Kathleen. "Developing the 'Hill Tribes' of Northern Thailand." In *Civilizing the Margins: Southeast Asian Government Policies for the Development of Minorities*, edited by Christopher R. Duncan, 116–49. Ithaca, NY: Cornell University Press, 2004.

Gladney, Dru C. "Representing Nationality in China: Refiguring Majority/Minority Identities." *Journal of Asian Studies* 53, no. 1 (1994): 92–123.

Glassman, Jim. "On the Borders of Southeast Asia: Cold War Geography and the Construction of the Other." *Political Geography* 24, no. 7 (September 2005): 784–807.

———. "Recovering from Crisis: The Case of Thailand's Spatial Fix." *Economic Geography* 83, no. 4 (2007): 349–70.

———. *Thailand at the Margins: Internationalization of the State and the Transformation of Labour*. London and New York: Oxford University Press, 2004.

Gleditsch, Kristian Skrede. *All International Politics Is Local: The Diffusion of Conflict, Integration, and Democratization*. Ann Arbor: University of Michigan Press, 2002.

———. "Transnational Dimensions of Civil War." *Journal of Peace Research* 44, no. 3 (2007): 293–309.

Global Witness. "Jade: Myanmar's 'Big State Secret,'" 2015. https://www.globalwitness.org/en/campaigns/oil-gas-and-mining/myanmarjade/.

Goodman, David S. G. "The Campaign to 'Open up the West': National, Provincial-Level and Local Perspectives." *The China Quarterly*, no. 178 (2004): 317–34.

Goss, Jasper, and David Burch. "From Agricultural Modernisation to Agri-Food Globalisation: The Waning of National Development in Thailand." *Third World Quarterly* 22, no. 6 (December 1, 2001): 969–86.

Gravers, Mikael. "Introduction: Ethnicity against State—State against Ethnic Diversity?" In *Exploring Ethnic Diversity in Burma*, edited by Mikael Gravers, 1–33. Copenhagen: NIAS Press, 2007.

———. *Nationalism as Political Paranoia in Burma: An Essay on the Historical Practice of Power*. London: Routledge, 1999.

Grundy-Warr, Carl, and Elaine Wong Siew Yin. "Geographies of Displacement: The Karenni and the Shan Across the Myanmar-Thailand Border." *Singapore Journal of Tropical Geography* 23, no. 1 (March 1, 2002): 93–122.

Guo, Xiaolin. *State and Ethnicity in China's Southwest*. Leiden; Boston: Brill, 2008.

Haacke, Jürgen. *Myanmar: Now a Site for Sino-US Geopolitical Competition?* SR015 LSE IDEAS. London: London School of Economics and Political Science, 2012.

Hall, D. G. E. *History of South East Asia*. London: Macmillan, 1981.

Han, Enze. "Bifurcated Homeland and Diaspora Politics in China and Taiwan towards the Overseas Chinese in Southeast Asia." *Journal of Ethnic and Migration Studies* 45, no. 4 (2019): 577–94.

———. "Borderland Ethnic Politics and Changing Sino-Myanmar Relations." In *War and Peace in the Borderlands of Myanmar: The Kachin Ceasefire, 1994–2011*, edited by Mandy Sadan, 149–68. Copenhagen: NIAS Press, 2016.

———. *Contestation and Adaptation: The Politics of National Identity in China*. New York; London: Oxford University Press, 2013.

———. "From Domestic to International: The Politics of Ethnic Identity in Xinjiang and Inner Mongolia." *Nationalities Papers* 39, no. 6 (November 1, 2011): 941–62.

———. "Geopolitics, Ethnic Conflicts along the Border, and Chinese Foreign Policy Changes toward Myanmar." *Asian Security* 13, no. 1 (January 2, 2017): 59–73.

———. "Transnational Ties, HIV/AIDS Prevention and State-Minority Relations in Sipsongpanna, Southwest China." *Journal of Contemporary China* 22, no. 82 (2013): 594–611.

Han, Enze, and Christopher Paik. "Dynamics of Political Resistance in Tibet: Religious Repression and Controversies of Demographic Change." *The China Quarterly*, no. 217 (2014): 69–98.

———. "Ethnic Integration and Development in China." *World Development* 93 (May 1, 2017): 31–42.

Hansen, Mette Halskov. *Lessons in Being Chinese: Minority Education and Ethnic Identity in Southwest China*. Seattle: University of Washington Press, 1999.

Harrell, Stevan. "Introduction: Civilizing Projects and the Reaction to Them." In *Cultural Encounters on China's Ethnic Frontiers*, edited by Stevan Harrell, 3–36. Seattle: University of Washington Press, 1995.

Heberer, Thomas. *China and Its National Minorities: Autonomy or Assimilation*. Armonk, NY: Routledge, 1989.

Herbst, Jeffrey. *States and Power in Africa: Comparative Lessons in Authority and Control*. 1st ed. Princeton, NJ: Princeton University Press, 2000.

———. "War and the State in Africa." *International Security* 14, no. 4 (1990): 117–39.

Herman, John. *Amid the Clouds and Mist: China's Colonization of Guizhou, 1200–1700*. Cambridge, MA: Harvard University Asia Center, 2007.

———. "Collaboration and Resistance on the Southwest Frontier: Early Eighteenth-Century Qing Expansion on Two Fronts." *Late Imperial China* 35, no. 1 (2014): 77–112.

Hiro, Dilip. *The Longest War: The Iran-Iraq Military Conflict*. London: Routledge, 1990.

Ho, Elaine Lynn-Ee. "Mobilising Affinity Ties: Kachin Internal Displacement and the Geographies of Humanitarianism at the China–Myanmar Border." *Transactions of the Institute of British Geographers* 42, no. 1 (March 1, 2017): 84–97.

Ho, Ts'ui-p'ing. "People's Diplomacy and Borderland History through the Chinese Jingpo Manau Zumko Festival." In *War and Peace in the Borderlands of Myanmar: The Kachin Ceasefire, 1994–2011*, edited by Mandy Sadan, 169–201. Copenhagen: NIAS Press, 2016.

Hobsbawm, E. J. *Nations and Nationalism Since 1780: Programme, Myth, Reality*. Cambridge, UK: New York: Cambridge University Press, 1990.

Holliday, Ian. "Addressing Myanmar's Citizenship Crisis." *Journal of Contemporary Asia* 44, no. 3 (July 3, 2014): 404–21.

———. "Ethnicity and Democratization in Myanmar." *Asian Journal of Political Science* 18, no. 2 (August 1, 2010): 111–28.

Holmes, Robert A. "Burmese Domestic Policy: The Politics of Burmanization." *Asian Survey* 7, no. 3 (1967): 188–97.

Hooghe, Ingrid d'. "Regional Economic Integration in Yunnan." In *China Deconstructs: Politics, Trade and Regionalism*, edited by David S. G. Goodman and Gerald Segal, 286–321. London: New York: Routledge, 1994.

Horowitz, Donald L. *Ethnic Groups in Conflict*. Berkeley: University of California Press, 1985.

Hsieh, Shi-Chung. "Ethnic-Political Adaptation and Ethnic Change of the Sipsong Panna Dai: An Ethnohistorical Analysis." PhD diss., University of Washington, 1989.

Hui, Victoria Tin-bor. *War and State Formation in Ancient China and Early Modern Europe*. New York: Cambridge University Press, 2005.

Hyun, Sinae. "Building a Human Border: The Thai Border Patrol Police School Project in the Post–Cold War Era." *Sojourn: Journal of Social Issues in Southeast Asia* 29, no. 2 (July 17, 2014): 332–63.

———. "Indigenizing the Cold War: Nation-Building by the Border Patrol Police in Thailand, 1945–1980." PhD diss., University of Wisconsin-Madison, 2014.

———. "Mae Fah Luang: Thailand's Princess Mother and the Border Patrol Police during the Cold War." *Journal of Southeast Asian Studies* 48, no. 2 (June 2017): 262–82.

International Crisis Group. *Building Critical Mass for Peace in Myanmar*. Yangon/Brussels: International Crisis Group, 2017.

Israeli, Raphael. *Islam in China: Religion, Ethnicity, Culture, and Politics*. Lanham, MD: Lexington Books, 2002.

Jain, R. K., ed. *China and Thailand, 1949–83*. New Delhi: Radiant Publishers, 1984.

James, Helen. "Myanmar's International Relations Strategy: The Search for Security." *Contemporary Southeast Asia* 26, no. 3 (2004): 530–53.

Jelsma, Martin, Tom Kramer, and Pietje Vervest, eds. *Trouble in the Triangle: Opium and the Conflict in Burma*. Chiang Mai, Thailand: Silkworm Books, 2005.

Jirattikorn, Amporn. "Aberrant Modernity: The Construction of Nationhood among Shan Prisoners in Thailand." *Asian Studies Review* 36, no. 3 (September 1, 2012): 327–43.

———. "'Pirated' Transnational Broadcasting: The Consumption of Thai Soap Operas among Shan Communities in Burma." *Sojourn: Journal of Social Issues in Southeast Asia* 23, no. 1 (2008): 30–62.

———. "Shan Virtual Insurgency and the Spectatorship of the Nation." *Journal of Southeast Asian Studies* 42, no. 1 (2011): 17–38.

Jones, Lee. "The Political Economy of Myanmar's Transition." *Journal of Contemporary Asia* 44, no. 1 (February 1, 2014): 144.

———. "Understanding Myanmar's Ceasefires: Geopolitics, Political Economy and State-Building." In *War and Peace in the Borderlands of Myanmar: The Kachin Ceasefire, 1994–2011*, edited by Mandy Sadan, 95–113. Copenhagen: NIAS Press, 2016.

Kampan, Palapan. "Standing Up to Giants: Thailand's Exit from 20th Century War Partnerships." *Asian Social Science* 10, no. 15 (August 2014): 153–68.

Karim, Mohd Aminul, and Faria Islam. "Bangladesh-China-India-Myanmar (BCIM) Economic Corridor: Challenges and Prospects." *The Korean Journal of Defense Analysis* 30, no. 2 (2018): 283–392.

Kathman, Jacob D. "Civil War Contagion and Neighboring Interventions." *International Studies Quarterly* 54, no. 4 (2010): 989–1012.

Keyes, Charles F. "Buddhism and National Integration in Thailand." *Journal of Asian Studies* 30, no. 3 (1971): 551–67.

Kiik, Laur. "Conspiracy, God's Plan and National Emergency: Kachin Popular Analyses of the Ceasefire Era and Its Resource Grabs." In *War and Peace in the Borderlands* of Myanmar: The Kachin Ceasefire, 1994-2011, edited by Mandy Sadan, 205-35. Copenhagen: NIAS Press, 2016.

———. "Nationalism and Anti-Ethno-Politics: Why 'Chinese Development' Failed at Myanmar's Myitsone Dam." *Eurasian Geography and Economics* 57, no. 3 (May 3, 2016): 374-402.

Kingston, Lindsey N. "Protecting the World's Most Persecuted: The Responsibility to Protect and Burma's Rohingya Minority." *The International Journal of Human Rights* 19, no. 8 (November 17, 2015): 1163-75.

Kipgen, Nehginpao. "US–Burma Relations: Change of Politics under the Bush and Obama Administrations." *Strategic Analysis* 37, no. 2 (March 1, 2013): 203-16.

Kiser, Edgar, and Yong Cai. "War and Bureaucratization in Qin China: Exploring an Anomalous Case." *American Sociological Review* 68, no. 4 (2003): 511-39.

Kiser, Edgar, and April Linton. "Determinants of the Growth of the State: War and Taxation in Early Modern France and England." *Social Forces* 80, no. 2 (2001): 411-48.

———. "The Hinges of History: State-Making and Revolt in Early Modern France." *American Sociological Review* 67, no. 6 (2002): 889-910.

Krainara, Choen, and Jayant K. Routray. "Cross-Border Trades and Commerce between Thailand and Neighboring Countries: Policy Implications for Establishing Special Border Economic Zones." *Journal of Borderlands Studies* 30, no. 3 (July 3, 2015): 345-63.

Kramer, Tom, Ernestien Jensema, Martin Jelsma, and Tom Blickman. *Bouncing Back: Relapse in the Golden Triangle*. Amsterdam: Transnational Institute (TNI), 2014.

Krasner, Stephen D. *Structural Conflict: Third World Against Global Liberalism*. Berkeley: University of California Press, 1985.

Kuah, Khun Eng. "Negotiating Central, Provincial, and County Policies: Border Trading in South China." In *Where China Meets Southeast Asia: Social & Cultural Change in the Border Regions*, edited by Grant Evans, Christopher Hutton, and Kuah Khun Eng, 72-97. Singapore: Institute of Southeast Asian Studies, 2000.

Kubo, Koji. "Myanmar's Cross-Border Trade with China: Beyond Informal Trade." Discussion Papers 625. Institute of Developing Economies, Japan External Trade Organization, 2016.

Kudo, Toshihiro. "Myanmar's Economic Relations with China: Can China Support the Myanmar Economy." Discussion Papers 066. Institute of Developing Economies, Japan External Trade Organization, 2006.

Kyaw Yin Klaing. "Understanding Recent Political Changes in Myanmar." *Contemporary Southeast Asia: A Journal of International & Strategic Affairs* 34, no. 2 (2012): 197-216.

Lacina, Bethany. "Explaining the Severity of Civil Wars." *Journal of Conflict Resolution* 50, no. 2 (2006): 276-89.

Lahpai, Seng Maw. "State Terrorism and International Compliance: The Kachin Armed Struggle for Political Self-Determination." In *Debating Democratization in Myanmar*, edited by Nick Cheesman, Nicholas Farrelly, and Trevor Wilson, 285-304. Singapore: ISEAS Publishing, 2014.

Latt, Sai S. W. "More Than Culture, Gender, and Class: Erasing Shan Labor in the 'Success' of Thailand's Royal Development Project." *Critical Asian Studies* 43, no. 4 (December 1, 2011): 531-50.

Laungaramsri, Pinkaew. "Commodifying Sovereignty: Special Economic Zones and the Neoliberalization of the Lao Frontier." In *Impact of China's Rise on the Mekong Region*, edited by Yos Santasombat, 117-46. New York: Palgrave Macmillan, 2015.

---. "Contested Citizenship: Cards, Colors, and the Culture of Identification." In *Ethnicity, Borders, and the Grassroots Interface with the State: Studies on Southeast Asia in Honor of Charles F. Keyes*, edited by John A. Marston, 143–62. Chiang Mai: Silkworm Books, 2014.

---. "Ethnicity and the Politics of Ethnic Classification in Thailand." In *Ethnicity in Asia*, edited by Colin Mackerras. London: RoutledgeCurzon, 2003.

---. "Women, Nation, and the Ambivalence of Subversive Identification along the Thai-Burmese Border." *Sojourn: Journal of Social Issues in Southeast Asia* 21, no. 1 (April 1, 2006): 68–89.

Leach, Edmund R. *Political Systems Of Highland Burma: A Study Of Kachin Social Structure*. London: Bell, 1964.

Lee, Melissa. "The International Politics of Incomplete Sovereignty: How Hostile Neighbors Weaken the State." *International Organization* 72, no. 2 (2018) : 283–315.

Lee, Sang Kook. "Behind the Scenes: Smuggling in the Thailand-Myanmar Borderland." *Pacific Affairs* 88, no. 4 (December 1, 2015): 767–90.

Leibold, James. *Ethnic Policy in China: Is Reform Inevitable?* Washington, DC: East-West Center, 2013.

---. "Positioning 'Minzu' within Sun Yat-Sen's Discourse of Minzuzhuyi." *Journal of Asian History* 38, no. 2 (2004): 163–213.

Lieberman, Victor B. "Reinterpreting Burmese History." *Comparative Studies in Society and History* 29, no. 1 (January 1987): 162–94.

Liew-Herres, Foon Ming, Volker Grabowsky, and Renoo Wichasin. *Chronicle of Sipsong Panna: History and Society of a Tai Lu Kingdom*. Chiang Mai, Thailand: Silkworm Books, 2012.

Lin, Hsiao-ting. *Modern China's Ethnic Frontiers: A Journey to the West*. Abingdon, UK; New York: Routledge, 2010.

Lintner, Bertil. *Burma in Revolt: Opium and Insurgency since 1948*. 2nd ed. Chiang Mai, Thailand: Silkworm Books, 1999.

---. "Recent Developments on the Thai-Burma Border." *IBRU Boundary and Security Bulletin* 3, no. 1 (April 1995): 72–76.

---. *The Rise and Fall of the Communist Party of Burma (CPB)*. Ithaca, NY: Southeast Asia Program, Department of Asian Studies, Cornell University, 1990.

Lintner, Bertil, and Michael Black. *Merchants of Madness: The Methamphetamine Explosion in the Golden Triangle*. Chiang Mai, Thailand: Silkworm Books, 2009.

Lovelace, Daniel Dudley. *China and "People's War" in Thailand, 1964–1969*. No. 8. *China Research Monographs*. Berkeley: Center for Chinese Studies, University of California, 1971.

Lovell, Julia. *The Opium War: Drugs, Dreams and the Making of China*. London: Picador, 2012.

Lu, Guangsheng. *China Seeks to Improve Mekong Sub-Regional Cooperation: Causes and Policies*. Singapore: S. Rajaratnam School of International Studies, Nanyang Technological University, 2016.

Ma, Jianxiong. "Salt and Revenue in Frontier Formation: State Mobilized Ethnic Politics in the Yunnan-Burma Borderland since the 1720s." *Modern Asian Studies* 48, no. 6 (November 2014): 1637–69.

Macfarquhar, Roderick, and Michael Schoenhals. *Mao's Last Revolution*. Cambridge, MA: Harvard University Press, 2006.

Mackerras, Colin. *China's Minorities: Integration and Modernization in the Twentieth Century*. Hong Kong; New York: Oxford University Press, 1994.

Mallet, Marian. "Causes and Consequences of the October '76 Coup." *Journal of Contemporary Asia* 8, no. 1 (January 1, 1978): 80–103.

Mangrai, Saimong. *The Padaeng Chronicle and the Jengtung State Chronicle Translated*. Ann Arbor: University of Michigan, Center for South and Southeast Asian Studies, 1981.

Marciel, Scot. "Burma: Policy Review." Diplomacy in Action. United States Department of State, 2009.

Marks, Tom. *Making Revolution: The Insurgency of the Communist Party of Thailand in Structural Perspective*. Bangkok, Thailand: White Lotus Press, 1994.

Marshall, Andrew MacGregor. *A Kingdom in Crisis: Thailand's Struggle for Democracy in the Twenty-First Century*. London: Zed Books, 2014.

Marx, Anthony W. *Faith in Nation: Exclusionary Origins of Nationalism*. Oxford; New York: Oxford University Press, 2003.

Masviriyakul, Siriluk. "Sino-Thai Strategic Economic Development in the Greater Mekong Subregion (1992–2003)." *Contemporary Southeast Asia* 26, no. 2 (2004): 302–19.

Maung Aung Myoe. *In the Name of Pauk-Phaw: Myanmar's China Policy since 1948*. Singapore: Institute of Southeast Asian Studies ; London, 2011.

———. "The Soldier and the State: The Tatmadaw and Political Liberalization in Myanmar since 2011." *South East Asia Research* 22, no. 2 (June 1, 2014): 233–49.

Maung Maung. *Grim War Aganist KMT*. 2nd ed. Yangon, Myanmar: Seikku Cho Cho Publishing House, 2013.

McCargo, Duncan. "Informal Citizens: Graduated Citizenship in Southern Thailand." *Ethnic and Racial Studies* 34, no. 5 (May 1, 2011): 833–49.

———. *Tearing Apart the Land: Islam and Legitimacy in Southern Thailand*. Ithaca, NY: Cornell University Press, 2008.

McCarthy, Susan. *Communist Multiculturalism: Ethnic Revival in Southwest China*. Seattle: University of Washington Press, 2009.

McCoy, Alfred W. *The Politics of Heroin: CIA Complicity in the Global Drug Trade*. 1st ed. Brooklyn, NY: Lawrence Hill Books, 1991.

McLynn, Frank. *The Burma Campaign: Disaster into Triumph 1942-45*. London: Vintage, 2011.

Meehan, Patrick. "Fortifying or Fragmenting the State? The Political Economy of the Opium/Heroin Trade in Shan State, Myanmar, 1988–2013." *Critical Asian Studies* 47, no. 2 (April 3, 2015): 253–82.

Middleton, Carl, and Jeremy Allouche. "Watershed or Powershed? Critical Hydropolitics, China and the 'Lancang-Mekong Cooperation Framework.'" *The International Spectator* 51, no. 3 (2016): 100–117.

Min, Brian. *Power and the Vote: Elections and Electricity in the Developing World*. New York: Cambridge University Press, 2015.

Min Zin. "Burmese Attitude toward Chinese: Portrayal of the Chinese in Contemporary Cultural and Media Works." *Journal of Current Southeast Asian Affairs* 31, no. 1 (January 1, 2012): 115–31.

Montalvo, Jose G., and Marta Reynal-Querol. "Ethnic Diversity and Economic Development." *Journal of Development Economics* 76, no. 2 (April 2005): 293–323.

Mueller, John E. "Presidential Popularity from Truman to Johnson." *The American Political Science Review* 64, no. 1 (1970): 18–34. https://doi.org/10.2307/1955610.

Mullaney, Thomas. *Coming to Terms with the Nation: Ethnic Classification in Modern China*. Berkeley: University of California Press, 2010.

Murashima, Eiji. "The Commemorative Character of Thai Historiography: The 1942–43 Thai Military Campaign in the Shan States Depicted as a Story of National Salvation and the Restoration of Thai Independence." *Modern Asian Studies* 40, no. 4 (2006): 1053–96.

———. "The Thai-Japanese Alliance and The Overseas Chinese in Thailand." In *Southeast Asian Minorities in the Wartime Japanese Empire*, edited by Paul H. Kratoska, 192–223. Oxford: RoutledgeCurzon, 2005.

Murphy, Ann Marie. "Beyond Balancing and Bandwagoning: Thailand's Response to China's Rise." *Asian Security* 6, no. 1 (January 22, 2010): 1–27.

Muscat, Robert J. *The Fifth Tiger: Study of Thai Development Policy*. Armonk, NY: M.E. Sharpe, 1994.

Mya Than. "Myanmar's Cross-Border Economic Relations and Cooperation with the People's Republic of China and Thailand in the Great Mekong Subregion." *Journal of GMS Development Studies* 2 (2005): 37–54.

Mylonas, Harris. *The Politics of Nation Building: Making Co-Nationals, Refugees, and Minorities*. New York: Cambridge University Press, 2013.

Nemoto, Kei. "The Concepts of Dobama ('Our Burma') and Thudo-Bama ('Their Burma') in Burmese Nationalism, 1930–1948." *Journal of Burma Studies* 5, no. 1 (March 30, 2011): 1–16.

Nyíri, Pál. "Reorientation: Notes on the Rise of the PRC and Chinese Identities in Southeast Asia." *Southeast Asian Journal of Social Science* 25, no. 2 (1997): 161–82.

OECD. *OECD Investment Policy Reviews: Myanmar 2014*. Paris: OECD Publishing, 2014.

Olson, James Stuart, and Randy W. Roberts. *Where the Domino Fell: America and Vietnam 1945–2010*. 6th ed. Chichester, UK: Wiley-Blackwell, 2013.

Østby, Gudrun. "Polarization, Horizontal Inequalities and Violent Civil Conflict." *Journal of Peace Research* 45, no. 2 (2008): 143–62.

Parameswaran, Prashanth. "US, Thailand Launch 2016 Cobra Gold Military Exercises Amid Democracy Concerns." *The Diplomat*, September 2, 2016.

Park, Joy K. "A Global Crisis Writ Large: The Effects of Being 'Stateless in Thailand' on Hill-Tribe Children." *San Diego International Law Journal* 10, no. 2 (March 22, 2009): 495.

Parnini, Syeda Naushin. "The Crisis of the Rohingya as a Muslim Minority in Myanmar and Bilateral Relations with Bangladesh." *Journal of Muslim Minority Affairs* 33, no. 2 (June 1, 2013): 281–97.

Perdue, Peter C. *China Marches West: The Qing Conquest of Central Eurasia*. Cambridge, MA: Harvard University Press, 2005.

Perera, Suda. "Alternative Agency: Rwandan Refugee Warriors in Exclusionary States." *Conflict, Security & Development* 13, no. 5 (December 1, 2013): 569–88.

Perry, Elizabeth J. "Rural Violence in Socialist China." *The China Quarterly*, no. 103 (1985): 414–40.

Platt, Stephen R. *Autumn in the Heavenly Kingdom: China, the West, and the Epic Story of the Taiping Civil War*. New York: Vintage Books, 2012.

Postiglione, Gerard A., ed. *China's National Minority Education: Culture, Schooling, and Development*. New York: Falmer Press, 1999.

Rajchagool, Chaiyan. *The Rise and Fall of the Thai Absolute Monarchy*. Bangkok, Thailand: White Lotus Press, 1994.

Ramsay, James Ansil. "Modernization and Centralization in Northern Thailand, 1875–1910." *Journal of Southeast Asian Studies* 7, no. 1 (March 1976): 16–32.

Randolph, R. S., and W. Scott Thompson. *Thai Insurgency: Contemporary Developments*. Beverly Hills; London: Sage Publications, 1981.

Ratanaporn, Sethakul. "Political, Social, and Economic Changes in the Northern States of Thailand from the Chiang Mai Treaties of 1874 and 1883." PhD diss., Northern Illinois University, 1989.

Ratchasomphan, Saenluang. *The Nan Chronicle*. Translated by David K. Wyatt. Ithaca, NY: Southeast Asia Program, Cornell University, 1994.

Renard, Ronald D. "Social Change in the Shan States under the British, 1886–1942." In *Changes in Northern Thailand and the Shan States 1886–1940*, edited by Prakai Nontawasee, 109–47. Singapore: Institute of Southeast Asian Studies, 1988.

Reynolds, Bruce. "Phibun Songkhram and Thai Nationalism in the Fascist Era." *European Journal of East Asian Studies* 3, no. 1 (2004): 99–134.

Rigger, Shelley. "Nationalism versus Citizenship in the Republic of China on Taiwan." In *Changing Meanings of Citizenship in Modern China*, edited by Merie Goldman and Elizabeth Perry, 353–74. Cambridge, MA: Harvard University Press, 2002.

Ritharom, Chatri. "The Making of the Thai–U.S. Military Alliance and the SEATO Treaty of 1954: A Study in Thai Decision-Making." PhD diss., Claremont Graduate School, 1976.

Rock, Michael T. *Dictators, Democrats, and Development in Southeast Asia: Implications for the Rest*. New York: Oxford University Press, 2016.

Rossi, Amalia. "Turning Red Rural Landscapes Yellow? Sufficiency Economy and Royal Projects in the Hills of Nan Province, Northern Thailand." *Austrian Journal of South-East Asian Studies* 5, no. 2 (December 30, 2012): 275–91.

Sadan, Mandy. *Being and Becoming Kachin: Histories Beyond the State in the Borderworlds of Burma*. Oxford: British Academy, 2013.

———, ed. *The War and Peace in the Borderlands of Myanmar: The Kachin Ceasefire, 1994–2011*. Copenhagen: NIAS Press, 2016.

Safman, Rachel M. "Minorities and State-Building in Mainland Southeast Asia." In *Myanmar: State, Society and Ethnicity*, edited by N. Ganesan and Kyaw Yin Klaing, 30–69. Singapore: Institute of Southeast Asian Studies, 2007.

Sai Aung Tun. *History of the Shan State: From Its Origins to 1962*. Chiang Mai, Thailand: Silkworm Books, 2009.

Salehyan, Idean. "Transnational Rebels: Neighboring States as Sanctuary for Rebel Groups." *World Politics* 59, no. 2 (2007): 217–42.

Salehyan, Idean, and Kristian Skrede Gleditsch. "Refugees and the Spread of Civil War." *International Organization* 60, no. 2 (April 2006): 335–66.

Sambanis, Nicholas. "Do Ethnic and Nonethnic Civil Wars Have the Same Causes?" *Journal of Conflict Resolution* 45, no. 3 (June 2001): 259–82.

Samudavanija, Chai-anan. "State-Identity Creation, State-Building and Civil Society, 1939–1989." In *National Identity and Its Defenders: Thailand Today*, edited by Craig J. Reynolds, 59–85. Chiang Mai, Thailand: Silkworm Books, 2002.

Santasombat, Yos. *Lak Chang: A Reconstruction of Tai Identity in Daikong*. Canberra: Australian National University Press, 2011.

Satawedin, Dhanasarit. "Thai-American Alliance during the Laotian Crisis, 1959–1962: A Case Study of the Bargaining Power of a Small State." PhD diss., Northern Illinois University, 1984.

Sautman, Barry. "Ethnic Law and Minority Rights in China: Progress and Constraints." *Law & Policy* 21, no. 3 (July 1, 1999): 283–314.

———. "Preferential Policies for Ethnic Minorities in China: The Case of Xinjiang." *Nationalism and Ethnic Politics* 4, no. 1–2 (March 1, 1998): 86–118.

Schendel, Willem van. "Geographies of Knowing, Geographies of Ignorance: Jumping Scale in Southeast Asia." *Environment and Planning D: Society & Space* 20, no. 6 (2002): 647–68.

Schoenhals, Michael. "Cultural Revolution on the Border: Yunnan's 'Political Frontier Defence.'" *The Copenhagen Journal of Asian Studies*, no. 19 (2004): 27–54.

Scott, James C. *Seeing Like a State: How Certain Schemes to Improve the Human Condition Have Failed*. New Haven, CT: Yale University Press, 1999.

———. *The Art of Not Being Governed: An Anarchist History of Upland Southeast Asia*. New Haven, CT: Yale University Press, 2009.

Setakun, Rattanaporn. "History of Chiang Tung." In *Things about Chiang Tung*, edited by Arunrat Vichiankiew and Narumon Ruangrangsi. Chiang Mai: Suriwongs Book Center, 1994.

Shan Women's Action Network and Shan Human Rights Foundation. *License to Rape: The Burmese Military Regime's Use of Sexual Violence in the Ongoing War in Shan State*. Chiang Mai: Shan Human Rights Foundation, 2002.

Shannon, Stephanie, and Nicholas Farrelly. "Whither China's Myanmar Stranglehold?" In *ISEAS Perspective: Selections 2012–2013*, edited by Kee Beng Ooi, 26–36. Singapore: ISEAS-Yusof Ishak Institute, 2014.

Shao, Dan. "Chinese by Definition: Nationality Law, Jus Sanguinis, and State Succession." *Twentieth-Century China* 35, no. 1 (2009): 4–28.

Silverstein, J. *Burmese Politics: The Dilemma of National Unity*. New Brunswick, NJ: Rutgers University Press, 1980.

Sirikrai, Surachai. "Thai-American Relations in the Laotian Crisis of 1960–1962." PhD diss., State University of New York, 1979.

Skinner, G. William. *Chinese Society in Thailand. An Analytical History*. Ithaca, NY: Cornell University Press, 1962.

Skinner, George William. *Chinese Society in Thailand An Analytical History*. Ithaca, NY: Cornell University Press, 1957.

Slater, Dan. "The Elements of Surprise: Assessing Burma's Double-Edged Détente." *South East Asia Research* 22, no. 2 (June 1, 2014): 171–82.

Smith, John Sterling Forssen. *The Chiang Tung Wars: War and Politics in Mid-19th Century Siam and Burma*. Bangkok: Institute of Asian Studies, Chulalongkorn University, 2013.

Smith, Martin. *Burma: Insurgency and the Politics of Ethnic Conflict*. London: Zed Books, 1999.

———. "Reflections on the Kachin Ceasefire: A Cycle of Hope and Disappointment." In *War and Peace in the Borderlands of Myanmar: The Kachin Ceasefire, 1994–2011*, edited by Mandy Sadan, 57–91. Copenhagen: NIAS Press, 2016.

———. *State of Strife: The Dynamics of Ethnic Conflict in Burma*. Washington, DC: East-West Center Press, 2007.

Sng, Jeffery, and Pimpraphai Bisalputra. *A History of the Thai-Chinese*. Singapore: Editions Didier Millet, 2015.

Solinger, Dorothy J. "Politics in Yunnan Province in the Decade of Disorder: Elite Factional Strategies and Central-Local Relations, 1967–1980." *The China Quarterly*, no. 92 (1982): 628–62.

———. *Regional Government and Political Integration in Southwest China 1949–1954: A Case Study*. Berkeley: University of California Press, 1977.

Soonthornpasuch, Suthep. "Socio-Cultural, and Political Change in Northern Siam: The Impact of Western Colonial Expansion (1850–1932)." In *Changes in Northern Thailand and the Shan States 1886–1940*, edited by Prakai Nontawasee, 148–74. Singapore: Institute of Southeast Asian Studies, 1988.

South, Ashley. *Ethnic Politics in Burma: States of Conflict*. London; New York: Routledge, 2008.

South, Ashley, and Kim Jolliffe. "Forced Migration: Typology and Local Agency in Southeast Myanmar." *Contemporary Southeast Asia: A Journal of International & Strategic Affairs* 37, no. 2 (August 2015): 211–41.

Steinberg, David I. *Burma: The State of Myanmar*. Washington, DC: Georgetown University Press, 2001.

Steinberg, David I., and Hongwei Fan. *Modern China-Myanmar Relations: Dilemmas of Mutual Dependence*. Copenhagen: NIAS Press, 2012.

Steiner, Zara. *The Triumph of the Dark: European International History 1933–1939*. Oxford; New York: Oxford University Press, 2013.

Stewart, Frances, ed. *Horizontal Inequalities and Conflict: Understanding Group Violence in Multiethnic Societies*. Basingstoke, UK; New York: Palgrave Macmillan, 2008.

Strate, Shane. *The Lost Territories: Thailand's History of National Humiliation*. Honolulu, HI: University of Hawai'i Press, 2015.

Strauss, Julia C. "Paternalist Terror: The Campaign to Suppress Counterrevolutionaries and Regime Consolidation in the People's Republic of China, 1950–1953." *Comparative Studies in Society and History* 44, no. 1 (2002): 80–105.

Stubbs, Richard. "War and Economic Development: Export-Oriented Industrialization in East and Southeast Asia." *Comparative Politics* 31, no. 3 (1999): 337–55.

Sturgeon, Janet C. *Border Landscapes: The Politics of Akha Land Use in China and Thailand*. Seattle: University of Washington Press, 2005.

———. "Cross-Border Rubber Cultivation between China and Laos: Regionalization by Akha and Tai Rubber Farmers." *Singapore Journal of Tropical Geography* 34, no. 1 (March 1, 2013): 70–85.

Sturgeon, Janet C., and Nicholas Menzies. "Ideological Landscapes: Rubber in Xishuangbanna, Yunnan, 1950 to 2007." *Asian Geographer* 25, no. 1–2 (January 1, 2006): 21–37.

Sturgeon, Janet C., Nicholas K. Menzies, Yayoi Fujita Lagerqvist, David Thomas, Benchaphun Ekasingh, Louis Lebel, Khamla Phanvilay, and Sithong Thongmanivong. "Enclosing Ethnic Minorities and Forests in the Golden Economic Quadrangle." *Development and Change* 44, no. 1 (January 1, 2013): 53–79.

Su, Xiaobo. "Development Intervention and Transnational Narcotics Control in Northern Myanmar." *Geoforum* 68, Supplement C (January 1, 2016): 10–20.

———. "From Frontier to Bridgehead: Cross-Border Regions and the Experience of Yunnan, China." *International Journal of Urban and Regional Research* 37, no. 4 (July 1, 2013): 1213–32.

———. "Nontraditional Security and China's Transnational Narcotics Control in Northern Laos and Myanmar." *Political Geography* 48 (September 2015): 72–82.

Summers, Tim. *Yunnan—A Chinese Bridgehead to Asia: A Case Study of China's Political and Economic Relations with Its Neighbours*. Oxford: Chandos Publishing, 2013.

Sun, Yun. "China, Myanmar Face Myitsone Dam Truths." *Asia Times Online*, February 19, 2014.

———. "China, the United States and the Kachin Conflict." Issue Brief. *Great Powers and The Changing Myanmar*. Washington, DC: Stimson Center, 2014.

———. "China's Strategic Misjudgement on Myanmar." *Journal of Current Southeast Asian Affairs* 31, no. 1 (2012): 73.

Supin, Ritpen. *The Princesses of Mangrai-Kengtung (Chao Nang)*. Chiang Mai: Tai Ethnic Art and Culture Center, Thakradat Temple, 2013.

Taylor, Robert H. "British Policy and the Shan States, 1886–1942." In *Changes in Northern Thailand and the Shan States 1886–1940*, edited by Prakai Nontawasee, 13–62. Singapore: Institute of Southeast Asian Studies, 1988.

———. *Foreign and Domestic Consequences of the KMT Intervention in Burma*. Ithaca, NY: Southeast Asia Program, Dept of Asian Studies, Cornell University, 1973.

———. *The State in Myanmar*. London: C Hurst & Co Publishers Ltd, 2008.

Tejapira, Kasian. *Commodifying Marxism: The Formation of Modern Thai Radical Culture, 1927–1958*. Kyoto, Japan; Melbourne, Australia; Portland, OR: Trans Pacific Press, 2001.

Thies, Cameron G. "Of Rulers, Rebels, and Revenue: State Capacity, Civil War Onset, and Primary Commodities." *Journal of Peace Research* 47, no. 3 (2010): 321–32.

———. "State Building, Interstate and Intrastate Rivalry: A Study of Post-Colonial Developing Country Extractive Efforts, 1975–2000." *International Studies Quarterly* 48, no. 1 (March 1, 2004): 53–72.

———. "The Political Economy of State Building in Sub-Saharan Africa." *Journal of Politics* 69, no. 3 (2007): 716–31.

———. "War, Rivalry, and State Building in Latin America." *American Journal of Political Science* 49, no. 3 (July 1, 2005): 451–65.

Thomas, M. Ladd. "Communist Insurgency in Thailand: Factors Contributing to Its Decline." *Asian Affairs* 13, no. 1 (1986): 17–26.

Thompson, William R. "Identifying Rivals and Rivalries in World Politics." *International Studies Quarterly* 45, no. 4 (December 1, 2001): 557–86.

Thornton, Patricia M., Peidong Sun, and Chris Berry, eds. *Red Shadows*. Vol. 12. *Memories and Legacies of the Chinese Cultural Revolution*. Cambridge, UK: Cambridge University Press, 2017.

Tian, Qunjian. "China Develops Its West: Motivation, Strategy and Prospect." *Journal of Contemporary China* 13, no. 41 (November 1, 2004): 611–36.

Tilly, Charles. *Coercion, Capital and European States: AD 990–1992*. Cambridge, MA: Wiley-Blackwell, 1992.

———, ed. *The Formation of National States in Western Europe*. 1st ed. Princeton, NJ: Princeton University Press, 1975.

———. "War Making and State Making as Organized Crime." In *Bringing the State Back In*, edited by Dietrich Reuschmeyer, Theda Skocpol, and Peter Evans, 169–91. Cambridge, UK: Cambridge University Press, 1985.

Tin Maung Maung Than. *State Dominance in Myanmar: The Political Economy of Industrialization*. Singapore: ISEAS Publishing, 2007.

Tinker, Hugh. *The Union of Burma: A Study of The First Years of Independence*. London: Oxford University Press, 1967.

To, James Jiann Hua. *Qiaowu: Extra-Territorial Policies for the Overseas Chinese*. Leiden: Brill Academic Publishers, 2014.

Toft, Monica Duffy. *The Geography of Ethnic Violence: Identity, Interests, and the Indivisibility of Territory*. Princeton, NJ: Princeton University Press, 2005.

Tollefsen, Andreas Forø, and Halvard Buhaug. "Insurgency and Inaccessibility." *International Studies Review* 17, no. 1 (March 1, 2015): 6–25.
Tsuneishi, Takao. "Border Trade and Economic Zones on the North-South Economic Corridor: Focusing on the Connecting Points between the Four Countries." Discussion Papers 205. Institute of Developing Economies, Japan External Trade Organization, 2009.
———. "Development of Border Economic Zones in Thailand:Expansion of Border Trade and Formation of Border Economic Zones." Discussion Papers 153. Institute of Developing Economies, Japan External Trade Organization, 2008.
———. "The Regional Development Policy of Thailand Its Economic Cooperation with Neighbouring Countries." Discussion Papers 32. Institute of Developing Economies, Japan External Trade Organization, 2005.
Tubilewicz, Czeslaw, and Kanishka Jayasuriya. "Internationalisation of the Chinese Subnational State and Capital: The Case of Yunnan and the Greater Mekong Subregion." *Australian Journal of International Affairs* 69, no. 2 (March 4, 2015): 185–204.
Turnell, Sean. *Fiery Dragons: Banks, Moneylenders and Microfinance in Burma*. Copenhagen: NIAS Press, 2009.
Turner, Alicia. *Saving Buddhism: The Impermanence of Religion in Colonial Burma*. Honolulu, HI: University of Hawai'i Press, 2017.
Unger, Daniel. "Ain't Enough Blanket: International Humanitarian Assistance and Cambodian Political Resistance." In *Refugee Manipulation: War, Politics, and the Abuse of Human Suffering*, edited by Stephen Stedman and Fred Tanner, 17–56. Washington, DC: Brookings Institution Press, 2003.
Vaddhanaphuti, Chayan. "The Thai State and Ethnic Minorities: From Assimilation to Selective Integration." In *Ethnic Conflict in Southeast Asia*, edited by Kusuma Snitwngse and W. Scott Thompson, 151–66. Singapore: Institute of Southeast Asian Studies, 2005.
Vella, Walter F. *Chaiyo!: King Vajiravadh and the Development of Thai Nationalism*. Honolulu, HI: University of Hawai'i Press, 1986.
Vila, Pablo. *Crossing Borders, Reinforcing Borders: Social Categories, Metaphors and Narrative Identities on the U.S.—Mexico Frontier*. Austin: University of Texas Press, 2000.
Viraphol, Sarasin. *Tribute and Profit: Sino-Siamese Trade, 1652–1853*. Cambridge, MA: Harvard University Asia Center, 1977.
Vogt, Manuel, Nils-Christian Bormann, Seraina Rüegger, Lars-Erik Cederman, Philipp Hunziker, and Luc Girardin. "Integrating Data on Ethnicity, Geography, and Conflict: The Ethnic Power Relations Data Set Family." *Journal of Conflict Resolution* 59, no. 7 (October 1, 2015): 1327–42.
Vreeland, James Raymond. "The Effect of Political Regime on Civil War: Unpacking Anocracy." *Journal of Conflict Resolution* 52, no. 3 (2008): 401–25.
Walker, Andrew. "Seditious State-Making in the Mekong Borderlands: The Shan Rebellion of 1902–1904." *Sojourn* 29, no. 3 (November 1, 2014): 554–90.
———, ed. *Tai Lands and Thailand: Community and State in Southeast Asia*. Singapore: National University of Singapore Press, 2009.
———. *Thailand's Political Peasants: Power in the Modern Rural Economy*. Madison: University of Wisconsin Press, 2012.
Walton, Matthew J. "The Disciplining Discourse of Unity in Burmese Politics." *Journal of Burma Studies* 19, no. 1 (June 17, 2015): 1–26.

———. "Ethnicity, Conflict, and History in Burma: The Myths of Panglong." *Asian Survey* 48, no. 6 (2008): 889–910.
———. "The 'Wages of Burman-Ness:' Ethnicity and Burman Privilege in Contemporary Myanmar." *Journal of Contemporary Asia* 43, no. 1 (February 1, 2013): 1–27.
Wang, Bing. *Ta'ang*. Documentary, Chinese Shadows, 2016.
Wang, Gungwu. *The Chinese Overseas: From Earthbound China to the Quest for Autonomy*. Cambridge, MA: Harvard University Press, 2002.
Webster, Donovan. *The Burma Road*. London: Macmillan, 2004.
Weinberg, Gerhard L. *Hitler's Foreign Policy 1933–1939: The Road to World War II*. New York: Enigma Books, 2005.
Weiner, Myron. "Bad Neighbors, Bad Neighborhoods." *International Security* 21, no. 1 (July 1, 1996): 5.
Wimmer, Andreas, Lars-Erik Cederman, and Brian Min. "Ethnic Politics and Armed Conflict: A Configurational Analysis of a New Global Data Set." *American Sociological Review* 74, no. 2 (2009): 316–37.
Winichakul, Thongchai. "Nationalism and the Radical Intelligentsia in Thailand." *Third World Quarterly* 29, no. 3 (April 1, 2008): 575–91.
———. *Siam Mapped: A History of the Geo-Body of a Nation*. Honolulu, HI: University of Hawai'i Press, 1994.
Wolters, O. W. *Culture, History and Region in South East Asian Perspectives*. Singapore: Institute of Southeast Asian Studies, 1982.
Wongsurawat, Wasana. "Beyond Jews of the Orient: A New Interpretation of the Problematic Relationship between the Thai State and Its Ethnic Chinese Community." *Positions* 24, no. 2 (May 1, 2016): 555–82.
Wongtrangan, Kanok. "Communist Revolutionary Process: A Study of the Communist Party of Thailand." PhD diss., Johns Hopkins University, 1981.
Woods, Kevin. "Ceasefire Capitalism: Military–Private Partnerships, Resource Concessions and Military–State Building in the Burma–China Borderlands." *Journal of Peasant Studies* 38, no. 4 (October 1, 2011): 747–70.
———. *Commercial Agriculture Expansion in Myanmar: Links to Deforestation, Conversion Timber, and Land Conflicts*. Washington, DC: Forest Trends, 2015.
Wyatt, David K. *Thailand: A Short History*. 2nd rev. ed. New Haven, CT: Yale University Press, 2003.
Wyatt, David K., and Aroonrut Wichienkeeo, trans. *The Chiang Mai Chronicle*. Chiang Mai: Silkworm Books, 1995.
Yang, Bin. *Between Winds and Clouds: The Making of Yunnan*. New York: Columbia University Press, 2009.
———. "'We Want to Go Home!' The Great Petition of the Zhiqing, Xishuangbanna, Yunnan, 1978–1979." *The China Quarterly*, no. 198 (2009): 401–21.
Yang, Kuisong. "Reconsidering the Campaign to Suppress Counterrevolutionaries." *The China Quarterly*, no. 193 (2008): 102–21.
Yawnghwe, Chao Tzang. *The Shan of Burma: Memoirs of a Shan Exile*. Singapore: Institute of Southeast Asian Studies, 2010.
Yoon, Won Zoon. "Japan's Occupation of Burma, 1941–1945." PhD diss., New York University, 1971.
Yun, Sun. "Chinese Investment in Myanmar: What Lies Ahead?" Issue Brief No. 1. *Great Powers and the Changing Myanmar*. Washington, DC: Stimson Center, 2013.

Zaiotti, Ruben. *Cultures of Border Control: Schengen and the Evolution of European Frontiers*. Chicago: University of Chicago Press, 2011.

Zhang, Wenyi, and FKL Chit Hlaing. "The Dynamics of Kachin 'Chieftaincy' in Southwestern China and Northern Burma." *Cambridge Anthropology* 31, no. 2 (Autumn 2013): 88–103.

Index

Tables, figures, and maps are indicated by an italic *t, f,* and *m,* respectively, following the page number.

Acemoglu, Daron, *Why Nations Fail,* 4–5
Africa, state building, 28, 29, 170n21
Akha, 47–48
Art of Not Being Governed, The (Scott), 3
Asian Highway system, 96, 157
Aung San Suu Kyi
   China ambassador meeting, 148–49
   China visit, 149
   election results and house arrest (1990), 103, 138, 144–45
   election victory (2015), 137–38, 154
   government, new, 155
   Rohingya crisis, 156

Bamar, 8–9
Bangladesh–India–Myanmar–China Economic Corridor, 161–62
bellicist theory, 27–29
borderland variations. *See also specific border countries*
   nation building, 26–27
   state building, 21–26, 22–25*f*, 23–25*t*
Border Patrol Police (BPP), Thai, 69
British colonialism
   China relations, 44–45
   Lan Na, 42–44
British colonialism, Burma, 8, 42–44
   consolidation, WW II, 50, 52–54
   Shan states, 45–47, 177n3
Brubaker, Rogers, 10, 34
   Nationalism Reframed, 34–35
Burma. *See* Myanmar (Burma); *specific cities*
Burma–China borderland
   militarization, Burmese state fragmentation, 63
   solidification, 1950s-1960s, 59

Chakri Dynasty, 7–8
Chiang Mai
   Burmese occupation, 39, 40–41
   KMT troop remnants and descendants, 55–56
   Lan Na principality (*see* Lan Na)
   local people, 173n6
   Shan nationalists and exiles, 119, 134
   Siamese military expeditions, 41
   size and importance, 99–100
   tax-farming revenue, 43
   wartime devastation, 48
Chiang Rai, 55, 70, 88–89, 100
Chiang Rung, 37–39, 48, 173n6
Chiang Tung, 37, 38–39, 40–41, 42, 48, 173n6
China. *See also* Yunnan Province; *specific cities and topics*
   borderland control, 10–11
   borders, sovereign control, 3
   British colonial relations, Qing Dynasty, 44–45
   ethnic groups, 8–9
   Ethnic Identification Project, 121–22
   ethnonationalist movements, 26–27
   GDP per capita, 21–23, 22*f*
   human development indicators, 21–23, 23*t*
   Myanmar, border trade, 105, 106*f*
   Myanmar, recent relations, 160–62
   nation building, 3
   nation building at borderland, 129
   nation building at borderland, Xishuangbanna Dai Autonomous Prefecture, 131–32
   state consolidation, WW II, 49–50
   Thailand, recent relations, 159–60

234 INDEX

China civil war, spillover and
  repercussions, 55–71
 borderland militarization and Burmese
  state fragmentation, 14, 63
 border region solidification,
  1950s, 14, 59
 spillover, 14, 56
 Thai northern borderline, irregular
  force along, 14, 67
 Yunnan Kunmin Incident and historical
  precedents, 55–56
China–Myanmar border, continual
 contestations, 137–56
 armed conflict, 2009+, 137–38
 China–Myanmar bilateral relations,
  changing, 144
 conflicts, renewed, 140–41
 conflicts, renewed, Kachin state and
  northern Shan state, 141, 143t
 conflicts, renewed, Kokang, 140
 conflicts, renewed, resource curse, 142
 Kokang, fight against Myanmar
  government, 137
 Kokang, vs. Crimea, 201n71
 Myanmar, 2015 election, 154
 Myanmar, political transition, 138
 Myanmar insurgencies, China's
  changing reactions, 150
 Twenty-first Century Panglong
  Conference, 137–38, 155–56, 162–63
China–Myanmar Economic Corridor, 162
China–Myanmar–Thailand border
 geography, 5–7, 6m, 7m
 history, 7–8
 people and ethnic groups, 8–9
China–Thailand border, irregular force
 along, 67
Chinese Cultural Revolution, Yunnan, 73
Chinese Nationalist Party. See
  KMT (Kuomintang, Chinese
  Nationalist Party)
civil war
 China, 14, 55–71 (see also China civil
  war, spillover and repercussions)
 geography in, 29
colonialism, British
 China relations, 44–45
 Lan Na, 42–44

colonialism, British in Burma, 8, 42–44
 consolidation WW II, 50, 52–54
 Shan states, 45–47, 177n3
colonialism, western
 China, British relations, 44–45
 China, French, 44–45
 China, Qing, 44–45
 Siam, 42–43
 Southeast Asia, upland, 42
 Yunnan–French Vietnam border, 45
Communist Party of Burma (CPB)
 borderland posting, 79
 collapse, 167n37
 insurgency, Thailand, 85
Communist Party of Thailand (CPT),
  borderland posting, 79
communist revolutions, borderland,
  15, 72–91
 Chinese Communist Party, 72–73
 Chinese Cultural Revolution,
  Yunnan, 73
 Communist Party of Burma insurgency,
  borderland, 79
 Communist Party of Burma insurgency,
  Thailand, 85
contestation, China–Myanmar
 border, 18
cross-border dynamics, 10, 172n43
cross-border trade, 103–9f, 103

Dai, 8–9
Deaton, Angus, *The Great Escape*, 4–5
development indicators. *See also* GDP per
  capita; *specific types*
 Myanmar, Kachin and Shan states,
  23–24, 24f
 Thailand, 24, 25f
Dobama Asiayone, 183n32
Doner, Richard F., 29
double-minority status, 10–11

East Asia. *See also specific countries*
 state building, 29
economic flows, transboundary,
  16, 92–117
 cross-border trade, 103–9f, 103
 economic development disparities,
  94, 95–99f

GDP per capita, northern Thailand and provinces, 98–99, 99f
GDP per capita PPP, 94, 95f
economic flows, transboundary, Myanmar
  border trade, with China, 105, 106f
  border trade, with Thailand, 107–9, 108f
  China, border trade, 105, 106f
  export partners, major, 103f, 103–4
  foreign investment source countries, by sector, 110–11, 111f
  foreign investment source countries, top, 109–10, 110f
  import partners, major, 103–4, 104f
  jade output, 102–3, 111–13, 112f
  Kengtung economic opportunities, borderline village, 92–93
  Myanmar, natural resource exploitation, 109, 110–14f, 116t
  Myanmar–China cross-border trade, through Gengma and Chinshwehaw, 105–6, 107f
  Myanmar–China cross-border trade, through Longchuan and Lwejel, 105–6, 107f
  Myanmar–China cross-border trade, through Ruili and Muse, 105–6, 106f
  poppy cultivation, Myanmar Shan and Kachin, 116t
  timber, Chinese imports of, 102–3, 113–14, 114f
economic flows, transboundary, Thailand–Myanmar cross-border trade
  through Mae Sai and Tachileik, 107–9, 108f
  through Mae Sot and Myawaddy, 107–9, 109f
economic flows, transboundary, Yunnan
  gross regional product per capita, 100 million Chinese yuan, 96–97, 97f
  gross regional product per capita, Chinese yuan, 96–97, 97f
education
  cross-border differences, 23–26, 24–25f, 25t
  ethnic language, China, 192n1
  ethnic language, Myanmar prohibition, 20–21

empirical materials, sources, 11–12
ethnic groups, 8–9. *See also specific countries and groups*
  borderland, on nation building, 10
  double-minority status, 10–11
Ethnic Identification Project, 121–22
ethnic language education
  China, 192n1
  Myanmar, prohibition, 20–21
ethnonationalist movements, borderland
  China, 26–27
  Myanmar, 26
  Thailand, 27
European state system, 27–28
external kin states, 34
  ethnic groups across state borders, 35
  of minority group, in nationalism, 34–35

Fourth Thai-Lao Friendship Bridge, 157

GDP per capita, 21–23, 22f
  Myanmar, 21–23, 22f
  PPP, 94, 95f
  tax revenues as percentage of, 21, 22f
  Thailand, 21–23, 22f
  Thailand, northern and provinces, 98–99, 99f
geography
  China–Myanmar–Thailand border, 5–7, 6m, 7m
  in civil war, 29
Golden Triangle, poppy/opium trade, 5–7, 114–15, 116t, 157
  Kengtung, 93
  KMT troops, opium smuggling, 66, 71
Golden Triangle Special Economic Zone, 157
Greater Mekong Subregion (GMS) Economic Cooperation Program, 95–97, 157–58, 187n8
  Myanmar, 102–3
  Thailand, 100
Great Escape, The (Deaton), 4–5

Hamilton, William, 82
Herbst, Jeffrey, 28

history. *See also specific countries and topics*
  China–Myanmar–Thailand border, 7–8
  state formation patterns, upland Southeast Asia, 36–54 (*see also* state formation patterns, upland Southeast Asia)
human development indicators, 21–23, 23t

identity construction, national, 120. *See also* national identity construction
Industrial Revolution, 4–5
internally displaced persons (IDP), KIA camps, 20

jade, Myanmar, 102–3, 111–13, 112f
Jingpo (Kachin), 8–9, 47–48, 129–30

Kachin (Jingpo), 8–9, 47–48
Kachin state conflict, 141, 143t
Kachin Independence Army (KIA), 1, 137–38, 143t
  internally displaced in area controlled by, 20
  Laiza territory, occupation and treatment, 2, 20, 118–19
  Myanmar–Thailand border, 2
  rebel group clashes, 137–38
  timber trade support, 113–14
Kachin Independence Organization (KIO), 1
Karen National Defense Organization (KND), 81–82
Karen National Union (KNU), 104–5
Kengtung, 172n105, *See also* Myanmar (Burma)
  Amazing Kengtung Resort, 36
  economic flows, transborder, 92–93, 107–9
  economic opportunities, borderline village, 92–93
  Golden Triangle, poppy/opium trade, 93
  KMT invasion, 56, 65, 66
  modern, 36–37
KMT (Kuomintang, Chinese Nationalist Party)
  Kengtung invasion, 56, 65, 66
  troops, evacuation and relocation, 58–59
  troops, Korean War era, 56–57
  troops, opium and war economy, 66–84
  troops, Shan State expansion, 58
Kokang
  vs. Crimea, 201n71
  fight against Myanmar government, 140
Konbaung Dynasty, 7–8
Kunming Military Region, 75–76, 77–78, 82–83, 90
Kuomintang (KMT). *See* KMT (Kuomintang, Chinese Nationalist Party)

Lahu, 8–9
Laiza, 1–2
  ethnic language education, prohibition, 20–21
Lancang-Mekong Cooperation (LMC), 157–59
Lan Na, 37, 38–39, 40, 41–42
  Bangkok centralizing control, 42–43, 174n44
  British colonialism, 42–44
Latin America, state building, 28
Law on Regional Autonomy, 122
Leach, Edmund, 47–48
Linter, Bertil, 82, 162–63
Lisu, 8–9
Luohei (Lahu), 47–48

Mae Hong Son, KMT troop remnants and descendants, 55
Mae Salong, 55
Malay, Southern Thailand, 86, 185n89
map, 6m
methodology, 11
Miao (Hmong), 8–9, 47–48
mountain people, upland Southeast Asia, 47
  Akha, 47–48
  Kachin (Jingpo), 47–48
  Luohei (Lahu), 47–48
  Miao (Hmong), 47–48
  Palaung, 47–48
  Wa, 47–48
  Yao (Mien), 47–48

INDEX   237

muang. *See* Tai principalities (muang)
Multiple Indicator Cluster Survey (MICS),
   development indicators, 23–24, 24f,
   168–69n4
Myanmar (Burma)
   2015 election, 154
   Amazing Kengtung Resort, 36
   borderland control, failure, 10–11
   border trade, with China, 105, 106f
   border trade, with Thailand, 107–9, 108f
   capital, move to Naypyidaw,
      145, 200n40
   ceasefire agreements, 169n6
   China, recent relations, 160–62
   China border contestations, 137–56
      (*see also* China–Myanmar border,
      continual contestations)
   China borderland militarization and
      state fragmentation, 14, 63
   China cross-border trade, through
      Gengma and Chinshwehaw,
      105–6, 107f
   China cross-border trade, through
      Longchuan and Lwejel, 105–6, 107f
   China cross-border trade, through Ruili
      and Muse, 105–6, 106f
   Chinese Communist Party, 72–73
   Communist Party of Burma insurgency
      against, 85
   development indicators, Kachin and
      Shan states, 23–24, 24f
   economic development, 94, 100–2
   ethnic groups, 8–9
   ethnic minority migration away, 119
   ethnic rebels, resistance, 3
   ethnonationalist movements, 26
   export partners, major, 103f, 103–4
   foreign investment source countries, by
      sector, 110–11, 111f
   foreign investment source countries,
      top, 109–10, 110f
   GDP per capita, 21–23, 22f
   human development indicators,
      21–23, 23t
   import partners, major, 103–4, 104f
   insurgencies, China's changing
      reactions to, 150
   jade output, 102–3, 111–13, 112f

   Kachin people, government soldier
      attacks, 118–38
   Karen National Defense
      Organization, 81–82
   KMT troops, evacuation and
      relocation, 58–59
   KMT troops, Korean War era, 56–57
   KMT troops, opium and war
      economy, 66–84
   KMT troops, Shan State expansion, 58
   map, 6m
   National League for Democracy, 103,
      137–38, 139, 144–45, 149, 154, 198n3
   nation building at borderland,
      Jingpo, 129–30
   nation building at borderland,
      Wa, 130–31
   natural resource exploitation, 109,
      110–14f, 116t
   Operation Paper, 57–58, 68
   political transition, 138
   poppy cultivation, Myanmar Shan and
      Kachin, 116t
   Sawbwa system, 36–37, 172n2
   State Law and Order Restoration
      Council, 94, 101–2
   State Peace and Development
      Council, 101
   Thailand cross-border trade, through
      Mae Sai and Tachileik, 107–9, 108f
   Thailand cross-border trade, through
      Mae Sot and Myawaddy, 107–9, 109f
   time period, 165n1
   trading partners, China, 103–4
   trading partners, Thailand, 103
   Wa, 47–48
Myanmar (Burma), British colonialism,
   8, 42–44
   consolidation, WW II, 50, 52–54
   Shan states, 45–47, 177n3
Myanmar–China borderland
   militarization, Burmese state
      fragmentation and, 63
   solidification, 1950s-1960s, 59
Myanmar National Democratic Alliance
   Army (MNDAA), 2–3, 26, 101–2,
   114–15, 137–38, 140–42, 143t,
   153, 154–55

narcotics, China–Myanmar–Thailand borderland, 114–15, 116t
national identity construction, 120
  China, 120–22
  Myanmar, 125–27
  Thailand, 123–25
nationalism, state, minorities, and minority group external kin state, 34–35
Nationalism Reframed (Brubaker), 34–35
National League for Democracy (NLD), 103, 137–38, 139, 144–45, 149, 154, 198n3
  Aung San Suu elections Kyi, 103, 137–38, 144–45, 154, 155
nation building, 4–5
  borderland variations, 26–27
  China, 3
  comparative borderland, 17
  definition, 5
  ethnic groups on, borderland, 10
  neighborhood effect, 9–10, 13, 33–35, 34t (*see also* neighborhood effect)
  Thailand, 3
  theories, 30
nation building across borderland, comparative, 118–36
  at borderland, 128
  at borderland, China, 129
  at borderland, China, Xishuangbanna Dai Autonomous Prefecture, 131–32
  at borderland, Myanmar, Jingpo, 129–30
  at borderland, Myanmar, Wa, 130–31
  at borderland, Thailand, hill tribes, 135–36, 197n108
  Kachin people, Myanmar soldier attacks, 118–38
  national identity construction, 120 (*see also* national identity construction)
  national identity construction, China, 120–22
  national identity construction, Myanmar, 125–27
  national identity construction, Thailand, 123–25
natural resource exploitation, Myanmar, 109, 110–14f, 116t

neighborhood effect, 9–10
  nation building, 9–10, 13, 33–35, 34t
  state building, 9–10, 13, 30–33, 32t
neighboring states
  power symmetry, 32, 32t
  relations, 32, 32t

One Belt One Road (OBOR), 158–59, 161–62
Operation Paper, 57–58, 68
opium cultivation, China–Myanmar–Thailand borderland, 114–15, 116t

Palaung, 47–48
Peng, Jiasheng, 137
people, China–Myanmar–Thailand border, 8–9
Political Frontier Defense (PFD), 75–76
power asymmetry. *See also specific topics*
  neighboring states, 32–33
power capabilities, 32, 32t, 33, 172n42
power symmetry. *See also specific topics*
  neighboring states, 32–33, 32t

Qing Dynasty, China, 7–8
  British colonial relations, 44–45
  state consolidation, WW II, 49

Red Flags, 79–80
Red Guards, 16, 73–74, 75, 76–77
  former, Han Chinese youth, 79
  recalling, after Mao, 84
  recruitment, 81–82
  Shan State crossing, 82–83
resource exploitation, Myanmar, 109, 110–14f, 116t
Ritchie, Bryan K., 29
Robinson, James, *Why Nations Fail*, 4–5
Rohingya crisis, 156

Sawbwa system, 36–37, 172n2
school enrollment rate, Yunnan Province, 24–26, 25t
Scott, James
  Art of Not Being Governed, The, 3
  on mountain people, SE Asia, 47–48
Shan, 8–9, 173n6
  nationalist movements, 82–84

INDEX 239

Shan states, 23–24, 24f
  British colonialism, 45–47, 177n3
  conflict, 141, 143t
  development indicators, 23–24, 24f
  KMT expansion into, 58
  language education, 20
Siam. *See* Thailand
Silk Road Fund, 158–59
Sino-Myanmar border. *See* China-Myanmar border
Slater, Dan, 29
Southeast Asia, upland, state formation patterns, 36–54
  mountain people, 47
  Sawbwa system, 36–37, 172n2
  state consolidation, WW II, 49
  Tai principalities (muang), 37, 173n6
    (*see also* Tai principalities (muang))
  western colonialism and local responses, 42
state building, 4–5
  Africa, 28, 170n21
  borderland variations, 21–26, 22–25f, 23–25t
  definition, 5
  domestic factors, 9–10
  East Asia, 29
  European state system, 27–28
  Latin America, 28
  neighborhood effect, 9–10, 13, 30–33, 32t (*see also* neighborhood effect)
  theories, 27–29
state capacity building
  bellicist theory, 27–29
  domestic factors, 29
state formation patterns, upland Southeast Asia, 36–54
  mountain people, 47
  Myanmar, Amazing Kengtung Resort, 36
  state consolidation, WW II, 49
  Tai principalities (muang), 37, 173n6
    (*see also* Tai principalities (muang))
  western colonialism and local responses, 42
State Law and Order Restoration Council (SLORC), 94, 101–2
State Peace and Development Council (SPDC), 101
Stubbs, Richard, 29

Tai principalities (muang), 37, 173n6
  Chiang Rung, 37–39
  Chiang Tung, 37, 38–39, 40–41, 42
  Lan Na, 37, 38–39, 40, 41–42
  political system, 37–38
tax revenues, as percentage of GDP, 21, 22f
Thai Border Patrol Police (BPP), 69
Thailand. *See also specific cities*
  21st century, Chinese support, 159–60
  21st century, domestic instability, 159–60
  borderland control, 10–11
  borders, China northern, irregular force along, 14, 67
  borders, sovereign control, 3
  Communist Party of Burma insurgency, 85
  counter-insurgency strategy, 90
  development indicators, 24, 25f
  economic development, 94, 97–100, 99f
  ethnic groups, 8–9
  ethnic minorities, highland population, 27
  ethnonationalist movements, 27
  European extraterritoriality, 8
  GDP per capita, 21–23, 22f
  GDP per capita, northern provinces, 98–99, 99f
  human development indicators, 23t
  Japanese invasion, WW II, 52
  Mae Salong, Yunnan Kunming Incident, 55
  map, 6m
  nation building, 3
  nation building across borderland, Shan, 132–34
  nation building across borderland, Tai/Shan, 131
  nation building at borderland, hill tribes, 135–36, 197n108
  nation building at borderland, Shan, 132–34
  nation building at borderland, Tai/Shan, 131
  Southern, Malay, 86, 185n89
  state consolidation, WW II, 49, 50–51
Thailand-China border, irregular force along, 14, 67

Thakin
  definition, 183n35
  thirty, 52
Thakin Ba Thein Tin, 82, 83–84, 183n35
Thakin Soe, 79–80
Thakin Than Tun, 83–84
Thirty Comrades, 52
Tilly, Charles, 27–28
timber, Myanmar exports to China, 102–3, 113–14, 114f
transboundary economic flows, 16. *See also* economic flows, transboundary
Twenty-first Century Panglong Conference, 137–38, 155–56, 162–63

United Wa State Army (UWSA), 130–31, 140, 154–56, 162–63
upland Southeast Asia. *See* Southeast Asia, upland
UWSA
  Chinese government support, 196n79
  Wa forced resettlement, 196n78

Wa, 47–48, 130–31
  United Wa State Army, 130–31, 140, 154–56, 162–63
wartime mobilization, 30
Western Development Program (EDP), 96–97, 97f
Why Nations Fail (Acemoglu & Robinson), 4–5

Xishuangbanna. *See also* Yunnan Province
  aristocrats' escape, 61
  aristocrats in new government, 62
  Chiang Rung, 38
  cross-border trade, 107–9
  Dai Autonomous Prefecture, 120–21, 131–32
  farm relocation, 77–78
  military recruitment, 79–80

Yao (Iu-Mien), 8–9, 47–48, 135–36
Yunnan–French Vietnam border, 45
Yunnan Kunming Incident, 55
Yunnan Production and Construction Corps (YPCC), 77–78
Yunnan Province. *See also* Xishuangbanna
  Chinese Cultural Revolution and, 73
  economic development, 95–97f, 97–98
  ethnic groups, 8–9
  gross regional product per capita, 100 million Chinese yuan, 96–97, 97f
  gross regional product per capita, Chinese yuan, 96–97, 97f
  Kunming Military Region, 75–76, 77–78, 82–83, 90
  map, 6m
  PRC founding (1949), 56
  school enrollment rate, 24–26, 25t
  state consolidation, WW II, 49